WHY WE GARDEN
STORIES OF A BRITISH OBSESSION

by the same author

non-fiction
Shanghai: Electric and Lurid City
Chinese Ink, Western Pen: Stories of China
Let the Credits Roll: Interviews with Film Crew

poetry
Round: Poems and Photographs of Asia

WHY WE GARDEN
STORIES OF A BRITISH OBSESSION

Barbara Baker

Aston House Press

First published in Great Britain in 2004 by
Aston House Press
8 Lower Mall
London W6 9DJ

Copyright © Barbara Baker, 2004

The moral right of the author has been asserted.

All rights reserved. No part of this publication may be reproduced, stored or introduced into a retrieval system, or transmitted, in any form or by any means (electronic, mechanical, photocopying, recording or otherwise), without written permission of both the copyright owner and the publisher of this book.

A catalogue record for this book is available from the British Library.

ISBN   0-9547501-0-1

Designed by Sherene Poon of earnes, Hong Kong
Printed and bound by Wing Cheong Printing And Paper Products Company, Hong Kong

In memory of my parents

CONTENTS

ACKNOWLEDGEMENTS ix
INTRODUCTION xi

PART I GARDENERS BY DESIGN

1. DAVID AUSTIN   Rose Specialist 3
2. CLARE BASSETT, NORMA BIRD, RHON ROGERS   Blewbury Cottage Gardeners 11
3. SARAH COOK   Head Gardener at Sissinghurst 25
4. DAVID DORWARD   Edinburgh Clock Gardener 31
5. DEREK HOSIE   Head Gardener at Cawdor Castle 39
6. DAVID MAGSON   London Square Gardener 45
7. ROBERT MURRAY   Landscape Contractor and Lawn Mower 55
8. DAME MIRIAM ROTHSCHILD   Wild-flower Gardener and Entomologist 61
9. GORDON ROWLEY   Plantsman and Succulent Specialist 71

PART II GARDENERS BY DEFAULT

10. DAVE COOKE   Temperate House Manager at Kew 83
11. SELINA DIX HAMILTON   Roof Gardener 91
12. CAROLYN ELWES   Galanthophile 97
13. ALISON GODING   Composter and Estate Gardener at RHS Harlow Carr 105
14. MIKE HANNA and JOSEPHINE MEWS   Belgravia Gardeners 115
15. JEAN HILL   Cliff-top Gardener 121
16. BUDDHA MAITREYA   Japanese Gardener 129
17. JANET OLDROYD HULME   Fruit and Vegetable Grower and Rhubarb Specialist 135
18. ROWAN VUGLAR   Community Gardener 145

PART III LATE DECIDERS

19. JAMES CREBBIN-BAILEY   Topiary Specialist 155
20. TERRY DAVIES   Allotment Gardener and Beekeeper 161
21. JULIET LACEY   Floating Gardener 167
22. JEKKA McVICAR   Herb Farmer 175
23. RORA PAGLIERI   Creator of a Highland Garden 181
24. HANNAH PESCHAR   Garden Sculpture Specialist 187
25. RICHARD PIM   Water Gardener 195
26. SARAH RAVEN   Cutting Gardener 201
27. KIM WHATMORE   Urban Gardener and Designer 211

PHOTOGRAPHY CREDITS 217

ACKNOWLEDGEMENTS

Once again I could not have written this book without my husband Robin. From putting up with me talking about it morning, noon and night, to taking brilliant photographs, his contribution was tremendous.

I owe many thanks to my editors, Rebecca Lloyd and Jacqueline Young. I am also indebted to Madeleine Marie Slavick who looked through a plethora of photographs and read the text: the opinions of Madeleine, a friend as well as a writer/photographer, were invaluable. I thank Miriam Rothschild for allowing me to use the photographs in her chapter: she retains the copyright for these. Others to whom I am grateful gave advice, suggested, or arranged interviews: Guy Cooper, John Grimshaw, Alexandra Lynch, Hannah Rogers, Marjorie Sweetko, Christine Thomas, Janet Uttley, Ayllie White and Allison Williams.

In a project such as this the people who should be afforded most thanks are the interviewees. It is unfortunate that owing to confines of space, some interviews could not be included. To those people, I apologize, but I thank them too. Everyone involved shared their stories with me and gave their time most generously. It is their words that make this book: words which both inform and captivate.

INTRODUCTION

There is an old Chinese saying that goes: 'If you want to be happy for a week, get married. If you want to be happy for a month, kill a pig. If you want to be happy for life, plant a garden.'

This last piece of advice has certainly been taken up in Britain, especially in recent times. Britain has been called a 'nation of gardeners' and gardening has been dubbed the 'nation's obsession'. This book is about living gardeners – not, as is often the case, garden designers, but the actual tillers of the earth. Moreover it's about why, rather than how, people garden: the pleasures and inspiration gained, as well as the obsession – because for many, gardening is more than a casual activity. There is an element about it which is beyond control.

According to *The Oxford English Dictionary* 'obsess' means 'haunt, harass, preoccupy and fill the mind'. But it is not just a negative thing. Juliet Lacey, the floating gardener  whom I interviewed, who owns barges near Tower Bridge, expressed it nicely when she said, 'I think about the gardens most of the time, even at night. I wake up thinking, "I'd better do that today. What a good idea!" And I rush out. It is a lovely, harmless obsession, which is beneficial to more than just oneself.'

The development of the nation's obsession has been a gradual one. Gardening is one of man's earliest pursuits. From the story of Adam and Eve onwards, there are tales over the centuries of how people have improved the soil, watered, planted and formed what garden historian and designer Penelope Hobhouse called 'a partnership between nature and art.' It is not appropriate here to give a history of British gardening, but a very brief summary of its development.

'Horti' (gardens) are mentioned in the Domesday Book of 1086. Apothecary, monastery and castle gardens flourished, and they were also mentioned in literature – in the fourteenth century by Chaucer; in the sixteenth, by Shakespeare. In the sixteenth century too, John Gerard's *Herball* was published, forerunning many books dealing  with the medicinal and culinary properties of plants, while garden design took on influences from abroad, particularly Italy. Seventeenth-century plant hunters brought back new plants to Britain, and garden designers came to prominence, culminating in the eighteenth-century landscape movement.

By the nineteenth century the craft of gardening widened: not only royalty and landed gentry, but poor people owned gardens in order to grow provisions. New housing and suburbs around industrial towns increased the interest in gardening and its fads and fashions. Where once there were yards for hanging washing and for providing a distance between the house and the outside 'privy', now even the smallest urban houses have back gardens in which many owners take pride and pleasure. Gardeners and authors such as Gertrude Jekyll, Edward Augustus Bowles, Vita Sackville-West and Beth Chatto all influenced the gardening scene. More and more plants became available, and currently gardening has never been more popular. Pressures of modern living increase, while horticulture is a multi-billion-pound industry. There are books, magazines, websites, radio and TV programmes, shows, centres, nurseries and societies in seemingly limitless numbers, all thriving.

Influential garden writer John Claudius Loudon might have been writing about villagers today when he described Bowness on Windermere in 1831. There a Mrs Starkey 'ornamented her own house and ground with many of the finest plants and shrubs, and offers seeds of young plants freely to every villager who will plant and take care of them.' Loudon continues, 'It is true, the working inhabitants of London and of manufacturing towns cannot be expected all at once to pay the same respect to flowers as the inhabitants of Bowness; but time will remedy this evil.' And indeed, Loudon's prophecy has come true: few people living in London today are evil enough to have no interest at all in flowers!

I have interviewed gardeners from the Cornish coast to the Scottish Highlands. I divided them into three sections – some are born gardeners, some attain gardening skills and some have gardening thrust upon them – but they all have several things in common. They specialize in an aspect of the art of gardening and are inspired by it; they are generous in sharing their knowledge and their stories; and they are eager to explain why they garden, and the different feelings it stirs.

There is definitely something soothing about seeing growth and being in touch with nature. In Virginia Woolf's novel *Mrs Dalloway*, it is said of the enigmatic Sally that, 'despairing of human relationships (people were so difficult), she often went into her garden and got from her flowers a peace which men and women never gave her.' Gardening definitely evokes different things in different people. To quote just a few more favourites of mine, Alan Titchmarsh, gardener, presenter and novelist, said, 'gardening can be the most rewarding thing in life – next to having children.' The more pessimistic poet Philip Larkin wrote, 'Anything that looks bright and positive I take to be a weed.' Judi Smith, owner of a North Yorkshire gravel garden wrote, 'I often say we used to have a life – now we have a garden.' Gardening can be frustrating, relaxing, therapeutic, addictive and obsessive. It is often all these at different times.

Gardening is unusual in that it can be done either as a job or as a hobby: there are both kinds of gardener in this book. Another distinctive feature of gardening is that it is never finished, and consequently gardeners are continually learning. It is reassuring that some (such as Kim Whatmore, an urban gardener) experience certain feelings of panic, but that in time this tends to dissipate. Conversely, sometimes lack of knowledge can actually be useful, aiding the creative side of gardening which appeals to many. Charles Jencks, who designed 'Landform' in Edinburgh (maintained by Robert Murray) asserts, 'Ignorance is the first thing you need before you can create a great garden. You need to be ignorant of thinking there is a right way to do it. If you think you know the answers you won't discover what you need to, but merely reproduce or replicate what has gone before.'

Most gardeners aim to combine use with beauty; many to combine work with contemplation; and some, pleasure with profit. Serious gardeners are usually devoted to their art and find restraint difficult. Few spend much time sitting in their gardens – they are compelled to get up and do something, even if it is just deadheading a flower. Gardens are in fact used for a myriad of purposes: they may be looked at, relaxed in, played in; they may be places of botanical research, or sustenance of the soul. It is also revealed in these interviews that gardens are places where babies are born (floating gardener), ashes scattered (cottage gardener), placentas buried (communal gardener), pictures painted (cottage gardener), haddock baked (composter) and follies invented (water gardener)!

It became apparent too, whilst conducting these interviews, that the difference between men and women gardeners was less pronounced than suggested by the usual stereotype of men enjoying practical handicraft, compost, lawns, and architectural plants but not being 'plantaholics', while women devote themselves to artistic creativity, cultivation, pastel shades and pretty flowers. Other findings were that a lot of professional gardeners are self-taught rather than trained, and that many professional gardeners do not garden much at home for pleasure. Nor do most modern architectural garden designers own minimalist gardens themselves. People interested in gardening tend to want their own gardens to evolve and develop, enjoying the changes.

The interviews bear out what famous horticulturalist and radio and TV presenter Geoffrey Smith voiced – a quote which perhaps gives a clue to the inspiration which is

common amongst gardeners: 'Your garden is your own personal artistic impression. Get someone else to do it, and you won't love it as much.... Seeing a picture that is in your mind only: that is the privilege that gardeners get.' And it is this inner vision which often *has* to be realized – whether by keeping the lawn perfect or creating some grandiose scheme. Gardens reflect the

xiii

vision of their makers. They may be filled with one kind of flower, overflowing with as many varieties as possible, places where a certain colour is banished, or where imagination runs riot. To me it is not surprising that the bottom of the garden is the place thought to be a fitting habitat for fairies: gardens can be magical and the feelings gained from tending them are unique.

But I have to admit that amongst the many feelings stirred in me, one is obsession. I was in Blewbury, on a fairly tight schedule, interviewing three gardeners, and became inspired by the plants in the first garden. I *had* to have some in my own garden, but London nurseries are not ideal for rarer cottage plants. I asked Norma Bird, one of the Blewbury gardeners, where her local nursery was; undeterred by the fact that it was eight miles away and difficult to find, and that I scarcely had time before my next interview, I beetled off there.

My interest in gardening started early. I grew up in a suburban house in London with a small garden, but even as a child, some of my happiest moments were spent there. I made rainwater soup with spaghetti rhododendron stamens and lupin pod peas, which my mother obligingly would pretend to eat. I spent solitary afternoons searching for caterpillars, ladybirds and other mysterious tiny things which eager eyes at low level could spot triumphantly. Eventually I would help my mother order bulbs and plants from catalogues, which I poured over gladly for hours. Each year the orders got a bit bigger, and I also managed to persuade her to buy a magnolia tree – a definite achievement in the strict regime where my sister and I never asked for anything.

Friends of my parents had a big London garden where we sometimes played. It was not only the unusual freedom, or the tricycles, which enthralled; the garden was magic. There was no lawn, but a path all around surrounded by trees, ferns, and flowering shrubs – many white and scented. The centre was sunken and had a statue and fountain. It was a grand place that could not be seen all at once, but which had secret corners and hidden wonders. Its atmosphere has always stayed with me.

Living first in flats with window boxes, then in Hong Kong with a balcony, it is only in fairly recent years that I have had a garden of my own. When we bought our house, most people would have been struck by the fact that it is right on the Thames. But I was captivated by the back garden. It reminds me of the secret garden in Francis Hodgson Burnett's story, being walled, overgrown, cottagey, and with a very friendly

robin in it. My desk is by a window overlooking the garden, and I spend a considerable amount of time gazing out and planning, as I am doing even as I write now. To start with, I was rather nervous of the garden, as one might be of a new baby; later I worried when I was away, not liking to miss stages of its growth and development, and now I cannot

 imagine my life without it.

Visiting so many varied gardens and talking with their passionate makers for this book has not just been informative, but a true pleasure. Choosing gardeners to interview was, however, rather a daunting challenge. My aim was to include interesting and different gardeners who excelled in a particular field, whether they were famous or unknown. These gardeners were not chosen because they were media celebrities or even because they had the most beautiful gardens. I interviewed them because of their enthusiasm and passion and because each had a different story and contributed something unusual, individual and intriguing. For me, these gardeners represent what is great in British gardening at the start of the twenty-first century. Together they offer an insight into a special way of life. Each gardener holds a fascination for me, and I hope will for you, too.

The aim of this book is to give a glimpse into the minds of 30 disparate gardeners. The patchwork of specialities together forms a whole tapestry or garden. In this way readers will readily identify with at least some aspects of their own garden as they read about those of others. In a book about gardeners rather than gardens, it was not possible to include every kind of garden, nor did I feel it necessary in each photograph to mention every plant by name. Similarly, where an interviewee used the Latin name for a plant this was retained, but common names for plants are also often used instead; for this book is essentially not about plants but people. What I found thrilling was when a gardener expressed exactly something I had thought but had never articulated. What I also found fascinating was, in the words of Alan Titchmarsh, 'The best gardens reflect the individual personality of the person who made them.'

Whilst writing this book I reread the poem 'The Garden' by Andrew Marvell (1621-1678). I found that many of the lines fitted the gardeners I had interviewed in an uncanny way. I have therefore quoted the relevant lines from the poem with each interview. As the chapters of my book might make one large garden, together the separate lines create this whole poem:

THE GARDEN

How vainly men themselves amaze
To win the Palm, the Oke, or Bayes;
And their uncessant Labours see
Crown'd from some single Herb or Tree,
Whose short and narrow verged Shade
Does prudently their Toyles upbraid;
While all Flow'rs and all Trees do close
To wave the Garlands of repose.

Fair quiet, I have found thee here,
And Innocence thy Sister dear!
Mistaken long, I sought you then
In busie Companies of Men.
Your sacred Plants, if here below,
Only among the Plants will grow.
Society is all but rude,
To this delicious Solitude.

No white nor red was ever seen
So am'rous as this lovely green.
Fond Lovers, cruel as their Flame,
Cut in these Trees their Mistress name.
Little, Alas, they know, or heed,
How far these Beauties Hers exceed!
Fair Trees! Where s'eer your barkes I wound,
No Name shall but your own be found.

When we have run our Passions heat,
Love hither makes his best retreat.
The *Gods*, that mortal Beauty chase,
Still in a Tree did end their race.
Apollo hunted *Daphne* so,
Only that She might Laurel grow.
And Pan did after *Syrinx* speed,
Not as a Nymph, but for a Reed.

What wond'rous Life in this I lead!
Ripe Apples drop about my head;
The Luscious Clusters of the Vine
Upon my Mouth do crush their Wine;
The Nectaren, and curious Peach,
Into my hands themselves do reach;
Stumbling on Melons, as I pass,
Insnar'd with Flow'rs, I fall on Grass.

Mean while the Mind, from Pleasure less,
Withdraws into its happiness:
The Mind, that Ocean where each kind
Does streight its own resemblance find;
Yet it creates, transcending these,
Far other Worlds, and other Seas;
Annihilating all that's made
To a green Thought in a green Shade.

Here at the Fountains sliding foot,
Or at some Fruit-trees mossy root,
Casting the Bodies Vest aside,
My Soul into the boughs does glide:
There like a Bird it sits, and sings,
Then whets, and combs its silver Wings;
And, till prepar'd for longer flight,
Waves in its Plumes the various Light.

Such was that happy Garden-state,
While Man there walk'd without a Mate:
After a Place so pure, and sweet,
What other Help could yet be meet!
But 'twas beyond a Mortal's share
To wander solitary there:
Two Paradises 'twere in one
To live in Paradise alone.

How well the skilful Gardner drew
Of flow'rs and herbes this Dial new;
Where from above the milder Sun
Does through a fragrant Zodiack run;
And, as it works, th'industrious Bee
Computes its time as well as we.
How could such sweet and wholesome Hours
Be reckon'd but with herbs and flow'rs!

PART I
GARDENERS by Design

DAVID AUSTIN
ROSE SPECIALIST

'Pat Austin', an entirely new colour break in English Roses. The inside of the petals is a bright copper, with pale copper-yellow on the outer sides.

'Yet it creates, transcending these'

Roses are one of the best-loved garden flowers and David Austin has been described as one of the world's foremost rose experts. He has hybridized and grown roses for more than 40 years; he introduced the uniquely charming 'English Rose', now sold all over the world; and he is proprietor of one of the UK's leading rose nurseries. He sells all kinds of roses, but it is the English Rose for which he is justifiably famed. This rose combines the form and scent of an Old Rose but is available in a greater variety of delicate, rich shades, and it repeat flowers like a Modern Rose. In the minds of many, English Roses are as near as you can get to perfection, and we have David Austin to thank for them.

What is less known is that David is an extraordinarily modest man. Proud of his family (one son has taken over much of the business side of the company, another is a lecturer and his daughter owns a herbaceous plant nursery), David himself is shy and slightly diffident. He still feels close to his farming background and enjoys contact with the earth, while at the same time his sense of the aesthetic is paramount. He has a love of fine books, sculpture and all things beautiful. I met him at his plant centre in Albrighton, in an office filled with trophies and copies of his books and catalogues in many languages. Later he showed me around his nursery and stunning rose gardens. He is a busy man, but gave time generously.

I started gardening when I was about four, when we had a house and farm up the road. My grandmother lived down here, where we live now, and she gave me a little garden, which was about 20 feet wide, but I expanded it! She had a very good gardener who used to come along with some seed in his hand and put it into my little hand. He never spoke, but in his silent way he encouraged me, and I would watch him and then go and do the same myself.

Another person who influenced me when I was young was James Baker, who was a great friend of my father's. My father was a farmer and James Baker had a nursery near here. James introduced lots of new varieties of hardy plants, but his chief fame was in buying and introducing George Russell's new strain of lupins. He also did work on delphiniums and phlox and many other herbaceous plants. That gave me the idea of hybridizing, so when I was about 12, I started playing around with different plants, putting pollen around and seeing what happened. I just liked the idea of hybridizing.

In his book *The English Rose*, Austin writes of 'Eglantyne', 'For me, this is perhaps the most charming English Rose... The flowers are saucer-shaped, with the petals turning up a little at the edges. The colour is soft pink and there is a delicious fragrance.'

When I left school (and for half my life) I was a farmer, but I chanced on George Bunyard's book on Old Roses. He was the first man to write a book on 'Old Roses' – prior to that there were just 'roses'. He listed 30 or 40 Old Roses in a really beautiful book, and it was he who started my passion for roses. It was also at around this time that I learned of Montagu Allwood's work with pinks. He crossed the Alpine pink with the perpetual flowering carnation, creating a repeat flowering pink. So the idea struck me that one might be able to do this with Old Roses and Modern Hybrid Teas.

I never really liked Modern Roses – they seemed stiff and harsh, though they had the advantage of flowering throughout the summer, whereas Old Roses only flower once in a season. But if one could cross them, one could keep the character, form, scent and charm of the Old Roses but get the repeat flowering of the Modern Rose, plus a much wider range of colour. Old Roses came in colours ranging from white to a kind of dirty crimson. People think of deep crimson as being an Old Rose colour, but it isn't really; that colour only came in at the turn of the last century. By crossing you would get some lovely pinks, blushes, a few whites, as well as yellows and crimson and all the colours of the Hybrid Teas and Floribundas.

So that is what I did. I was still farming for a living, but in my spare time, I got my first box of about 20 little rose seedlings. They all 'damped off' and I never saw them. By that time we were living in Shrewsbury and I had put a greenhouse up and eventually I got a handful of seedling roses, which I took down to Graham Thomas, a well-known horticulturalist. At around the time of Bunyard's

David Austin sitting in the Renaissance garden with 'Heritage' growing on the wall behind.

book, people like Constance Spry and Vita Sackville-West were beginning to collect Old Roses, but Graham Thomas got together a collection of about 1,200 varieties of Old Roses. I still remember seeing them all for the first time and it was a *fantastic* sight.

One of the seedlings I showed Graham was the rose that we eventually called 'Constance Spry'. He introduced it in 1961, first through Hillings Nursery, where he was the nursery manager. It took about ten years from my first attempts at hybridization to selling 'Constance Spry'. It was a marvellous rose and became extremely popular, although, being a first cross, it only flowered once a season. Later I got a range of about eight varieties that were reliably repeat flowering and they were the basis of what we now call the English Rose. They weren't terribly good, and we probably introduced them a bit too soon.

At that time no one was interested really. Graham had left Hillings and become head of the National Trust Gardens. So I thought, since I had the land here, I would use it and I would make a little catalogue, and put some small ads in the papers and that is how we started. Now we have expanded and expanded so that we grow about a quarter of a million seedlings a year from which, in about eight

The impressive Renaissance garden is devoted entirely to English Roses.

years time, we will get about six new varieties. It is a *long* process of selection over those years – and what we are particularly keen on is the *look*.

I think every flower breeder should breed for his particular sort of flower, so if you are growing a lily, it is something quite different to a rose. The rose traditionally has a certain beauty, which it really lost because it got too commercialized and too harsh, hard-edged and straight. We always look for graceful, strong stems and flowers of the old type, which can vary from cupped in shape, to shallow-cupped like a saucer. Others are rosette-shaped with tightly packed petals, or the petals may turn downwards, to provide a more domed flower. Some of the very nice ones are semi-double, or they can be single: instead of one form, we get a whole range of forms.

English Rose bushes have a natural, shrubby growth, and may be of all sizes. Some will arch, some will be nice and bushy, some recent ones have a more open look. I am very keen on these; they have a kind of airy growth, a bit less crowded, almost like in a Chinese painting. I like variety. Most people can grow roses in their gardens, and because they can flower throughout the summer, I think if they were all the same, one could get a bit tired of them. As it is, there are so very many variations that it is wonderful.

In a garden it is best not to plant roses where you have had them before, or if you do, remove the soil to another part of the garden and replace it. Roses build up disease in the soil, and although they can live quite happily while they are there, a new plant coming in wouldn't have a very good chance. The other thing I would say is that they tend to look better in groups rather than dotted around. They make more of an impression that way. Also, because a rose is grafted on to a stock, it tends to grow in a fan-shape from one point, unlike an ordinary shrub, which comes up all over the place, so it tends to look better if there are about three. Of course, advising people to put roses in groups of three is also good from a business point of view! A friend of mine once asked, 'Why don't you tell people to put them in groups of five?'

In the old days, people had large gardens and a bed of roses, but that is not so common now. Then you would have 15 or more roses to a bed so you could get a continual display. But if you just have one plant, from one point in the soil, you are asking a lot of it to produce a really good display of flowers all by itself. My wife has the garden at home. It was one of my great sacrifices to say, 'You can have the garden.' I never had time to do it in the early days. There is so much to breeding – the complexity is enormous, and roses are a business as well as my interest. We have about 70 staff. I have got a very good breeding manager, and his assistant, and selectors, and I am mainly up there doing breeding. We also have various advisors, like a man who used to work for a perfumery, who comes about twice a year and describes the scent of the flowers for us. I would almost like someone to help

David stoops to smell the rose named for his wife, 'Pat Austin', which he describes as 'a lovely flamey rose, but never gaudy'.

David shows a sample of rose pollen collected for hybridizing.

with describing the colour because actually that is quite difficult to do, too.

The descriptions of scent can sound slightly affected, rather like wine, but it adds to the interest, and if you are in the business, you may as well describe something thoroughly so that people will want to try it. For instance, in the catalogue we might write that a rose is clear pink; or warm pink in the centre, shading to pale pink at the edges; with a strong myrrh fragrance; or a suggestion of almond and lilac; or apple and cinnamon, or whatever. We make a point of selling all kinds of roses here: Modern Hybrid Teas and Floribundas, Old Roses, Wild Roses and some Miniature Roses as well as both shrub and climbing English Roses.

English Rose is a good name, I feel, because roses are very much an English thing. A Scottish lady once said to me, 'You know there are four countries in this country of ours!' She didn't like the rose being English, but I wouldn't have the cheek to call it British, and I feel it really is *our* flower – although it does extremely well internationally. It is the national flower of America, and the Japanese love it and most of Europe too. We have catalogues in many languages. Other growers and nurseries can grow English Roses when they have paid their little bit of royalty. It is a comparatively new thing to patent plants, and it has been marvellous; it has advanced farm crops enormously too, and without the royalties we couldn't possibly breed on the scale we do.

In the old days you would breed a rose and everyone would seize hold of it if it were a good one, especially the Dutch. They reckoned if they could get one rose plant within 12 months by grafting, then, by multiplying by 50 each time, they could take it to 1,000,000 by propagating. We actually don't do any grafting: we do budding of the commercial crops and seeding of the trial crops in the field. First we search for two parents, which will combine certain virtues. We plant the parents in the greenhouse and take pollen from one variety and put it on another – that is hybridizing.

By the autumn the plant will have bright pods of seeds, and those seeds will be sown. Then the plants start the perpetual struggle to get chosen! From May to July the plants will flower, and from those plants we will select about 10,000 of the most promising. Al-

A field of trial roses stretching to the horizon with an irrigation machine on the right.

though, actually, the less hopeful ones often turn out to be the best, because you can't see the growth at that stage, so we keep them as well, in a different field. So about 500 to 1000 will go on with the 10,000, which get preferential treatment and get ahead. If some unexpectedly become better from the reserve field they will be added to next year's lot. Each year we have to rotate the fields where we plant new roses. And each year we go on refining the plants we have.

The attitude that we take here is to grow roses for their beauty: it is the look of the rose that matters most to me. But having said that, they must grow, and disease is a big problem. We have got one rose, called 'The Mayflower', which, as far as we know is entirely without disease, but I don't know many garden roses that are. Plant breeders often do choose graceful plants with good foliage, but I doubt that they consciously aim for that; they tend to aim for disease resistance, vigorous growth, quantity of flower, stronger fragrance, brighter colours, bigger flowers. They think, 'That's a bright colour, much brighter than the last one', or, 'Oh, that's a bigger flower.' It is all quantitative. But you would never paint a picture according to its size – that is not what makes it a good picture, or a good rose. There is something else, which you can't really put into words, which is just something you *like* about the thing, and *that* is really what you should be looking for.

There is a kind of softness, which I think suits the rose better, and it is not only to do with colour. Actually we have got some brighter varieties now. To start with I went right away from any bright colours, but lately, I have realized that you need some orangey shades. The danger is that people are attracted to the bright roses and end up with a garden full of clashing colours. But if they are used properly, a few brighter colours can form a highlight, a tiny splash that brightens a border of pastels. So they need do no harm at all and are useful to have. In fact I named one after my wife, 'Pat Austin'. It is a lovely flamey rose but it is never gaudy. It is a strong copper colour, darker on the inside of the petals and more copper-yellow outside.

David leans on the gate leading to the pergola walk. The rambler rose is 'The Garland'.

One of the beauties of a rose is that there are a lot of petals that are rather thin, and the light glows between them, giving all these colour effects so that a rose seldom looks the same twice. The light is very important. I think one of the reasons why the rose is so popular is that if you have a daisy, it is really just that, even though it might be very beautiful. But a rose has all this variation about it and every stage of growth is different too. Scent is very important also. We try always to start with original parents that are both disease-resistant and scented. So we have tried to breed and improve the flowers more and more over the years.

'Mary Magdalene' exemplifying 'One of the beauties of a rose is that there are a lot of petals that are rather thin, and the light glows between them, giving all these colour effects so that a rose seldom looks the same twice.'

What I enjoy most is dreaming up the new crosses. You can do that at your leisure, or as you go around selecting you can decide what rose you might cross with another. Thinking of where you go next and selecting are both exciting: it is rather like backing horses – suddenly a winner turns up. My wife might feel that I think about roses an awful lot of the time, but actually I am not bothered at all by things like Chelsea gold medals. I would be very glad if there were no such thing as a flower show. It was quite fun to start with, but I have got to the stage now where I could do without it. They take a lot of time.

I still have a lot of ideas. I am modelling myself on an American rose breeder called Ralph Moore. He is a remarkable man who is 96 and still crossing roses – that's what I'd like to do if I lasted that long! My son is very much involved with the business and he has two sons who we hope will keep things going too. There is a lot more still to be done: another generation of work before you can begin to be satisfied. You see, the rose is always capable of greater beauty.

2

CLARE BASSETT, NORMA BIRD, RHON ROGERS

BLEWBURY COTTAGE GARDENERS

Thatched roofs and hollyhocks (right) form a quintessential cottage idyll. Also seen here, in Norma Bird's Garden, are *Clematis* 'Blue Boy', blue *Campanula lactiflora* 'Pritchard's Variety' and yellow *Verbascum* 'Gainsborough'.

'When we have run our Passions heat, Love hither makes his best retreat'

Cottage gardens are my favourites, and you could not hope to find better examples than those that abound in the romantic village of Blewbury in Oxfordshire. Of course cottage gardens do not necessarily have to have a cottage, but it is an added bonus if they do. Nor can all gardens attached to cottages be rightly described as cottage gardens if they are not in the traditional 'old-fashioned' style (secluded, intimate and overflowing with generous, informal planting) but Blewbury delights in both. Called 'this venerable village' in its Saxon charter, Blewbury has streams passing through its older parts, and many of the houses are thatched and timber-framed. The buildings are linked by a network of footpaths, some of which are also bordered by thatched cob walls. Blewbury also boasts its own snowdrop, found by Alan Street and named 'Blewbury Tart' (see interview 12 with Galanthophile, Carolyn Elwes).

One day each year the gardens of Blewbury are open to the public for charity as part of the National Gardens Scheme. On 22 June, 2003 six gardens were open in Blewbury and none disappointed. It is a privilege to be welcomed to these private spaces and talk to owners who are passionate about what they do. Gardener and TV presenter Rachel de Thame wrote about the scheme, saying, 'Admiring plants and exploring gardens holds a special fascination for the British, and garden visiting is a long-established national pastime.... It's enormous fun to be allowed to take a peak at gardens that are normally hidden behind private houses, and I have spent many idyllic afternoons strolling around the back gardens of complete strangers.' Since my visit to Blewbury, the village was discovered by Rachel and television and featured on *Gardeners' World*.

Each garden and gardener in Blewbury is distinctive, and it was so difficult to pick just one that I decided to interview three cottage gardeners – a painter, a plantaholic and a propagator. They have in common that they are all female, eloquent, generous and non-competitive. More intriguing are their differences in approach and priorities, such as what gives them most pleasure, or their attitudes to going away on holiday. Clare Bassett is an artist and this is manifest in her planting and whole outlook. She regards her garden as a painter does a canvas, but despite colour-themed beds, her garden is comfortable and feels 'lived in'. Norma Bird's garden takes your breath away. The luxuriant planting is everything one expects of a perfect cottage garden, bursting with flower and foliage, and Norma is a proud plantswoman, meticulous as well as effusive. Rhon Rogers has a romantic idyll, picture-postcard front garden, but a more formal back, and is herself more formal in appearance. Yet her joy comes from propagating and nurturing – her plants replacing her now grown children.

Opposite: The white and yellow border by Clare's studio. On the wall are Rosa 'Iceberg' and R. 'Alberic Barbier'. Other plants in the border include oenothera (low yellow flowers near front) and eremurus (deep yellow spires). Behind are pale yellow digitalis and the silver leaves of cynara (top right).

CLARE BASSETT

Opening my garden for the first time this year was a pleasure as well as a strain. Actually, I was so filled to the brim with gardening that afterwards I felt I didn't want to go near it. So I spent about two weeks ignoring the garden and then was amazed when I turned round and looked at it and felt, 'Oh, my God, I've lost control!' Removing yourself from the garden is not satisfying, because you lose that connection with it. It is like when you come back from holiday and you look at it and think, 'This isn't mine any more! I haven't been following the process, so I have lost where I am in it.' Then because you have lost that connection, you don't want to know, and feel you can't deal with it. But then you do start again.

I have lived here about 12 years and my house is around 300 years old. When I arrived the garden was fairly basic – it was reasonably well kept, but it wasn't the owners' prime interest. It had the lawn, and several trees, and an 'orchardy' feel which was nice. We still have some of the trees, but several were on their last legs and died off and so we started to establish borders. I began with the one nearest to the house and planted lots of daffodils and snowdrops, and as that developed I thought, 'It's lovely having these yellows and whites together, so I'll use that as the basis of this border and keep it like that (with some silver and gold too), throughout the seasons.'

I planted a white 'Iceberg' rose to grow up the side of my studio, which I am lucky enough to have in the garden, and when I saw something like a yellow hemerocallis I put that in. I just played with those colours and now it always looks good throughout the year. That was what really got me going on the idea of colour in the garden. The border opposite, which is shady, was just a bank of nettles, so I

Clare's studio is in the middle of her garden so from her window she can see damson trees, buddleia and her husband's vegetable plot.

slowly dug them out, and extended the border two or three feet into the lawn. We dug up lots of flinty rock and stone, so my husband made a little dry wall, and we raised the bed up, giving that area a slightly different character. It is the least colour-coordinated part because it is governed by shade, so I have gone for shape, with things like fatsia and aruncus. The back of the garden is south facing and used to just have a privet hedge and, beyond that, a place for the cars. Now the border takes up the whole back part of the garden and I have used mainly blues, reds and pinks.

I think that being an artist, the prime thing about the garden is its visual impact. My main interest is not in knowing the botanics of the plants; it is more how they look together. A lot of it is hit and miss and experimentation. To start with I knew what looked nice, but not what worked, but gradually I have got to know what will grow well. Still, what strikes me when I walk into a garden is, 'Those shapes look good together. That upright looks good with that horizontal.' If someone said, 'Design a scented garden' I would be really bored. What is important to me is what it does to your *eyes*. I choose plants, like for example delphiniums, because they are tall and striking and the colours are strong but not brash; they are wonderful flowers. I like plants that make quite a statement.

It is lovely also, to have the studio as my

workplace in the garden, because I can nip out for half an hour here and there. To me gardening is leisure time. I enjoy creating a picture and the sensual feeling of the earth. I like standing back and seeing a new plant as it starts to take its place amongst the other flowers. I also like fiddling with it – moving things around (not always at the proper time). You sit and look at it and think, 'Something is not right.' And you hum and hah and then you think, 'I know, that shouldn't be there, and I need one of those!' So you dig up some poor little unsuspecting plant and move it and think, 'Yes, that's right!'

I get itchy fingers and feel I want it to be right – not so much right as opposed to wrong, but to feel comfortable. I want to feel relaxed when I look at the garden. I get very impatient and frustrated with myself when I can't figure out why it isn't hanging together, or why it looked better last season when I haven't altered anything. But maybe one plant is too big now and another too small, and the balance has gone. So it is a constant, ever-changing, organic process. You can't just sit back, like with a painting, and say it is finished.

Gardening is also a bit unpredictable; you can get wonderful surprises of plants that have self-seeded. I don't have a greenhouse and am not a propagator (like Rhon is). I am very cavalier about the real names of things although I feel I should know. And I don't feel the need to have one of everything or the newest variety. I also don't go by rules of drifts, or having three of a plant any more. You find your own compromise. I actually quite like having one 'spot' plant here and there, like a bright orange poppy. I have one little corner where I tried to plant every colour to see how it looked. Each year it is a bit different and some years it works better than others. Sometimes too, in say, July, a lot of things are going over, and the whole thing looks like a jumble of nothing much and you feel you need something strong to come up and distract from all the mess that is going on.

Working in the garden for me is an end in itself. I get satisfaction from that. And if I sit in the garden, I don't read a book; I look at the borders because that gives me pleasure. Every morning after I have got up, the first thing I do is walk round the garden to see what has come

Clare looks out and considers her garden. By her feet are the seed heads of wild, self-seeded poppies.

out and what it looks like today. But I can never just sit back and enjoy it as a given, because I know it constantly needs to be worked at – particularly if you are going to open it to the public. This year I had to make decisions about the garden and get on and do things I had put off before, which was satisfying. But it meant a lot more work and took a lot of hours. And you get slightly neurotic, worrying if anyone is going to notice all the little bits of bindweed that you have missed, and does it matter? But then 90 per cent of the people enjoy what they see, and I loved the day.

It is a bit like having an art exhibition. You do all this work, and you are the only person who has seen it. Then you put the work up on the wall and you suddenly see reactions from a third party, which is interesting, and gives confirmation of the things you like. People tend to respond the same way, whether with pictures or the garden. They say they liked the things I like and then make no comment about the things I am less sure of myself. One's own judgement is usually right. Then also, as with a painting, if someone sees other people looking and liking one particular plant, they will look at it too.

Keeping the garden nice is a bit easier now that my children are teenagers, but I have never been one to say, 'You can't play football in the garden,' so I have watched the prize rose have its head kicked off. And they had no sense of where their feet were, so if they lost a ball in the border, they would just walk straight through to get it. I did try to train them to look for the brown bits of earth between the green things! But since the children have grown we have dug a pond and I love sitting there. You dig a big hole and put a beautiful lining down and fill it up with water and it is just a puddle and I remember everyone saying, 'Give it a year, and it will all develop.' But I couldn't really believe it.

Anyway I bought some little irises and some oxygenating plants and it is one of those things that has been pure fascination to me. I have a little bench down there which I sit on in the evening and after a year the pond was heaving with life and plants. It is a wonderful little ecosystem, which is a real pleasure. You can watch the dragonflies and see the frogspawn and the little fish and it's lovely. So I would definitely have some water in my next garden. Another thing I would do in my next garden is to deal with the verticals first, and think not only about borders, but also about the backdrop. I am always curious to move on; every ten years or so I have started somewhere else. It is like a new project. I can imagine not having a garden, but then I would have a patio brimming with pots. I would always have something going on.

A lovely patch of pink, blues and whites. Towards the front are white *Geranium pratense f. albiflorum* (right) and blue *Anchusa* 'Loddon Royalist' (centre). Behind is pale pink *Linaria* 'Cannon J. Went'. Towards the back on the left are the small dark pink flowers of *Knautia macedonica*. Lilac-pink *Campanula lactiflora* 'Loddon Anne' (left) and blue delphiniums (right) add height as well as colour to the back of the border.

NORMA BIRD

Allegedly, this is the oldest house in the village, built of crook construction, somewhere between 1475 and 1525. We have lived here 16 years. Before that it was a weekend cottage with a high, extremely thick hedge, which hid the cottage from the front, and there was just grass with a forsythia tree in the centre at the back. Now it is so full that whenever I buy a new plant all the rest of the plants have to stand up straight and put their hands in their pockets so you can get the next one in! That's when you do the damage with your bum – backing out of the bed you might snap an alstromeria.

I think I have always gardened, even from the first flat that we had in London. My mother was from farming stock and certainly she knew the names of all the wild plants, and that became part of my year – knowing the may blossom, the snowdrops, the primroses and bluebells – and the excitement of finding them. Then I did a biology degree at university, which involved a lot of botany, and rather like bird 'twitchers', naming and finding wild flowers was my sort of stamp-collecting hobby. I still collect plants. I don't have a greenhouse, because I wouldn't want to waste the space, but I know a lot of very good plantsmen and nurserymen throughout the country and I will travel a long way to a new nursery. I get very excited with the anticipation of finding something that I don't know, which might grow in my garden, even though it seems so full already.

An obsessional side of me comes out, so that visiting a nursery is almost like a drug. There is a mixture of sometimes wanting a certain colour somewhere, and also a knowledge of what grows where. I like the garden to

Norma beside an informally packed border to the side of her house. From left to right are: blue/grey *Eryngium alpinum* 'Amethyst', lilac pink *Scabiosa graminifolia*, maroon *Allium shaerocephalon*. The white spires of *Epilobium angustifolium* complete the effect.

envelop me. I am not at all fussed about neatness and tidiness, although if you call it a garden, rather than just a botanical collection, there has to be a certain form and structure to it. The received information is that we have 'outside rooms' and I think that is where the idea of tidiness comes from. Like if someone comes to your house, you have got to be very tough to not care if there are some knickers in the middle of the dining-room floor!

My garden is too small to have separate rooms and is really just one room. But, like a room, I arrange the garden according to certain conventions. For instance, you wouldn't expect to open the door to a room and have the television facing you three feet away in the middle of the carpet. Also, I don't just think of plants on the floor like the carpet, I think of the garden as having walls, and pictures, which might be spotlit, so you look up in your room. Then you also have furniture, which has to be in proportion to the amount of space you have. As you go round a room, you see people's personality by their photographs and knick-knacks, and those are the individual plants. You can't have vistas in a small garden, so you have little desire lines, which the eye will follow. For instance, if you come in through the gate your eye will be drawn along by colour and height.

When I moved here to this house, we had one van of furniture and two with my plants from the other garden. If I left this garden now there would be three vans. After all, plants are jolly expensive and they are a passion – I couldn't leave them! Other people might have more ordinary plants like roses and delphiniums, which you can replace, but some of mine are really unusual. I don't recognize 'cottage plants' as a category. Traditionally cottagers would have hens in a coop, and maybe a pig and a beehive, and no way would I have that. I wouldn't have a town garden here, in as much as I have a wildlife pond but I wouldn't have a fountain, or metallic objects – and I do lean towards the romantic in my planting. If I had a mentor it would be Graham Stuart Thomas. Some people go to bed and read food recipes, I read books about plants, especially his. He had grown 90 per cent of what he wrote about, and if you had a small garden and just chose the plants that he gave stars to, you would do well. If you haven't a lot of space you want the *best* form of everything – the one which has perfume as well.

I could never grow vegetables, because just when they are ripening in this country, you are away on holiday. I don't mind leaving the plants, and I don't really mind if the odd thing dies, so I am not obsessional in that way, but nevertheless I could not imagine being without a garden. I asked a friend who is a painter, 'If you were on a desert island, and no one saw your work, would you still do it?' And my friend was unsure, because there is some-

The front garden, overflowing with densely tiered plants. Amongst them are blue *Triteleia laxa* (front), white *Gypsophila paniculata* 'Bristol Fairy' (bottom left), grey/blue *Amsonia salicifolia* (bottom right behind triteleia), red hot pokers *Kniphofia* 'Jenny Bloom' (a coral variety, middle left), peach *Alstromeria Ligtu* hybrids (middle right) and blue delphiniums at the back.

thing about art which needs to be shared. For me, gardening is not like that. I think if I was on a desert island I would still be out looking for plants and putting them close around my hut and putting them in combinations so that they pleased *me* as I walked out of the dwelling place. I like the colour, the form, the overall smell. Sometimes it is just a smell of green.

There is also the creative side to gardening, which is always a year away. Whatever you do now, you will have probably forgotten by spring and then you get a wonderful surprise when you see the hellebore you planted which looks so good next to something else. It is also very forgiving; you can do all sorts of things that are wrong but that can usually be put right. Lots of people think they are not going to like gardening, but in the end it drives them. And it is also a sort of solace. For me the wildlife in the garden touches on the naturalist in me. The plants satisfy the *collector* in me. And most people are collectors and are scientists if we weren't always told we weren't, and I have discovered, a little to my surprise, that we are all artists too.

One thing I don't use the garden for much is to sit down and read: yesterday afternoon was the first time this year that I have sat and read there. Whatever I am wearing or doing, and wherever I am going in the car, I always have a filthy thumb nail, because I am always twiddling. You have always got deadheader's thumb nail! There is that obsessional side to it. There is an excitement in going out there and seeing what is coming on – who's come out, who's done well this year, as well as the housework side, which can be boring. Sometimes I'll think, 'I'm just going to leave it now, and let it do.' And then you see that quite a nice phlox has just come out and something else is really taking up too much room, and you really ought to cut that down, and can you be bothered or not?

When people come round they often say, 'I could never do this because it is such a lot of work.' Then I say, 'They are all herbaceous perennials, so to me, that is not a lot of work compared to growing everything from seed each year. Also, the more densely it is planted, the less you notice the weeds. I do my weeding in February, when an hour is worth six in April in this part of the country. I also put six inches of manure on then, so I don't have to water so much later, and the rest is tweaking and twiddling.' Then that person I have been talking to might go round to Clare, who has worked so hard opening her garden for the first time this year, and they might hear someone say to her, 'It is a lot of work, isn't it?' and they will say, 'Oh no! these are herbaceous perennial plants. They're not much work at all.' And poor Clare will be upset, because of course it is hard, really.

My aim, I suppose, is to get to a point where I don't have to do any more and it will all be perfect – whatever that means. Meanwhile I think to myself, 'There is a little hole there at the back; I wonder what shrub I could get in there that would go between those other two plants?' So there probably never will be an end to it. There are always things I *must* have, and if you are organized, and know when something will be cut back, and where something else will come, you can find the spaces.

I know where everything is because it is all on a database! I have spreadsheets, and call the beds A, B, C and so on, and then there is back, middle and front. I list each plant alphabetically under the Latin name, with its position, height, colour and form (whether it

Norma smells a buddleia and enfolds other of her favourite flowers: pink pelar-goniums, yellow *Kniphofia* 'Little Maid' and orange *Potentilla* 'Gloire de Nancy'.

is a double variety or whatever). Then I divide the year into weeks so I can put the time it starts to come out as week 15 or whatever, and bloom end when I would cut the plant down. So I know what should be out in any week, in what height and colour, in any of the beds. It also helps me to know if something has died, and where I can put something else.

My husband, Richard, will say, 'But you've already got loads of pink flowers, why do you want another one?' He doesn't quite understand the 'must have' nature of it. He never goes in the garden! He cuts the grass, bless him, but that's it. I made the pond and laid the patio myself, but I like acquiring new skills –

the garden fulfils so much. Whatever horrid things are happening, I can get pleasure from growing plants. One of my biggest scary nightmares is that something happens where I have to go to hospital for two months. There are two problems: I would come out grey, because I dye my hair; and there would be nothing left of my garden and it would be covered in convolvulus. I don't know which would be worse! But it makes you realize the ephemeral nature of it all. Within a very few months it would be lost – which is perhaps all right.

Richard's father's ashes and my father's and my mother's ashes are all in the garden. It may sound morbid to some, but it is quite a nice feeling. I don't have any supernatural beliefs, but rather than having a grave up north somewhere that you can never get to, it is better that they are here. My mother's birthday was 1 March; her favourite flowers were daffodils, and so she is where they are, in that bit of the front bed, and I think of Mum there. My father was July, so he is with the hot July things, and Richard's father was May, and his mum is 94 and she knows she's coming here as well! She is a flamboyant personality and she wants to be in the centre of the front bed.

I am not sentimental about where I am buried. Someone else will own the garden then, and probably wouldn't like it at all if they had to have my ashes here, but I don't mind. I don't have any feelings of possessiveness about the garden when I am not here – that it *must* go on. It is like the house: you feel you are a caretaker for a while, and leave your impression on it and then the next people come and look after it and do their own thing. You get used to the fact that things are always changing in gardening – that is the whole nature of it. It is a delight.

RHON ROGERS

To start with this garden was really a play space for my children, with dens and a climbing frame in it. Now it is a place I look at, and relax in. Gardening enables me to cut off from my day-to-day work, which is pressured, as a schools' advisor with the local education authority. Some people come to decisions in baths: I very often think more clearly in the garden, when I am sowing seeds or pricking out. So it is therapeutic for me. I also *love* watching seedlings grow. In January, when I am planting in the propagator, I will come down first thing in the morning and lift the top off the propagator, and that elation when you see the germination is extraordinary. The seedlings are like my babies, and the devastation if they 'damp off' is like bereavement!

There is definitely a maternal aspect to gardening for me. Actually, almost all the keen gardeners in Blewbury are women. It might be because of the 'cottagey' nature of most of the gardens. I think most men take to the harder-edged part of gardening – they seem to like straight lines, so they are good with lawns and hedges. My husband loves building and creating, and something like digging a pond and lining it gives him satisfaction. To my mind, there are usually two kinds of men gardeners: the ones that focus on plants, who seem to have quite a feminine side to them, like, say, Christopher Lloyd; and those more interested in the whole design element, like, say, Diarmuid Gavin. I cannot relate to Diarmuid Gavin. Although I can appreciate what he does, I could not live with one of his gardens.

I have lived in this house for 15 years, and when we arrived the large beech trees and a couple of shrubs were here. Other than that there was one border filled with Hybrid Tea roses, which were just brown sticks most of the year; a thin bed of petunias; and a small vegetable patch beyond the greenhouse. It has

One of Rhon's greatest joys is seeing the first signs of germination. Here she smiles at a Salvia argentea *amongst some of the other plants she propagates, such as digitalis, aquilegia, nicotiana and verbascum.*

Rhon's charmingly picturesque front garden. White Rosa *'Alberic Barbier', pink* Rosa *'Albertine' and* Clematis viticella *'Etoile Violette' grow against the house, while the rest of the garden includes* Campanula persicifolia *(on left by the gate) with* Centrantus ruber *'Albus' behind. On the right is a clipped mound of* Buxus sempervirens *with pink* Phlomis italica *behind.*

undergone a big change. I put in the plants I want to grow – bulbs, perennials and annuals – and then saw how I could put them together in arrangements that pleased me aesthetically. My background as a *young* person was art, and although I have long given up painting, I have found that putting colours together in plants gives me the same satisfaction that I used to get 30 years ago from painting.

I only started gardening more seriously about eight years ago, when I could get rid of climbing frames and have ponds instead of paddling pools. At that point putting colours together was really using pastels, because they were easy on the eye and easy to blend to give a kind of haze or shimmer, which I like. Then I moved into putting yellows with certain mauves and lilacs to bring them alive and heighten them, and gradually I got braver and braver with colours. I was inspired by Christopher Lloyd's writing and the red border at Hidcote, and I created a little red area here, which is at its best in late August. I also started to like some apricoty colours, and slowly began to let orange into the garden, which I thought I would never, ever do! So as I have got older I have used colours that not only blend and match, but also ones which compliment each other, and that zing. Eight years ago I would have probably told you they clashed, but now they seem to sing against each other.

One of my challenges here was to create a pond area in the dry shady place under the beech trees where the children's den had been. I have managed to put plants like sedges, which actually look as though they belong in a woodland or wet area, but which will survive in dry shade. Early spring bulbs do quite well too, before the leaves are out on the trees. I

Near the back of the house are some hotter colours. Here *Lilium* 'Red Velvet' is planted in a pot (front right) by the grass *Stipa tenuissima*. Behind are self-sown *Papaver* 'Mother of Pearl' and the tall seed heads of nectaroscordum, while the tree to the right is *Acer palmatum* 'Bloodgood'.

like a mix of plants in the garden, and that is where my seed sowing comes in. In January I sow annuals like *Salvia* 'Coral Nymph' and *Nicotiana langsdorfii*, or things like gaura, which you may lose in the winter. Then later, in June and July, I sow my biennials, like foxgloves, as well as some perennials to go into the beds in the autumn.

Generally, I am not obsessive about collecting particular new varieties, or *having* to have something immediately. You do meet people who collect plants almost in the same way as they would collect something in the house. For me the garden is more part of a whole. Occasionally I will put something in and then have to take it out again because there wasn't really enough room, and the plant will have to be rejuvenated in what I call my little 'hospital bed' down near the patio.

I can't imagine life without a garden. I could have done as a young person living in town, and for a while later a garden was just for sunbathing in. But once I started fiddling around a bit with gardens, the passion developed. My mother was a very good gardener and I realize that I learnt an awful lot from her. I hadn't been interested as a child, and yet I knew how to take a cutting without looking it up in a book, and knew what depth to plant individual seeds at. I must have just learnt by listening to my mother, and my grandmother was a good gardener too, so I suppose it is now in my genes. If I didn't have a garden I would be like my mother now – she is not able to move, and misses her garden passionately. I think she misses that more than being able to watch television or read a book. You can at least have an audio book, but there is no real substitute for gardening.

I only like to be away from my garden for a week. Phil, my husband, always wants to go away for longer, but I never do. On around the sixth day I start to get itchy and need to know what is going on in my garden. I let someone else water, but I wouldn't let anyone else garden. You see, I know where everything is and I also allow a lot of self-seeding, and I am not convinced that someone else would know what a treasured young plant looks like, and they might pull it up. Even now, I'll come back and find that too much water has been put on my seedlings and they have all floated off to one side of the pot, but you have to accept those sorts of things.

When I *am* away, I love looking at other people's gardens and hate to go on conferences where I can't get out to the nearest garden. For instance, I went to one in Gloucestershire recently, very near Hidcote, and I couldn't get out, but could see the sign for Hidcote! Once I went on an inspection a whole day early so I could go to Rosemoor. Knowing that visiting gardens is a pleasure is one of the reasons I open my garden. And because I work full time, I can't really do any voluntary work, and gardening is something I do anyway, and by opening for charity I can give something back. Most people are really interested in the plants and are great. I have never caught anybody taking any cuttings or anything. Sometimes people ask for a little seedling, and that is fine. Actually, not many of my best friends are gardeners with the sort of passion that I have, and so it is nice to meet people coming into your garden and talking plants!

One interesting and irritating thing that visitors sometimes do, though, is to try to exploit some element of competition in the

A rare chance to relax for Rhon, sitting on the small paved patio beside the back of her house.

gardens. So they will say to an owner of one that they like that garden better than the others. But that is not what we are about. We are open for charity, for the 'Yellow Book' scheme, and we are all individual. In fact we try to help each other and after the open day we usually all go out for a meal together. I would be upset if the garden wasn't looking as good as it could have done, but I also have a full-time job so I haven't got the time to worry about it in the build-up time. We are not competitive and we all like each other's gardens, though we all come at it from slightly different angles. Like, I suppose, Norma comes from her botanical, scientific background and knows a tremendous amount about, for instance, why plants are chlorotic, whereas I just think, 'Oh, it's gone yellow!'

What I enjoy best about gardening is the growing part of it. And I love all seasons. There is nothing that compares with the first snowdrops and aconites of the year. Then my heart lifts when the alliums come out, and I also enjoy the autumn with the redness that comes from things like dahlias. This is not an easy garden, because it is up off the road and very dry, and it devours compost. That is Phil's part. Once we went on a garden tour of Dublin and we were in the Dillon garden, and Helen herself was showing us round, and there was no sign of Phil, or of her husband Val either. They were later found discussing compost! While we were looking at the *wonderful* plants, they were behind the house looking at the compost heaps. But it is a really important part that Phil plays here, because without his compost, I couldn't grow the sorts of plants I grow.

Some things will grow almost anywhere, like Miss Willmott's ghost, in the front garden. There was a notable, English gardener called Ellen Willmott [1858-1934] who thought that every garden should have the silvery-blue plant called *Eryngium gigantium*. She used to go round with a pocketful of seeds and sprinkle them into other people's gardens, unbeknown to the owners. Then after she had gone the ghost of Miss Willmott appeared, and once you have got one, you will have it forever. The spiny plant was said to match her personality, and it is still known today as Miss Willmott's ghost! But not everything is so easy to grow, and one of the things I don't subscribe to is that you *have* to grow plants to suit your conditions. You can change your conditions.

You know how people with curly hair want straight hair, and vice versa? Well, people with chalk soil want to grow acid plants. So what I have done in a couple of places in the garden, again, with Phil's help, is to change the conditions. In one case I sank a bath into the grass and filled it with lots of drainage and ericaceous compost and then I was able to grow *Tropaeolum speciosum* [nasturtium] up the big hedge. In another place I wanted to grow some shade-loving but acid-loving plants, and we dug out a small, very deep area, and again put in drainage and ericaceous compost. So you can create little different areas in your garden. We have a scree; the hot area; an apricot one; a cool space along by the shed; a pond; a ferny area; dry shade; and a little tapestry area with jewel-like dark blue and dark red plants. I enjoy all the different parts, but the best thing of all is seeing plants happy!

3

SARAH COOK

HEAD GARDENER AT SISSINGHURST

A view of the orchard from the top of the tower in which Vita Sackville-West had her study.

'Such was that happy Garden-state'

The famous writer and gardener Vita Sackville-West and her husband, Harold Nicholson, who was a designer as well as a diplomat, made Sissinghurst Castle Garden in Kent when they moved there in 1932. Their son, Nigel Nicholson, who still lives there, tellingly describes the garden overall as 'a portrait of a marriage' and its individual parts as 'a series of intimacies.'

With its romantic setting and atmosphere, its combination of informal planting within a formal framework, its 'garden rooms' and its white garden, Sissinghurst is one of the most copied flower gardens in the world. Now the property of the National Trust, the inspiration which made the garden lives on through the talents and skills of succeeding head gardeners – in particular, Pam Schwerdt and Sibylle Kreutzberger and, since 1991, Sarah Cook.

Sarah is full of enthusiasm, modest and funny. Her joy in her work is evident in all she says; she uses 'we' rather than 'I' and talks of the gardeners who work with, rather than under, her. She joked that she must have been drunk when she agreed to be interviewed, and when I mentioned taking some photographs, suggested, 'Maybe you could just have my eyes peeking out from behind a bush with a caption "Spot the shy gardener".'

I always liked gardening, from the time that I had my own little plot of garden as a child. Later I did all sorts of things, but in the mid '70s, I decided I really would like to be a gardener and I worked on a private estate for three years, which confirmed that this really was the career for me. Next, very luckily, I got a job at Kew Gardens, not as a student, but as a gardener. At that time, and probably still now, Kew was very good for training staff as well as students. I did day-release City and Guilds for a year and then did what is now the M. Hort., so I was able to get qualified whilst working there.

I stayed four years at Kew, working in the alpine and herbaceous department. I was interested in hardy herbaceous plants that grow in England rather than in tropical plants which grow in greenhouses, and I liked the outdoor aspect of gardening which I found very appealing. After Kew I came to Sissinghurst for four years, working with the previous two head gardeners [Pam Schwerdt and Sibylle Kreutzberger], and then I went to Upton House as head gardener for just under three years, and then I came back here as head gardener when Pam and Sibylle retired.

Sissinghurst is a twentieth-century garden on a scale with which lots of people can identify, particularly because it is designed in rooms. It's a garden with which people can actually engage; and I would also call it a great work of art. With any garden you can look at the whole picture, or the plants, or the structure, but at Sissinghurst the whole is more than the sum of the parts. One of the really good things about it is that the garden rooms have got different characters and feelings, and also Vita aimed to make different parts of the garden perform best in different seasons, so

Sarah writing notes about what could make a good plant association with the dark crimson *Rosa* 'Baron Girod de L'ain', a repeat-flowering Old Rose.

you need the whole for year-round interest. Vita worked really hard at this, and I feel that having bits of your garden coming into prominence and going again over the year is something that a lot of people could learn from.

Gardening this way you are putting plants together that really make good neighbours, because you are not dotting bits of colour all over the garden for the whole year. We are keeping this up: we have read and, I hope, analysed what Vita and Harold were doing here, and although we put our own interpretation on to that, we want to keep the garden feeling mid-20th century. We try to make sure we don't follow fashion. It would be very easy at the moment to put in loads of grasses or make the cottage garden into a tropical garden, which is not the feel it should have at all. The cottage garden does have a lot of reds and hot colours and it could look terribly modern but we really try to make sure it is of the right period although we do use new and modern plants. Vita was very much a *gardener*, so we want to carry on gardening it in that sort of style, and that definitely involves experimenting and keeping the thing moving.

I think if you tried to keep the garden as a museum piece you would lose the meaning of it. So we feel very strongly that gardening is as important as the end result. It isn't important to be a woman gardener because it is both Vita and Harold's legacies which are important. In fact if you look at the garden, Harold Nicholson had the most lasting part, because he designed the really strong structure with the vistas and the walkways. Our aim is to keep it in the style of Vita and Harold; we don't ever think one or the other. It is the two together which make it great, and the tension between the two characters – her romantic side with the overflowing flowerbeds, and his classical side with the vistas and straight edges.

People sometimes say, 'Oh, the hedges are cut far too straight and are far too manicured,' but in fact that is how it should be, because they planned it to have this contrast. Some people remember the garden from the '50s when Vita and Harold were getting quite elderly and the hedges had 'gone' a bit and the whole place was romantic, and you didn't get the romantic/classic contrast. Pam and Sybille had a programme of cutting all the yew hedges back and replanting some of the box hedges so that the structure was crisp again. That is actually frightfully important to the design of it.

We look at all the bits of style that are Sissinghurst: the classic versus romantic; the seasonality; the old-fashioned roses, with their muted colours, which are terribly important because Vita loved them; and the hot colours in the cottage garden. So we work within quite strict rules, which we wouldn't change. Some people ask if I would like to do whatever I wanted, but unfortunately I am not a rich landowner, so I have to be an employee. I think people get muddled up between employed gardeners and garden owners. I can't afford not to have a job, and I have a job that I *love*.

I don't have my own garden because I don't have time, and I find plenty in this garden to keep me absolutely thrilled day-in, day-out. For instance, if you are working within this strict regulation, you have to be really aware of what is going on in the gardening world about you, so you don't follow

The bed to the south of the rose arbour in the White Garden contains some wonderfully harmonious planting. At the back the statue of the little virgin stands beneath a weeping silver pear echoing the silver leaves of *Stachys olympica* in front.

fashion by mistake. So there is loads of interest to be had from it, and really growing plants is such fun anyway, that it is not as restrictive as you might think. I don't ever feel the temptation to plant something absolutely unsuitable somewhere! I do sometimes think, 'That would make a nice combination if I had my own garden, although it wouldn't work *here*.' So I store up ideas for the future, but really, as an employed gardener, I've got a smashing job.

Trying new plants and new combinations – all things that Vita used to do – is thrilling. Lex, [Alexis Datta] the assistant head gardener, and I work together, massively, on the planting. Much as Pam and Sibylle used to do, or, probably, Vita and Harold, we wander around with bits of plants, and say to each other, 'Shall we put it there?' or 'This bit of the garden doesn't look nice, how shall we make it better?' So we are still two people sparking ideas off each other, and having robust discussion, and it makes it so much more interesting and part of the enjoyment.

When Lex and I first took over from Pam and Sibylle, we said, 'Well, it will take us five years to ruin it!' This was in 1991, and we felt after the first five years that we certainly hadn't ruined it, so we were pretty pleased about that, because it was a jolly hard act to follow. I think we have developed and changed things and brought them on, but maybe we feel particularly proud of trying to get beneath the skin of the place and doing it within that. Keeping it lively and interesting is what we are aiming at, and I would like to think we've done it. Some people, of course, think we haven't – that we have made a disaster of it – but we are fairly happy with most of what we have done. And in the nature of gardening, you are never happy with all of it. It is part of the fun, thinking, 'Well that didn't quite work, let's change it', and it is good thinking about why a plant didn't grow very well somewhere, and finding out why, and trying it somewhere else, say, against a wall.

The different buildings of Sissinghurst add a lovely setting for the garden. Vita and Harold saw the garden as a man-made work of art within the traditional Kent countryside, so the farm and the countryside, which surround the garden, are as important to the garden as having the correct frame on a picture. We have got woods and wildlife, and I get great pleasure from driving down the drive and

One of the things Sarah enjoys about her job is constantly looking to see which plants might work well together. Here she considers *Campanula* 'Hidcote Amethyst' with *Allium cristophii*. Whilst she was holding the campanula, a member of the public told her off for picking the flower.

The most renowned part of Sissinghurst is the White Garden. Here the tower is seen through a veil of *Crambe cordifolia* with the contrasting large sensual flowers of *Paeonia* 'Duchesse de Nemours' below.

seeing the sunlight on the bricks and knowing that it is a nice estate. We also have a tower here from which you see the garden in its frame and get a strong idea of the design, which is fabulous. Pam and Sibylle worked really hard to make sure that the car park was hidden from the top of the tower.

I think that some very flat gardens, where you don't get an overview, can be a bit claustrophobic, but the spaciousness of the top and the lower courtyard here, before you go into the intimate bits, gives you a sense of space, which I think is a good design principle – not enclosing people too quickly. Another really good thing about Sissinghurst, which you don't get in many gardens open to the public, is that you actually go in through the front door. With gardens which have one house as their main access, you don't usually go in the way it was designed. And I think, even if you are just going round your own garden, it is quite important to take your friends round the right way.

At Sissinghurst you progress from one area to another and see the differences. Many people, particularly in spring, try to have a patch of colour from, say, tulips, in each part of their garden and that really does look dotty, as in spotty; whereas the lime walk in Sissinghurst is just an eyeful of knockout. So I might advise people, particularly with spring things, to corral them together. I love all the seasons. August is the quiet time in the garden here because when it was designed, Vita and Harold used to go cruising in August, and other people with similar gardens would go shooting. So August is my least favourite time in the garden and it is always hot and dry then, too.

There are no jobs in the garden that I dislike. I really like going down drains – when there is all that water glugging away, and then you let the water out and the beds are really wet and you have some good fun then! But my really favourite job is wandering round with Lex deciding where to put the plants for the following year, or which bits to change. I also love pruning the roses. But I have to say, I even like raking leaves, because you are always looking around to see what is going on around you! And it is nice talking gardening with the people who visit. Or you might be forking a border, and although you are making sure not to fork out your rarities, you are also looking at the bed thinking, 'Wouldn't that look nice *there*.' I like the fact that the actual mechanics of gardening give you plenty of time to do the thinking and the planning.

We obviously buy new plants, but then we bulk them up for the garden here, and there are quite extensive greenhouse facilities behind the scenes. That gives us some jobs to do in the wet weather. Another brilliant thing which Pam and Sibylle started was they planted over an acre of hazel coppice. Every year we coppice about a fifth of it so we have a constant supply of lovely pea sticks for staking our plants. For anyone with a large garden, I would suggest that they keep about six hazel bushes in a part of it, and you could cut one down to ground level each year in rotation. Grass doesn't grow very strongly under hazel, but in Upton House, where I worked before, they had a lovely spring bank with little daffodils and oxlips and cowslips growing under hazel in a kind of naturalized area. You wouldn't get any nuts, because you need older wood, but you would get a jolly good crop of pea sticks.

When I reach retirement age I shall certainly have my own garden. I can't imagine not gardening, having done it all my life. We try to encourage the next generation of gardeners by giving all children who come here a packet of seeds. I would encourage everybody to give their children their own little bit of garden – although they shouldn't turn them into professional gardeners if they want to be looked after in their old age; they would be better off making their children accountants or solicitors! But for me, having a bit of a hand in the history of this garden is a great honour, really. I am also working somewhere that I love. And enough other people like the garden for me to feel jolly pleased to be working here. We didn't design it, but we are really lucky to work somewhere that was designed, and works, so well.

A backdrop of brick wall and leaded windows, with an overflowing, unevenly banked border of purple flowers, is quintessential Sissinghurst. In the foreground is *Clematis* x *durandii*, behind it *Delphinium* 'Black Knight' and on the wall the Bourbon rose, 'Madame Isaac Pereire'.

4

DAVID DORWARD

EDINBURGH CLOCK GARDENER

It is only the clock face and motif that have a prescribed design. The remainder of the space is up to David to fill.

'How well the skilful Gardner drew Of flow'rs and herbes this Dial new'

David Dorward is smiley, kind and gentle. He chose to be called the Edinburgh Clock Gardener, although in fact he works for the council and has many duties, but it is the planting and maintenance of the famous floral clock in Princes Street Gardens which affords him the most pride and pleasure. The clock is a horticultural extravaganza: a working timepiece, made of plants, set on a hillside, beside the flight of steps at the Mound entrance. With Scotland's climate, the clock is only there in the summer months and has to be replanted every spring, taking three gardeners four weeks.

The clock was built by James Ritchie & Son (Clockmakers) Ltd., and is the oldest floral clock in the world. In 2003 it celebrated its centenary, and a replica was shown for the first time at Chelsea Flower Show. In Edinburgh, the date for completion was 10 June, which proved a tough deadline, but it was met on time. Since 1973 the hands have been driven by an electrical mechanism and a mechanical cuckoo now marks the hours and quarters. The clock has a different design each year (usually publicizing organizations or events, such as the founding of the Royal National Lifeboat Institute or the Golden Jubilee), but it is always made up entirely of carpet-bedding plants – over 30,000 of them!

Of course, carpet bedding is not to everyone's taste. Artist William Morris described this mode of planting in 1882 as 'an aberration of the human mind' and continued, 'When I think of it even when I am quite alone I blush with shame at the thought.' However, if one is a devotee, then the Edinburgh clock is one of the finest examples. The dial is three and a half metres (11 feet 10 inches) in diameter. The hands are covered in plants too. Fully planted, the minute hand weighs 36 kilogrammes (80 pounds), and the hour hand weighs 23 kilogrammes (50 pounds). The central portion of the clock face is planted and grown in wire baskets, which are then placed in position, and more flowers are planted around and clipped to the required height and shape. It is a painstaking job, which, to avoid crushing any flowers, must be accomplished from long ladders stretching across the whole face of the clock. I visited David at the end of May 2003, when planting was near completion and the hands were due to be placed on the spindle.

Opposite: This is the world's first floral clock – it began ticking on 10 June 1903 with an hour hand only. Planting is a very painstaking job, involving the use of long ladders to avoid crushing any plants.

WHY WE GARDEN | David Dorward

I am the charge-hand gardener, which is like the foreman, and I have nine permanent staff who I am responsible for, and four seasonal staff, and any trainees from government schemes such as the long-term unemployed. I have been with the council since 1978, man and boy! I used to help my dad in my granny's garden and my interest came from that. I left school at 16 and, in those days we got sent to college to do a four-year apprenticeship, so I did a City and Guilds course in Fife. After college, in 1982, I got assigned to Princes Street Gardens, and I have been here ever since. There were various grades and I started as a craftsman gardener, being given specific tasks, with an assistant gardener and gardener under me.

But even during my apprenticeship in the early '80s I had begun to assist with the clock. We were sent to different places throughout the council: there was a tree and shrub nursery, glass houses, and bedding plant and cut flower production at the Inch nursery, which is where our main nursery is now. We were also sent to golf courses, sports facilities, and the forestry department, to give us a sounding in horticulture and some idea of what field we would like to be in. I quite enjoyed plant production, but due to cost cutting the nurseries around Edinburgh were closing and getting centralized, and the people who had worked in the other nurseries got the chance to go to the new one. This meant there was no opportunity for me to be placed there, so, fortunately, they were looking for someone to come here at the time, and I was able to get the place.

To start with, when I helped with the clock I would just break up the plants ready for Jimmy Ford, the gardener at the time, to plant. When I had got my confidence in that, he would maybe give me another little task to do so that my confidence increased. It is so different from just getting a tray of plants and putting them in the ground. But even then there was a great satisfaction in helping with the clock, and over the years it became easier, and you began to understand the bigger picture instead of just concentrating on one small bit you were doing; you could see it

Planting takes three members of staff four weeks and involves the use of 35,000 carpet bedding plants. These are grown at Inch nursery and brought to the clock site as tiny 'plug' plants. Here David takes out a *Pyrethrum* 'Golden Moss' ready for planting.

develop in your mind in front of you. Also the interest of the people of Edinburgh, who walk through the gardens every day, and who like to see the progress of the clock day-by-day, make you realize it is something special.

Jimmy Ford would have known that I had a certain aptitude for it and enjoyed it, before he retired. Now I have been in charge of the clock, on my own, for the last six years, and I have faced several challenges. Every year is different, celebrating a different anniversary, and a design comes down from the office – last year a royal coat of arms – which can be very difficult to do. All I receive is a black and white drawing, so I decide on the plants, the colours, everything. You have a continuous stock of plants at Inch nursery, which are your palette of paints.

When the frost comes in October, the clock goes back to the nursery and the guys there break it all up and put the plants back into individual cells in trays, and they are kept frost-free over the winter, until it is time for me to use them again in the spring. Many of the plants are used again or divided up and propagated. The clock face itself is the same every year – we can't change the numbers – but the top and bottom lettering and the dates and the badge are all different. Societies submit an idea, and if it is accepted it goes ahead, but they don't sponsor the clock in any way. A coat of arms will have a certain set of colours in it, and we choose the plants as best we can to correspond with those colours, bearing in mind that we need plants that are compact and don't grow too tall. It can be quite difficult, but we can't spray-paint the plants!

The main plant we use is *Pyrethrum* 'Golden Moss', which gives us the letters and numbers. 'Golden Moss' is quite labour-intensive because it needs trimming every 10 to 14 days to define the shape, whether it be an outline of a motif or the numerals on the clock. We also usually use lobelia, sempervivum, echeveria and sedum. When the clock started in 1903 all the plants were put directly into the ground at the site, but management decided that to save time, it would be better to plant baskets at the nursery and transfer the baskets into the gardens. So now we go to the nursery and do the planting there, which takes about two weeks, and then bring the baskets back. Then we hollow out the surface of the soil to create a saucer shape, which is also a precision job, so the baskets sit exactly correctly and the gaps between them are equidistant all the way round. All this, because of the slope of the site, is done whilst balancing on a ladder! But it is only the actual clock that is done with baskets; the rest is planted directly into the ground.

There are so many baskets involved, and so many joins in the baskets, that if you have something with a lot of detail, inevitably the design will cross over the baskets and it is just as easy to do it directly into the ground. It would be nice to have a free hand and do a design myself, but we do have a certain scope. We have the clock and a motif, but what we have in between is up to us. Last year's clock, for the Jubilee, turned out really well. Every year you learn a little bit more and can refine your skills, and the one at Chelsea this year was exceptional, I thought.

To do this job, patience is definitely needed, and also a vision of what is going to be there at the end of it all, when you are looking at a bare bit of soil. Every plant needs to be in exactly its right place, which is why it is different from normal bedding. Last year, because the badge was so detailed, I made a grid on the ground with strings, and drew each part freehand on the ground before I planted it.

It takes about four weeks to plant the whole site, and then it needs maintaining every day. Apart from the clipping, we water the clock by hand, with a hose with a fine rose, or with a watering can. We looked at irrigation systems, because we had a new irrigation system in the gardens last year. The clock mechanism is all sealed up in a box under ground so it is unaffected by water or anything. But the problem was how to water the hands, and also the flow of water coming out could be quite damaging to some of the plants. Because there are so many plants in a small area, they need water, but then the succulents don't like too much, so there is a fine line to keep it ticking over!

As the clock is such a tourist attraction, we can only really be there from 8 a.m. until midday, because people get upset if there are ladders there when they want to get a photograph! The ladders are quite easy to manage – in all my years I have never seen anyone fall off the ladder and into the plants. I think the clock is positioned as it is on this site because, if it was laid flat, you couldn't appreciate the work. But the hands are difficult to put on because they are very heavy, and it takes four men. Lead weights are used to counterbalance the minute hand: it is two and a half metres long and has to sit evenly.

The plants are lovely to work with, because when there is a sprinkling of rain, or a drop of water on them, the colours seem to me to intensify. There is a satisfaction at the end of the day when you have done a section, and you stand back and look at it and feel, 'We're getting there!' I have a love for the job,

and the public interest in it is tremendous, too. Although when people see me working, they often ask, 'Where's the Castle?' or 'Where's the nearest toilet?' But this year, because of Chelsea and coverage in the papers and on TV, people say, 'Oh, is this the one that was at Chelsea?' and they ask about the plants, and how long it takes to do the job.

Sometimes, if people have seen pictures of the clock, they imagine it differently. Last year a Texan came up to me when I was working overtime on a Saturday, and he asked [David puts on a very good Texan accent], 'Where can I find a flower clock?' and I answered, 'You've found it; it's just here!' But he countered, 'No, no. You don't understand. It's on a hill. It's on a hill with a castle.' So I said, 'Look, there's the Castle up there.' But he insisted, 'No, no, no. It was *big*.' Then I asked the gentleman to come round and have a look, which he did, and said, 'No, no, no – *that's* not it!' And off he went.

So sometimes working at the clock can be a sanctuary from the rest of the gardens, and sometimes it isn't! Actually, there is nothing better than working at home, in your own little garden away from it all, with no public pestering you. In my garden the front is mostly lawn, and the back is lawn with heathers and conifers. On one side I have a rose bed and I also have a water feature. I don't have carpet bedding at home, but people could try it out in their gardens if they found a nice design that was not too complicated. Then you would need to mark out the ground to scale and be careful of the heights and colours of the plants. But largely this sort of thing is done as municipal planting. Weston super-Mare, Eastbourne and Blackpool used to have carpet bedding in their public parks, but because of

WHY WE GARDEN | Derek Hosie

The Edinburgh clock is positioned on a hill, beside the flight of steps at the Mound entrance of Princes Street Gardens. The castle looms dramatically behind. The mechanism for the clock is housed in the base of the Alan Ramsay monument (right). No plant can grow too big, and all must be of the same height, requiring frequent clipping – done with shears.

At the end of the year, I am sad to see the clock go away. While it is here, I wake up wondering if it is still working and hoping there has been no vandalism. Once the clock is up and running and the hands are on and the cuckoo is fully functional, people like to take a souvenir home with them! So they will maybe make for the cuckoo and try to pull it out of its box, but inevitably they will walk over the clock to get there, so there can be quite a bit of damage. Or they try to change the time and spin the hands around. Now we've got a new mechanism, with a slipping clutch, so that if the hands are spun there is no actual damage done.

It goes in phases: sometimes there is no vandalism at all, and then there will be two or three nights in one week where something will happen. Then it can be a bit soul-destroying. But there is always stock in the nursery to replace the plants if necessary. We increase the stock all the time, because we also get other local authorities asking if we can supply them with plants, and from year to year we never know what the motif is going to be. There is always a challenge.

I certainly enjoy doing the floral clock; I think it is a great honour to be doing it. I could see myself doing it full-time. If someone came up with the money, and said, 'Come away with me, and we'll just do clocks and carpet bedding', I would be quite happy to do that. But actually our duties are wide and varied here. Unfortunately we have to control the litter as well, so we have to empty the litter baskets and sweep the paths. That is our first priority in the morning, and it can take a lot of time, particularly during the Festival. Because of all the fast-food chains around, obviously on a nice day people want to come

the economic climate nowadays it is just not viable for them to have a dedicated squad of men doing it. They would rather have things like geraniums and marigolds, which require a minimum of maintenance and are quick to throw out afterwards.

out and enjoy the gardens, but they leave all their litter behind, which is quite a problem. We also have to do grass-cutting, maintenance of the rose beds and other summer and spring bedding.

A lot of major events are held in the gardens as well, such as Hogmanay, and Winter Wonderland in the East Gardens, which can be quite damaging to the gardens. I think of this place as my own back garden in some ways, and that is why it upsets me when they have events here and it gets damaged. I can't quite understand why people do that and I wish the council were more sympathetic towards the gardens. The trouble is that it is such a marvellous setting. I don't think there is anywhere else in the world where you have something like this in your city centre, with the Castle there. But it was good for the morale to go down to Chelsea this year and have so many people show an interest in the clock. The people were so nice, and we were so well received. Let's hope it goes as well here. Touch wood, we've had no disasters as yet.

Next day I returned to Princes Street and found David looking worried, but he patiently explained the situation.

It's going wrong because I said there were never any problems! We got the clock hands pre-planted, except for two small spaces for handling, and gingerly lifted them into position as usual. We had two ladders suspended over the clock face and we positioned both hands on the spindle in the centre. But the hands did not engage! The clockmaker from Ritchie & Co. duly arrived but still the minute hand swung round freely, despite all his efforts, and we could not get the clock to work.

Then I had to loosen the nuts and we had to lift the hands off again. Now the gearbox, which is only three years old, may have to be removed, which would mean lifting out the central baskets of flowers! It will be difficult, as the clock is planted from the centre out, and it is virtually complete all round now. This has never happened before. With hindsight, we should check the mechanism each year before planting. The timetable will be very tight now, but I hope all will be well. A double whisky might be in order tonight!

Few people would be aware of David's problems, as the floral clock was working and perfect on the appointed day.

An electrically driven mechanism was introduced to the clock in 1973. For 100 years the clock has been maintained by James Ritchie & Sons, Edinburgh Clockmakers. Here, very unusually, Derek is joined by his assistant (top) and a representative from James Ritchie & Sons (bottom) to remove the hands in order to get the clock working.

5

DEREK HOSIE

HEAD GARDENER AT CAWDOR CASTLE

A laburnum tunnel borders the stepped holly maze, which was planted in 1981, when Derek first arrived to work at Cawdor Castle, seen in the background here.

'Where from above the milder Sun Does through a fragrant Zodiack run'

Derek Hosie is employed by the Dowager Countess Cawdor, who is very interested in gardening and has a lot of input – so it is lucky that he gets on so well with her. The name Cawdor is romantically linked by Shakespeare with *Macbeth*, and the castle, dating from the fourteenth century, is steeped in history, and is said to have two ghosts. The grounds are full of variety, incorporating three lovely gardens (flower, walled and wild), extensive woodland and a nine-hole golf course. Cawdor is further north than Moscow, but it is blessed with fertile soil; a climate tempered by the Gulf Stream; plentiful rain; long summer days; and head gardener, Derek Hosie.

It was a special pleasure to be personally shown round the garden by Derek. His enthusiasm, gained from watching the garden develop for more than 20 years, and his appreciation of nature, colour and the seasons, was heartwarming. Yet although Derek loves gardening, it has not taken over his whole life. He is a man with many hobbies, although admittedly they are all outdoor ones. But at the end of each day, when he locks up his greenhouses, Derek walks in the garden and often sits a while, spending his free time, to enjoy the fruits of his labour.

WHY WE GARDEN | Derek Hosie

I have worked at Cawdor Castle for 22 years. I came here as assistant gardener, and about three years later I became head gardener. I have always been interested in gardening, even as a child. I used to work in my father's garden when I was eight, and I took it over when I was about 12! We lived near Clydebank, where every wee house had its garden: privet hedge on three sides and a bit of lawn, and the other half veg, and sometimes flowers. When I took over, I did away with the veg garden and made it all flowers. I used to go down to the local park and get their spare bedding plants. I never, ever, wanted to do anything else. I had my job lined up even before I left school, as an apprentice in horticulture with Glasgow Parks.

I always had a dream of being head gardener on an estate in the country. It was always in my mind. So when I finished at Glasgow Parks, I worked at a private residence for about two years and then went to my first private estate, near Perth, for around a year. From there I moved to another estate, but after two and a half years the owners died and I was made redundant, and I came here. We used to holiday up here, near Nairn, and I know the area well and I like the climate, so I thought, 'I'll go up there', and I am still here!

Working at Cawdor is a constant challenge because there is always something new going on. We have three gardens here: the top garden, the wild garden, and the bottom garden. I've made the bottom garden, along with the owners – I planted it all, except the maze. It used to be a huge, walled vegetable garden, but it is now divided into several parts. There is a holly maze bordered by laburnum tunnels, and a knot garden with a seven-pointed star and parterres planted with Gallica

Derek points out a new planting of mixed dwarf dahlias. The more formal top flower garden near the castle is kept much the same as when it was designed by Sir Archibald Campbell. But to extend the seasons Derek does clear beds to plant more of the old varieties.

roses, white iris, lavender, standard gooseberries and a mixture of herbs. There is also a thistle garden with about 28 varieties of eryngeums, and we are always trying to get more; and a white, or paradise garden. On the first day I arrived here, in 1981, the maze was just being planted. It used to be just little sticks! Then in its time, it has been up to a seven-foot block, but then the late Lord Cawdor decided on the present staircase-effect.

I am lucky that I have been here so long, because I have watched everything grow and mature. Not a lot of people hang around long enough to see that. And I have quite a free hand in the bottom garden. It was designed (except for the maze, designed by the late Lord Cawdor) by the Dowager Countess Cawdor and some designers, and it has many symbolic meanings. In contrast, the top flower garden is a historic garden and much must be kept the same, but even here, I have made several changes to the borders and to the roses. It is a formal garden with some French influence and was laid out by Sir Archibald Campbell in the early eighteenth century. Nowadays, however, since we open the gardens to the public, we have tried to extend the season of colour and scents to give pleasure from early spring onwards. So we have introduced bulbs and ornamental trees. But in the top garden, although I might bring in more species of primulas or meconopsis, I would not use any modern varieties of old plants.

Behind the Castle, between it and the Cawdor Burn, is the wild garden, which was only planted in the 1960s and is an informal mass of azaleas, rhododendrons and daffodils set amongst tall old trees. There is a 750-acre mixed deciduous wood, dating from about 1670. In it is a redwood dating from 1853 – in those days you paid ten guineas for one seed. The scents and colours in this garden, too, are stunning. So there are many different areas for people to see, and for Lady Cawdor and her guests to stroll in. Hopefully they are given pleasure – that's the secret.

The large Victorian-style vegetable garden at Auchindoune, where the Dowager Countess Cawdor lives when the Castle is opened to the public.

The last garden I look after is in a different location altogether, at Auchindoune House, a short drive from here. It is where the Dowager Countess lives in the summer and is a smaller house dating from the 1920s. I have redone all that garden, too. There is a large vegetable garden there now, although it is the Dowager Countess who tells me which vegetables she wants to have growing there. We had to get a digger in; we took rocks out weighing three to four tons each, and made new paths and beds. Then because Jack Cawdor, the fifth Earl, went with Frank Kingdom Ward, the famous plant collector, on an expedition to South East Tibet in the 1920s, and brought back many plants, we are re-creating a wild Himalayan garden.

On that expedition they found *Primula florindae*, named after Kingdom Ward's first wife, and *Primula cawdoriana*, named after the Earl of Cawdor – but in Britain there are only about two people who have grown *cawdoriana* successfully in recent years. It is almost impossible to grow, and it doesn't grow outside very well, and unfortunately we do not have a specimen. It was also Kingdom Ward who brought back the seed of the blue poppy (*Meconopsis betonicifolia*) – it was a good expedition. So for years we have said we would redo this garden at Auchindoune, but it is only in the past two years that we have been doing it in earnest. Now we are trying to create a garden with Himalayan plants of good origin and from wild collected seed. There are some quite rare plants in here now, and it is satisfying to see it develop from scratch. Auchindoune is really a private garden, but it is open to the public by appointment.

There is such variety here. As well as the gardens, there is a golf course to look after, and I have two greenhouses where I raise plants for the gardens and also grow all the indoor pot plants for the whole year. That is a job in itself, particularly in November and December when it is the tail-end of everything, and there is not enough daylight to bring on the next season's plants. But I have found success with heat-treated amaryllis bulbs, where you can get three massive heads in a pot to look stunning at Christmas, and they will still be on the go in June if grown in succession.

I place all the pots in the castle. Once I was there alone and did hear footsteps in the long corridor, but I never saw anything. So I finished what I was doing and left! The building is over 600 years old and has always been owned by the one family. Lady Cawdor is very good to work for. She is very interested, and I have worked here so long that, in a funny kind of way, I know what she is thinking a lot of the time. I have become psychic! I can come to work one day and say to the boys, 'The cherries need picking today', and Lady Cawdor's chef will come down and say, 'I want cherries today', and I'll have them already picked! There are seven gardeners now in the two properties – there used to be just three. But we are all quite happy. The head gardener before me stayed for 20-odd years, too.

I rise at 6.50 a.m. and am over here by 7.25 and give the men their orders. I might start working in the greenhouse with the pot plants, doing a variety of things before 9.30 a.m. I still do weeding and mundane jobs. I am not so keen on cutting grass these days, but I still cut the majority of the hedges myself, and I am the one who usually goes up the scaffolding – probably because I am so light. Hedges are special. When you have planted them and nurtured them over the years you are loath to give someone else a pair of trimmers, because once a mistake is made it takes years for it to grow back again. But fortunately I have got some good men who work with me, and gradually I am becoming bolder and giving more of the work to them. There is a limit to what one can do oneself, and there is more to do all the time.

When we are open to the public we like to get all the jobs using weed killer or machinery like strimmers done before they come in, so that there is no danger. People mainly ask the names of plants, and where they can buy them. They ask, 'Is it easy to grow? Can I raise it from seed? Can I get some seed here?' We do give away some seeds if we have them. I still have a soft spot for the greenhouses: I like propagating plants; I like rearing difficult plants from seed. The climate is very good here, so there are not many plants we can't grow. There are sometimes bad frosts, so we have had tender plants killed – the secret is not to grow them, although there is always the wee urge to grow something different.

The moss gardens in Japan inspired Hugh Cawdor, the sixth Earl of Cawdor, to get me to try to grow moss here, and it worked reasonably well – until we had a drought or the birds scratched it out to use for nests, and we switched to bluebells instead. I enjoy refining and introducing new elements to the planting. One day we might achieve the status National Collection of eryngeums. We applied about 15 years ago, but our collection was very young at that time and we didn't have time to pursue it. But I still collect eryngeums, and I go through catalogues and seed exchange schemes and try to get new ones: it has been a long-term interest. All plants are fantastic, but they don't live forever, so we are always looking for something else that will have scent and keep going for as long as possible.

I like challenges and I like things to go my own way. I have time-scales and I hate to be waylaid by them, and I don't like the weather to upset my plans. In my early days I used to shout at people, but I have found that shouting doesn't get you anywhere. But I run a tight ship; I like to keep it like that. When the tourists come, in the peak of the season, we get extremely busy and there is a lot of wear and tear on the grass, especially if it is wet. When it is at its busiest I tend to stay out of the main gardens, and work more in the greenhouses or the vegetable garden – there are always plenty of other things to do here. There are only two days in the week, Monday and Friday; the rest is a blur!

I never thought I would be here this length of time. Now I feel I would quite like to still be here when I retire. I have recently moved house and have my own garden at home now, and it is looking very good, although I don't say I always look forward to looking after it. But in the main, gardening is therapy. To me, gardening is my job, a hobby, an interest, and it is a way of life. I don't know anything else. I read books on horticulture all the time, I go to other gardens, but sometimes it can get too much. I find that at certain times of the year you can overdose on gardening and you want no more! Then enough is enough and you

A break from work in the garden.

must have a holiday. I do military plane spotting as one of my hobbies, and also I drive a rally car. I actually built the car! I also like photography, and I love fishing. I regularly go for picnics on the west coast, too, and like the sea; they are all outdoor pursuits.

I like all times of year. Spring is a fantastic time, but so is autumn and so is winter when it is snowing and there is frost on the branches. When you are outside all the time, you can't beat seeing the different seasons: it's superb. The colours in the sky in the winter – clear blue skies by day, and then the sunsets. Then in spring you have all the different greens, and the buds burst. And in summer it is just a riot with all the flower colour, and in autumn the leaves are fantastic. All the seasons are good. I love the cold and frost and working outside – I still appreciate it.

A lot of people who live in the country take it for granted; but I never take it for granted. I come over here at night to shut the greenhouses up, but then I am here an hour or more. Some evenings I work, but some evenings I just go for a walk when no one is here, and it is calm on a warm balmy evening, and the scents are amazing. I often take a seat and just listen to the birds and look about me. And you know that you are the only person here, and you can enjoy it. Time just melts away. Then I drive the short distance to my house and I look at the clouds and the sky and see the differences each night. Some people don't

Derek smiles contentedly by a stream in the wild garden at Auchindoune. Behind him are bluebells, pink *Rhododendron yunnanense*, a red rhododendron hybrid and a large planting of irises.

even see the red squirrels and the wildlife. I suppose they are blinded by the rush of modern-day life.

I couldn't work here if I didn't like it. I must have a challenge, and the challenge here, is keeping it going, because it has got so big, particularly with the other garden, too. I am a perfectionist, and I want to keep it *all* clean and smart and make sure it gives people enjoyment. It is not straightforward every year. We raise almost all the plants here ourselves, and occasionally nature plays its hand and something gets devastated; or a mouse or rabbit wreaks havoc. But I'm glad I didn't do anything else – although you will never be rich gardening.

Gardening is an unrecognized skill. Some places more than others – not here at Cawdor. You are left alone here. The Dowager Countess could go away for a month and wouldn't phone me up; she would just know that the garden would still be maintained in the same way. Some gardeners are treated quite badly and are not given the wage rises they should get. But there would be few gardeners if they did it for the money. You either like it or hate it, but anyone can get into gardening. And you are never too old to learn: in fact when you garden, you must learn something new every day. When I was at school, a lot of people said, 'What do you want to do gardening for?' But when I look back at my class at school and think who is happy, I bet not many are. So many people do jobs they can't stand. I couldn't go to work from 7.30 a.m. to 5.30 p.m. and not be happy.

6

DAVID MAGSON

LONDON SQUARE GARDENER

David dead-heading an 'Iceberg' rose growing by his large greenhouse on the south side of the square.

'Insnar'd with Flow'rs, I fall on Grass'

David Magson delights in the address 'The Temple, Edwardes Square', for traditionally the gardener lives in the lodge, built in the Greek Revival Style, at the south gate of the garden, which was laid out in 1820. An Act of Parliament was passed in 1819 for the paving, cleansing, lighting, watching, watering, planting and improving of Edwardes Square. Additionally a fine of £5 was to be imposed for suffering swine to wander upon its footways and carriageways. Now the secluded three-and-a-half acre site has a dense border of shrubs to maintain privacy, serpentine paths, extensive lawns, flower beds, a charming rose pergola, a croquet lawn, tennis court and children's play area, but dogs are not suffered to wander in the garden.

A house in Edwardes Square, built between 1811 and 1819, is what an estate agent might call a highly desirable residence in Kensington, one of the smartest and most expensive London Boroughs. An added attraction is that every resident is entitled to a key to the pretty, private square garden in the centre. As London developed in the 18th and 19th centuries, squares became a popular feature, making the city unique and offering social, visual, environmental and economic benefits. The construction of London's terraced houses and squares is one of England's greatest contributions to the development of European town planning. Some people have lived in the same house in Edwardes Square for years, bought when property was cheaper. Most users of the square, especially children, seem friendly, and all know David, frequently calling to him by name.

David is welcoming, quiet and unassuming. Though keen to be interviewed, it was only after I had met him three times that I learnt that he had been head gardener to the Prince of Wales at Highgrove! And while both positions require a degree of tact and discretion, Edwardes Square appears to be a real contrast. Used relatively little by the residents, and with no outside visitors to the square (unlike the organized tours, booked months in advance to Highgrove), David sometimes sees nobody all day. The garden he maintains now is prestigious but small, and managed by committee which means that changes happen slowly. David is proud of the garden, but unlike many gardeners is not compulsive or obsessive, and though he lives on site he has outside hobbies.

When I was about seven or eight, living in Yorkshire where I was born, I used to help a guy who was only in his 20s but had been involved in a motorbike accident, so he was paralysed from the waist down. He was a cartoonist and lived with his parents in a huge bungalow with a massive garden that wrapped around it, and his father did the vegetables and he and I did the rest of the garden. He had a little bubble car and I would sneak in the back and we would go to the garden centre. It was just fun.

At school I did cookery, but they wouldn't let me do it as an exam, because I was a boy, which was extremely irritating. So I worked in a big kitchen in a hotel in Blackpool for two years, which was enjoyable, but I realized it wasn't for me – it was such hard work, especially for a young man. You would start at 8 a.m. and finish at 10.30 p.m., having a lot of responsibility piled on you. Then an offer of a gardening job came up and I took it. My next-door neighbour worked for a landscape gardener and he told me he needed someone to help. So I started landscape gardening and garden maintenance, and after about a year he encouraged me to go to college, and so I did a national certificate in horticulture for a year and went on to do the diploma for another three years.

As part of the course I went to Ness Botanics [Liverpool University Botanic Gardens] and also to Hidcote Manor, where I worked in the winter, which was fantastic. But when I went back to college, I began to think, 'Oh my God, what am I going to do?' because there are so many things you can do in horticulture! Then one of my lecturers approached me and said, 'You've been head-hunted to go for an interview at Highgrove. Are you interested?' I answered, 'Yes, of course!' So I went to the interview and was interviewed by Rosemary Verey [late *grande dame* of gardening] and a Commander, who both liked me and asked me if I would go back for a second interview.

When I went back I was interviewed by the Prince, sitting out on the terrace in the blazing sun – it was such a hot day and I was petrified. He said he wanted someone who knew the basics about how to look after a garden, nothing really fancy. He very quickly put me at my ease and I got the job of assistant gardener! I never actually found out how I had got head-hunted. Later on I got to know Rosemary Verey: she could be quite fierce but she had a heart of gold and treated me really well. She had a soft spot for me and I liked her. She would come to Highgrove quite a lot,

The front of the Grecian-style temple where David lives.

David framed by a topiarized golden privet.

advising and implementing schemes.

Prince Charles is a very, very keen gardener. The second he arrived home, he would walk straight through the house, out of the French windows at the back and into the garden. He liked to see every change and development and would talk to the gardeners quite a lot. In the early years, when he was more of an amateur, he relied on people like Rosemary Verey and others to get ideas. He is a very eclectic gardener and likes to gather ideas from many people, like Sir Roy Strong, who designed all the hedges and topiary. A lovely eccentric couple called Isobel and Judith Bannerman designed his stumpery and some other features; they were nice to work with. And Lady Salisbury designed a beautiful little rose garden for him, which has all been changed now as the garden has developed.

He designs more himself these days, I think, now that he has got his gardening feet. But while I was there I would suggest things, either by writing a letter or verbally. If he thought it was a good idea, he would say so, and if he thought it wasn't, he would say, too. But he was very diplomatic. He did get angry if things didn't go quite right, or if, say, a tree blew down, he would get upset. He liked to get out into the garden at weekends and do weeding and he was great with his handsaw, lopping off branches and things like that. I stayed eight years. I was assistant gardener for two, and then the head gardener left and I was promoted to his position.

Like here, I had a house on the estate, but I felt very much part of the staff there and we wore a uniform. There was also definitely a divide between the indoor and outdoor staff, but I was very friendly with the indoor staff and they were a lot more relaxed when the Prince wasn't there. A lot of the staff went with him, but the ones who stayed behind were more friendly when he wasn't around. When he was in residence we used to keep out of the way of the house because everyone was stressed. He was always busy with something happening or guests coming: he has a very busy lifestyle. If the Prince was working at Highgrove, they would set a phone out and a table and lounger, and all his paperwork and letters, and he would do his work in the garden. He didn't want to sit inside. We had extension points in the garden where he could plug in the phone and he would do everything from outside. It made me feel a bit awkward and we would tiptoe around him.

Prince Charles also has a kitchen gardener, Dennis, who is very much his own man and keeps himself to himself. So we didn't get too involved with growing specific things for the table. We were more involved with big maintenance jobs in the kitchen garden, like clipping the big box hedges, which was a *huge* job because there were miles and miles of box hedges and we would have to go and help do that. The kitchen gardener had some part-time help from a lady who worked in the stables, and I think it is pretty much the same now. There were not enough gardeners, but as well as maintenance, we designed beds and new planting schemes. The terrace was quite formal and I always did *big* pots overflowing with colour and we fed them and watered them and they always looked fantastic. The Prince liked red and purple, especially in the tulip walk. It was stunning, especially in the first year that we did it.

I enjoyed my time at Highgrove, but eight years is quite a long time to be somewhere and I think I just wore myself out. Also I wanted more staff but they wouldn't give them to me, and the garden was getting more and more complicated as the years went by and it had to be kept perfect. We started with having one visit a week from gardening groups who wrote in. Then that increased to a visit a day, and finally two visits a day and a shop, and I felt it started to get a little bit out of hand.

When I left I went on a world tour and took quite a bit of time off. I went to New York, Australia, the Maldives, Bali, everywhere. I came back and did a few little gardening jobs to save some more cash and then went back to Australia and stayed in Melbourne for six months, which I thought was fantastic, and I toyed with the idea of living there. But I came back, about five years ago, and was staying with friends and didn't want to outstay my welcome, so I was desperately looking for a

The Temple seen from the back. David looking out at the square.

job and heard about this place. It was on the job list of the Professional Gardeners' Guild, so I sent off my CV. In the meantime I had to come down to London for an interview for a job I wasn't that interested in, so I just popped by here, and the head gardener was here, Polly, so I just called out to her through the railings.

She let me in and we had a walk round and she said, 'I've seen your CV; I remember you worked at Highgrove and had a big portfolio with photos and design drawings. Come and have a cup of tea and a chat!' She was leaving Edwardes Square because she and her husband wanted to start a family and the house isn't big enough; there is only one bedroom and a little box room downstairs. So she told me all the ins and outs of the job and I was totally blown away by it. To be truthful it was the *house*! The garden needed quite a lot doing to it, so that was a *challenge*. Everyone complains about the city, but actually I had always wanted to live in London: I had always lived in the country so I wanted to give it a go and see what it was like. I don't know of any other squares where there is a house attached. At first I was a bit sort of 'la-di-da' about my address, but now I just write it and don't think about it – but I was smitten when I got the job.

In some London squares you can buy or rent a key, but here they are very proud of their square and want to keep it to themselves and only people who live on the streets surrounding the garden are allowed a key. At the weekend it can be busy but during the week it is always peaceful. You can walk out of the gate and be in Kensington High Street in less than a minute, and yet it is so quiet here. There are some problems with the garden being in the middle of London, such as deliveries. I usually get two big lorry-loads of mushroom compost, which makes a huge difference to the garden. The compost is delivered to a space in front of the gates by my house, but they are redeveloping that area and I am going to lose the space and then getting bulky things into the garden will be a nightmare.

I am the only full-time gardener here. It took a bit of persuading, but I managed to get a part-time gardener twice a week to help me. She is from the Women's Flower and Garden Association based in Cirencester, near Highgrove, so I knew that the students there were really good. When I worked at Highgrove they were just paid a basic wage and in return they got training. The previous gardener at Edwardes Square didn't have a huge budget, but just as I arrived on the scene the bank balance went up because the committee came into some money through a deal with a developer. So now there is some money, although they are very careful with it. Polly had spent a lot of time on the perimeter, getting the planting of shrubs right, so I just got here at a good time and could get stuck in to redeveloping the borders.

None of the actual layout of the informal paths and the lovely walkway round the outside has been changed. You still feel you could be in the countryside when you walk around the edges, and then you emerge in to a

Opposite left: The rose tunnel in June. The white roses 'Mme. Alfred Carriere', 'Rambling Rector' and climbing 'Iceberg' are underplanted with English and French lavender, rosemary, purple sage and yellow origanum.

Opposite right: The rose tunnel still looks lovely some months later with lavender, purple *Verbena bonariensis*, yellow *Anthemis* 'E. C. Buxton', purple-red *Lychnis cornaria* and mauve erigeron in flower.

huge expanse of grass. But the paths were black, flaking tarmac and we have had them all redone in resin-bonded gravel. The tarmac also went all through the rose tunnel and it has been replaced there with York stone, which looks much softer. There were huge arguments about that between the residents!

Many of them dislike change, although sometimes residents want something in particular and it is just best to be polite. Some would love to have a swimming pool and a hard tennis court, which would ruin the garden. Others resent the fact that dogs are not allowed, and they always give me a hard time about it even though it is not my decision. But they won't get me on their side over that issue: it would be me who would end up clearing the mess! There were ructions, too, when I took out a big hedge in front of my house so that I had a view out. Someone will always be against change – the opposite of Highgrove where change was always happening.

Any major decisions have to be put before the residents' committee and I tell them exactly how much something will cost and how long it will take to do, and then they decide. If it is just a case of changing a few shrubs around in a border I will go and do it. But it makes it a bit harder that I don't have one boss and decisions always take a long time to get made. On the other hand I do feel I am my own boss to a certain degree. There is a garden representative who is re-elected every third year and the committee members change round, too. So even if an awkward person got elected, who was really interfering, at least it would not be forever. I am lucky in other ways, too. Few squares have their own greenhouse and I can do a lot of propagating of annuals and things like half-hardy salvias and fuchsias.

I like the herbaceous and shrub borders the best, and creating big splashes of colour. The residents love flowers and I get my reward when they tell me they like it. And even people who don't come into the garden get the benefit, because all they have to do is look out of their windows. It is mainly families that use the square, and some people bring their lunch or use the tennis court. The garden is now a lot fluffier and prettier than it used to be and I think maybe that has made more people come in. In the autumn we strip some turf off the lawn and build a bonfire and have a professional company who come in and do a big evening fireworks display which is absolutely amazing. It is very loud because it echoes round the square. Every other year we have another large party: we have a big marquee and the residents can hire as many tables as they like and be as grand or as simple as they like. This year the garden looked completely magical.

We had a big marquee at the end for dancing, but because the weather was unsettled, everyone went out and bought little gazebos or marquees which they could put up. There is a table plan, but it is flexible. It is a little competitive in that some families go absolutely overboard and have private caterers but others just have a simple affair. I go overboard by putting lighting everywhere, and with fairy lights all over the place the garden looks stunning. It is adults only (there is a separate children's party); not quite black tie, but pretty smart. I just float around and drink masses of champagne! The local police come too because the music and lights attract people who try to jump over the railings and gatecrash. About five guys were desperate to get in this year. They tried the main gate first and then they tried to jump over the railings. We followed them around but they were so persistent – it was like a game.

One of the funniest things that happened to me was in my first year here. It was about

The west gate looking into the square.

five in the morning and I was lying in bed with the window open on a hot evening and I heard the gate rattle right beneath my bedroom. I jumped up and looked out and two guys jumped over the gates and nearly killed themselves. They picked themselves up from the heap where they landed and they were wearing dinner jackets, with their bow ties dangling down their dress shirts. Then they disappeared, so I got dressed and rushed out and I could hear singing. They were perched on top of the children's play area, smoking a joint, singing their heads off, as high as kites!

I just stood and watched them for a while, but I thought, 'I better tell them to leave, before they wake up all the residents', so I went over and said, 'Excuse me, gentlemen, you are being quite loud!' I shook the keys and started walking and they followed me like two little sheep. I opened the gate and they walked out, and one turned round and said, 'Oh, I'm so sorry!' and off they went. They couldn't have been more polite. I think they were very well chilled with what they were smoking! There was another incident this summer at about 11 p.m., when I heard a noise and came into the square and there were about six people doing yoga, getting themselves into all these weird positions! I felt really rotten asking them to leave, because they weren't really doing any harm, but they had jumped over the railings to get in.

But on the whole it is all fairly quiet here. There are occasional incidents of vandalism when kids come into the square, but not much. Generally people know me and stop and have a chat, which is nice. Otherwise it can get lonely. Having the student twice a week made all the difference to my morale as well as it being useful to have another pair of hands if you have a really big job on. Also you can throw ideas off each other and it is nice having someone to work with. I couldn't do it if I was on my own Monday to Friday – it would drive me up the wall, because of it being so quiet. You can be in here all day and you don't meet a soul sometimes.

You can get very protective of the garden, and I have to try not to be. Now that I have got it more or less how I want it (although there is still a lot to do), when the kids come and play football, it would be easy to get wound up and start screaming and shouting at them. So I have to take a step back from it. I put the hours in, and I go visiting gardens and garden centres at weekends, but I wouldn't say I was obsessive. I knew the head gardener at Powys Castle, who is retired now, and it was just his *life*, but I have other interests. One of my biggest hobbies is going to the gym and I also enjoy swimming. It is a relief and I also meet other people.

We open the garden to the public one day a year for the National Garden Scheme, which makes me work ten times harder – the garden will be scrutinized then not only by residents but lots of other people and gardeners. There is also loads to do in the winter: replanning borders and masses of pruning. I have made two red borders, which is probably a bit of an influence from Hidcote. And we have added to the underplanting of the rose tunnel, which has been very successful. The first year I was here I wanted to make a huge impact so I ordered something like £800-worth of bulbs and planted daffodils around the trees and everywhere. It looked stunning in spring with carpets of yellow, and people were blown away, so I have been augmenting them a bit every year.

It is odd: I once saw this garden from an upstairs window of the garden representative's house, and it looks like a forest! I don't know how it works because there is a huge expanse of grass in the middle, which somehow you don't see. I was amazed. It is part of the private nature of the garden. The residents like to show off the garden, but they want to keep it their little piece of paradise. They don't want it to be really well known and to have visitors all the time. They like to feel that it is theirs, and private. I am lucky to share it with them, and generally I feel very settled and happy here.

Children enjoying London Garden Squares Day when, unusually, the garden is open to the public for one Sunday.

7

ROBERT MURRAY

LANDSCAPE CONTRACTOR AND LAWN MOWER

It is not surprising that Robert doesn't talk much to the public while he is working. With narrow paths like these 'you have to look down all the time to make sure you are catching all the bits of grass from every angle, and you really have to concentrate.'

'To a green Thought in a green Shade'

Robert Murray is no ordinary grass cutter. He is a trained horticulturist, and whilst burly and tattooed, he is also thoughtful and sensitive. Robert's large frame and strength are necessary to his work, for he maintains one of the most dramatic and unique grass sites – Landform Ueda, designed by Charles Jencks for the Scottish National Gallery of Modern Art in Edinburgh. The turf sculpture, also known as an earthwork, is an S-shaped mound (over 18 feet high) with three sweeping lakes, and undulating paths of grass, which remind me of rice terraces in Asia, with their interaction of sun and water.

Architectural historian Charles Jencks and his late wife Maggie Keswick filled the gardens of their Dumfriesshire home with similar features. Maggie wanted to dig out a place for the children to swim, and would have flattened the spoil, but Charles made the mounds: a double helix and a snake. In Edinburgh, Landform Ueda is an expression of the intervention between man and landscape. Its shape refers to geometries expressed in natural features such as waves and geological formations, and to science and the Catastrophe Theory in its folds (like the way two different liquids fold into each other when stirred). But Landform has also been likened to the home of the Teletubbies! It forms part of the landscape connecting two galleries and is a setting for sculpture, as well as a work of art in its own right. At the same time it affords views over the city, a place for sunbathing or contemplation, and ideal slopes for children to roll down.

In May 2004 the Scottish National Gallery of Modern Art was awarded the £100,000 Gulbenkian Prize for Landform. Out of four nominees it was the unanimous choice of the judges to win this, the biggest arts prize in Britain. It was claimed that the joy and excitement of seeing Landform was like falling in love, and that it changed the whole way in which people related to the gallery. Landform was said to have a calming quality as well as a wonderful participatory effect. The museum can now do as it chooses with the money — it does not have to spend it on the upkeep of this magical outdoor sculpture.

Three thousand square metres of turf were used to create Landform Ueda, which opened on 1 August 2002. In years gone by, grass was cut by sheep, cattle, and teams of gardeners armed with scythes. The enormity of the task meant that only the wealthy could own lawns. In the 1830s, Edward Budding adapted a machine used to run over woven cloth to give it a smooth finish, so that it could cut grass. Suddenly all the Victorians began to grow lawns as there was now a cheap and efficient means of mowing them. Currently, turf mounds have become fashionable garden features. Few people, however, would have the vision to create a concept as lovely as the Landform. As soon as I saw a photograph of it in 2002, I wanted to go there.

Opposite: *Landform Udea* is itself a work of art in front of Edinburgh's National Gallery of Modern Art. Its designer, Charles Jencks also designed gardens around the Imperial War Museum North in Manchester, yet to be installed, and he has been commissioned to design a public park in Milan.

The Landform is a bugger to cut but you want it to look good for the Gallery. I have worked as a contractor for the Galleries here for eight years, maintaining the grounds and doing hard landscaping, such as making paths, fencing and doing turfing. I have always been in gardening. When I was younger I had a real passion for horticulture – I enjoyed plants. So when I first left school I went to 'the Botanics' [Royal Botanic Garden Edinburgh] and then I worked for the university for two years before I went self-employed. So to start with I was surrounded by hundreds of different plants, and I was learning, but when you go self-employed you lose some of the horticultural part. You are doing it to make money and you are in commercial horticulture then.

But I have been fortunate to work in some beautiful places. I used to do a lot of work for Historic Scotland and I still do some other contract work in the quiet times, but there is normally some sort of project going on here. This place has been revamped over the last few years, with quite a lot of landscaping going on, so it is quite high-maintenance, and the Landform was put in less than a year ago. Charles Jencks and his head gardener came up. The head gardener is a real character, and I got on quite well with him. He is the one that did all the tiering, and for some reason he insisted on digging it by hand! But most of it was built by contractors, and now I maintain it.

Basically, to have a good lawn, you need a good weed killer and feed, you need to scarify or rake it, aerate, water and mow it. Feeding with a fertilizer will make it greener and grow more thickly, which helps to minimize weeds and moss. Late spring is the best time to feed, and if the lawn gets heavy wear it will need feeding every six weeks until mid-summer. So far [the end of May] we have fertilized the Landform three times and we will probably fertilize it about six times altogether.

Small patches of weeds in a garden can be pulled up by hand or spot-treated with a weed killer. Larger areas can be treated with a selective lawn weed killer. Moss grows if the lawn is shady, compacted, damp or too short. That's one of the reasons you need to aerate the lawn by spiking it. Then you can treat the moss with a moss killer, and when it has died, rake it out. With a large lawn, you would use an electric scarifier, where basically the blades split the grass up. Scarifying is also used to remove the thatch and cut the rhizomes of the grass, which allows it to thicken up.

Areas of lawn that get heavy traffic get compacted and need aerating to improve drainage. In a small garden you would do this by pushing a garden fork into the ground about six inches deep and push it backwards and forwards to make air channels in the earth. Then you need to do that all over the lawn at intervals of about six inches. That's also a good time to brush in a top dressing of loam and sand. We probably won't aerate the Landform. I tried to scarify most of it in the winter, but it is quite difficult to do, as you can imagine, getting the machine up the banks.

The same problem applies to mowing. Of course I can mow the flat areas driving a flail mower; then I use a Marquis for running the paths – they are often used on bowling greens and are machines you push along while walking. But the sloping banks require brute strength! I use a Flymo for them, and tidy it off with a strimmer. So altogether I use four machines to cut the Landform. I can cut the whole lot, though, in about four hours.

During long dry spells, people should mow less often and avoid feed because it will scorch the grass. Actually, watering can harm it too, encouraging the grass to root closer to the surface, making it susceptible to drought. Mowing should really be done little and often, with the blades set at around one inch high to help protect the grass from damage. I have to say, though, I don't cut my own lawn at home as regularly as I should – when I get home I'm tired! In summer, garden lawns really need cutting at least once a week

Above: Robert in conversation. His physical strength enables him to cut the steep slopes of the Landform.

Opposite: Despite having taken a course in garden history at Harvard, Jencks had no interest in gardens until he met his wife and had a family. Then he created *The Garden of Cosmic Speculation* at his home, and a new language of land forms, 'relating us to nature through new metaphors presented to the senses', was born and is very evident here, in Edinburgh too.

unless there is a drought and the grass is exposed to constant sun. Last week I cut the Landform on Friday but then this Wednesday they had some 'do' on at the Gallery and they wanted me to do it again, so it mucked up my schedule a bit. But it reflects on me if anything in the grounds looks bad or untidy.

I take a great deal of interest in the grounds up here. I don't just look at it as a contractor coming to maintain it; I look at it as mine. It doesn't bother me when children slide down the banks of the Landform, but it can do a wee bit of damage if it is wet and they are climbing up. I wish it was a slightly more durable turf. This is a mix [a mixture of rye, fescues, and bents], which is what you would use on bowling greens, but I don't think it should have been used here. Rye grass is the most suitable for a lot of wear and tear because it is vigorous and tough with coarse leaf blades. The turf used elsewhere in the grounds is more durable and can come back a lot faster.

The turf for the Landform was chosen by an architect [Terry Farrell & Partners], which realistically was not a good idea. I think it should look a bit lusher. We add bits of seed, and if there are large areas of repair to do, we put more turf in. There was a lot of waterlogging at the start, which caused the turf to go yellow-brown, where other turfs [with less fescues] might not have done that; a hardier turf will keep green a bit longer and can take more of a beating. For the number of people who will walk through here in the summer, these paths could get worn.

People try to talk to me while I am mowing, but I have a machine going, so I try not to talk to them! It would mean turning the machine off, and it is a pest, so I prefer just to cut the grass. And although I find it quite easy to cut, some bits are more difficult. Like you can't walk on the top tier, so I have to hang the machine over. You also have to try to keep your angles right. Ideally they should all be really sharp and you should be careful and take a bit of time. You are cutting the grass with a kind of strap and so you have to look down all the time to make sure you are catching all the bits of grass from every angle, and you really have to concentrate. But I have cut it 28 times now, so I could cut it in my sleep! Thankfully, I don't actually dream about it. There are some gardening jobs you do dream about, but not this one, probably because it doesn't take that long. If it took a couple of days, like, say, turfing, you can dream you are still doing it.

I think the most gruelling piece of grass that I have cut is the Mound in Edinburgh. That's all banking work, so it is hard. But I have cut really nice places in and around Edinburgh – Melrose Abbey, Dryburgh Abbey and Linlithgow Palace. My favourite place was Dryburgh because I think it is so beautiful. There is the old ruin and big beautiful trees and it is all in the middle of nowhere. Melrose was difficult because it was all wee bits and pieces. Caerlaverock Castle in Dumfriesshire was also hard, because it was all banking work as well – mainly strimming.

It was interesting cutting these places, but it wasn't fun, like when you go round as a tourist. When you are spending maybe three hours travelling down there, offloading, cutting, and maybe trying to do another place or two in the same area, you have spent about 12 hours and still have to drive back. It is a hard shift. Linlithgow, with three Flymos, would take about four hours cutting – and we would have about five or six machines going at once there. Here at the Galleries I do all the cutting myself, but I often get someone to do the strimming for me. And then when the grass is done, I'll go off and do another job and another job.

It's nice but it is tiring. As long as my boss doesn't give me any hassle, I am quite happy. I will probably carry on contracting. I enjoy working up here. I spend so much time here, I do think of it as mine. And my boss is good and we will walk around and say, 'How can we improve certain sections of the grounds?' And then if I suggest something he will allow me to do that. So now I spend most of my time up here, maintaining the place almost like a full-time job. I had a much bigger business before – loads of contract and private work – but I found I could make just as much money doing two or three places.

This is quite an 'arty' place, where people don't really talk to you. I've been here eight years, and yet I don't really know any of the staff here except for the immediate people who I have to deal with. The rest, such as the people who work in the Gallery, don't mix and there is no kind of closeness. It is like Edinburgh as a whole: people don't really mix. So I don't get many comments, but on the other hand I don't have anyone who tells me what to do, except my boss, who is with the buildings department (roof, electrics, that sort of thing), and he is great.

It has taken years to get to know the grounds properly and maintain them to a high standard. At the moment I just employ one person, although if there is a big job on, I can bring in more people. It is a nice place to work. It's surreal. You are in the middle of a busy city centre, and yet a stone's throw away is this quiet place where it is relaxing to work. That is what I enjoy about it. And I like to spend time to do the job well and take some pride in what I am doing. What was strange was that through the year we did quite a lot of maintenance on the Landform before it actually opened to the public; then suddenly there were all these people here, and I thought, 'What are they all doing in my garden?'

8

DAME MIRIAM ROTHSCHILD

WILD-FLOWER GARDENER AND ENTOMOLOGIST

'Farmers' Nightmare' – a mixture of seeds collected from deserted airfields by Miriam Rothschild. These 'weeds' include ferverfew, cornflower, marigold, corncockle, poppy, daisy and flax.

'And, till prepar'd for longer flight, Waves in its Plumes the various Light'

Miriam Rothschild is a remarkable woman. Granddaughter of the first Lord Rothschild, she was educated at home and was awarded an honorary Doctorate of Science by Oxford University. Influenced by her father Charles, her interest in wild life and wild flowers is intertwined. She has published numerous important scientific papers as one of the world's foremost experts on fleas, and on subjects including butterflies, birds, ecology and conservation. She has written several books, worked at Bletchley as a code-breaker during the war, is a mother to two adopted, and four of her own children, and was a farmer and a pioneer of wild-flower gardening. Go into any bookshop and browse through books on wild-flower gardening and it is likely that the foreword or preface is written by her or that she will be cited in the text.

Miriam Rothschild's own garden in Northamptonshire is an outstanding example of wild-flower and grassland gardening and of the abundance of nature in almost all forms. Driving to meet her is an adventure in itself. Leaving the main road, an unmade road through fields becomes a mud track through woodland, bearing signs saying 'Private, Keep Out'. Deer run over the track, which branches in various directions to reach cottages. I remember Miriam Rothschild's directions over the phone when she warned, 'If you don't break the axle, you should eventually reach my house, and then you will think, "Surely no one can live there!"' For although the house is huge, it is completely overgrown, and with a large wooden front door and a ramp a bit like a drawbridge, it has similarities to both a castle and a witch's house.

I was shown into a handsome library. Wood burned in the large fireplace and wood panelled the walls. A generous sandwich lunch was laid out with drinks of every kind, including strange bottles of sloe gin. When Miriam Rothschild entered in a motorized wheelchair, the ramp at the front of the house was explained. At 95, with failing vision, she is understandably sometimes cross through frustration. But her mind is completely active, and when she talks of her joy in gardening and in wildlife, her whole face lights up in a smile.

Miriam Rothschild in her garden in 2003. She is still a campaigner for conservation and a testament to the success of wild-flower gardening.

WHY WE GARDEN | Dame Miriam Rothschild

I was born in this house, which my grandfather built for my father. My father met my mother, who was Hungarian, while he was collecting fleas in the Carpathian Mountains! He was allowed six weeks holiday a year from the Rothschild bank and he always took it in summer, in Hungary. I was born a year after my parents married. I worked out that I was conceived in Portugal. When I was young the gardens here at Ashton Wold were quite formal. There were rose gardens and areas of Edwardian bedding plants, huge herbaceous borders, a walled kitchen garden (the soil was brought from around Bournemouth by train!) and numerous greenhouses containing fruit, cacti, water lilies and orchids. After my father's death, in 1923, instead of 14 gardeners there were eight (now there is just one), but the gardens remained beautiful until my mother's death in 1940. During the war the house was taken over by the Red Cross. Garden walls were pillaged, pergolas collapsed and the garden was ransacked. I lived in a cottage in the village, and I returned to the house at the end of the war, with my husband, George Lane. Later we were to live in Oxfordshire, with Ashton merely a holiday home, but we returned in the '70s, when my taste in gardening had completely changed, and I had become a wild-flower gardener.

I got interested in gardening when I was extremely young, when I could hardly walk and would hang on to the pram. We were at Tring [Hertfordshire], where my grandparents lived, and where we spent every winter, and I was walking next to the pram as usual and I looked down at the ground, and there were these marvellous people, the white violets! I fell in love with them straight away, and have remained in love with violets ever since. I was *extremely* lucky, because in the ordinary way one would have just lost the feeling pretty soon, but my father was an *excellent* naturalist. He was a banker by profession but he was interested in all sides of the natural world: insects, birds, flowers, grasses, trees. He brought us up to love natural history, although I was the only one of the family who *really* took to it. My brothers and sisters liked drawing and painting wild flowers but were not really interested in the flowers themselves. But I stuck to it and, like my father, got immense enjoyment out of wildlife.

My father had a large collection of cacti that I loved, and when I was seven, I began a collection myself in a tiny miniature model greenhouse which he made for me. I became fascinated with the growth of these cacti. Some of my father's cacti were 20 feet tall, and I used to wonder, if I watched them, if I would see them grow! It was a semi-physical relationship with the cacti. Then my interest in plants and insects developed when I went to Hungary with my parents. They went first to visit my mother's family, and second because the fauna and flora of Hungary were virtually unknown and my father was *so* keen on it. There were so many insects and butterflies, and as a child, you didn't have any difficulty hunting for them. My father built a ranch next to my mother's home in Hungary and set up an entomological centre there. I followed him implicitly then.

But when my father died, when I was 15, I was so depressed that I gave up everything to do with natural history. I was no longer interested in it from the point of view of study, or collecting, or anything – it was finished for me. For two years I never opened a book about natural history, and I decided to become a writer. I took to reading translated

Russian novels and all the classical novels and poetry. The only slight arousal of my interest in natural history was in Wiesbaden, where my mother went to have the spa baths, which people had in those days to improve their health. I went out in the fields and saw the autumn crocus – colchicum – in flower. I had one or two days when I would sneak out and gather a few of these so-called crocuses: of course they are nothing to do with our crocus. That was the tinkle of the bell which suggested I wasn't entirely finished with it.

But my real interest was aroused when my brother came home from Harrow school with a holiday task of dissecting a frog and describing its blood system. He said to me, 'Oh hell, I can't do this damn thing. Will you help me?' I, like a good sister, said yes. We chloroformed the poor frog in a big jam jar and then we dissected it with the help of a book, and I was absolutely dumbfounded how *beautiful* the blood system was in this frog, and how wonderful the veins all looked. I was *completely* taken over. From that moment onwards I went back to zoology and botany as subjects of study. I was ready to be captured.

My father had been a great man on butterflies and so the first thing I did was read his papers on the subject. Even during his life he had made us go out with butterfly nets when we went for walks. But I came back to it with a fresh outlook. I no longer went mad on collecting, like stamps, but was more interested in animals' life histories. So in a way, the gap of two years proved a benefit. My interest in insects became more scientific, as my father's had been when he discovered the flea which carried the plague most effectively. My interest in flowers was related to my interest in insects, because I was interested in all pollinating insects as well as the insects and parasites which damage flowers. But whereas my interest in insects was scientific, my interest in flowers was sentimental and aesthetic.

In addition, gardening holds for me a physical pleasure. I enjoy the act of digging, and preparing soil and getting it through a sieve. I even like mowing when it is absolutely necessary. It is difficult to interpret one's physiological functions: but gardening made me feel fresher, happier, more energetic and more like someone who could *achieve* something, rather than just talk. The reason I wanted to make this garden into a wild-flower one was because I loved nature – on the whole, I didn't like artificial things. But there have always been multiple sides to my interest in gardening – I am also a keen conventional gardener.

I am very fond of pond gardening and greenhouse gardening. I have had an enormous amount of fun out of ordinary straightforward gardening. And also, you can mix the two. I have planted up a lot of wild roses in the garden, as if they were ordinary cultivated roses. In fact I have now got eight species and sub-species growing in a horticultural manner in my kitchen garden. I don't know whether I am pleased or ashamed of having won a prize from the Royal Horticultural Society for having grown gooseberries, and amaryllis, which are typically horticultural! And I think one of the things I liked best of all in the garden was a really artificial greenhouse with tanks filled with rainwater where I grew the famous blue water lilies. My father collected the seed from a lake in Africa, and my word they are beautiful! I think they are one of the most beautiful flowers in the world.

So I can confess that my interest in both plants and wildlife isn't necessarily confined to

This photo, taken by Miriam Rothschild (a truly multi-talented woman), shows Queen Anne's lace in early morning light at Ashton.

the British Isles. On a visit to America I was absolutely fascinated by humming-birds. Then I saw an advertisement in the newspaper asking 'Do you want to breed humming-birds?' Anyway the writer let me have two live birds, which were amongst the first to come into this country – I think it is banned now. Of all the miracles in the world, I think humming-birds win the first prize. They flew around free in this library. The curtains were flowered chintz, and the humming-birds recognized the flowers and would try to take nectar from the centre of the chintz flowers! I had special feeding bottles for the birds, so I used to hang them in the middle of the flower on the curtain, and the humming-birds always fed from them. I could move the bottles from flower embroidery to flower embroidery and the humming-birds would find them. It was a marvellous game we used to play!

You had to feed them every four hours with a mixture of New Zealand honey and baby food. I became an appendage to the humming-birds, really. I couldn't go out or do anything, so after a while I gave them to the zoo, where they were quite happy. But they were the first humming-birds to hibernate in this country. When winter came they tucked themselves behind the wooden shutters in the dining-room next door and went to sleep for the winter. This was a revelation to me, because I never thought a bird could hibernate, but they did. For me, any form of natural life is wonderful.

Another interest, which I had early on, was that I always liked to decorate the house with flowers. There were certain orchids which I thought went well with old bindings. So in the library, where there were tooled leather bindings, I used to put a vase with a 'Vanda' orchid in front of the books – that beautiful orchid which is heavily scented. I did that completely consciously. Then I found that certain trees which flowered very early, like the ash, seemed to suit a certain place in the bookshelves where travel books were. In those days I took an infinite amount of interest and trouble in decorating the library and certain other spots in the house. Funnily enough I think part of my interest in wild flowers grew from flowers on trees. I remember so well finding holly very attractive in vases. I think I could see a development from wild woods into gardens.

But it wasn't until I was about 65, that the two spheres of aesthetic and scientific interest in gardening merged. So, when I returned to live in Ashton Wold in the '70s, I planted the whole of the front of the house with creepers! There was already Japanese quince — which is now 100 years old or more — lilac and ivy. Now there is also a jumble of Virginia creeper, clematis, wisteria, roses, honeysuckle, buddleia, laurel, and spring and autumn flowering broom, which only grows a few feet high in the garden, but mine grows almost to the top of the roof! I allow everything to grow tall, losing any hint of suburban decoration. My house is a tenement house! Various birds, mice, bats and the occasional rat share the ivy with me.

This year in the courtyard we had two nests of the spotted flycatcher, and a blackbird. We also had a rat or two, which I wasn't so pleased about, because they take the eggs. In the old days we would have a cloud of house martins nesting under the eaves, mixed with bats. We had the long-eared bat, which is a charming animal that flies slowly so you can watch and listen to it. My favourite birds which nested here were the goldcrests, but we had all sorts. But when I put the food out for the birds in the morning there are always squirrels on the bird tables eating it all up. We have far too many for good gardening too. They dig up all the bulbs in the garden except daffodils, which are poisonous to squirrels.

My latest experiment now is to crush the bulbs of the daffodils in a container, so I make a daffodil-bulb soup, which can be spread on the tulip bulbs, so the squirrels won't eat them! There is one other person in the garden who has a better way of getting rid of the squirrel. We have got some foxes in the garden that actually catch squirrels. We have seen them carrying them off in their mouths. That seems fair play, if you see what I mean. Otherwise we would have to shoot the squirrels because they were doing too well — nothing else would survive — so we don't interfere with the foxes. But luckily the squirrels don't eat the wild flowers.

Anyway, when I was back here in the '70s, I turned the hothouses to cold-houses, growing oxlip, harebells and primula in pots

A view from the library steps, looking out onto the snow-covered garden and fields beyond. Just out of sight, along the library wall are trays and tables of food for birds and wildlife. To the left, parts of the garden are left undisturbed to encourage wildlife habitats.

and trays. In the grass area surrounding the house, I planted dwarf narcissi, tulip species and other bulbs, which could mingle with the wild flowers – the seeds of which I collected on local derelict airfields. I also let the four old grass tennis courts, the croquet lawn and the bowling green grow. We didn't mow them (they are now mown once a year in September), and soon they were wild-flower meadows by themselves! The seeds were imported by birds and squirrels so I didn't have to do any proper gardening there. All I had to do was pull out the trees! The squirrels planted fertilized nuts, and you got perhaps 30 little trees growing in a year. So you had to get rid of those or it would have soon turned into another bit of the wood.

Then I began to think of ways to promote the idea of growing wild flowers, and decided that the best way would be to find a stretch of the countryside where you weren't interfering with anything by planting them, and do just that! It struck me that the road verges were there to be cultivated. I started scattering seed on newly laid roads when the verges were bare. I would dig the surface if there was anything on it, naturally with the council's permission and understanding, and scatter seed collected from the airfields. People thought I was another nutcase!

But I carried on regardless, and next I thought to myself that all my wild flowers were hay-field flowers; why not put in some others? So I began looking at what grows in other crops and found all these lovely things like poppies, feverfew, flax, cornflowers, corncockles (which almost died out because they are poisonous and people did away with them) and marigolds, which were brought into the country from France with wheat. So I started to line the gravel paths here with these, although they need sowing each year. When I realized how popular these flowers were, I promoted the scheme further by making up little seed packets, with a nice picture on the front. I named the mixture 'Farmer's Nightmare', because it was flowers which farmers considered weeds.

It all took off by itself really. People saw how pretty the wild flowers were and how low in maintenance. Anyone can grow wild flowers in a very simple way: if you have a large area of grass, or a bare bank, you can just leave it alone and let it develop. Seeds are just brought in by birds and squirrels. You can also collect seeds from walking in the country and just scatter them around. If you have some bare patches amongst your herbaceous border, or round your lawn, or near the house, you can sow a mixture of seeds, and with very little cultivation you can get a wonderful show.

I always ran about six schemes simultaneously, some of them almost commercial and some very 'airy fairy'. I was always busy and never had time to do anything in sufficient detail. On the one hand I was growing wild flowers outside, on the other, I was breeding butterflies in a greenhouse. At the same time, I was working for the government on the flea's role in transmitting myxomatosis in rabbits, and exhibiting wild flowers at Chelsea, where I won some medals. I also won a gold medal from the Royal Horticultural Show in Westminster Halls, which was more interesting and important than Chelsea, which is a popularization of the whole thing really. I did most of it by myself, but I also had the help of a young mathematician who was hoping to go to college and was very keen on gardening. He used to come up and help plant rows of primroses and cowslips with me. And I got some advice from Terry Wells, who was the best wild-flower man in this country on grasses and things of that sort.

Because I was doing so many things together, the gardening all happened in a slightly sketchy way, and it is an awful thing to say, but I can't remember the year when I started to advise Prince Charles on his gardens. The Duke of Gloucester's children live near here, and I don't know if Prince Charles remembers going there, but that is where I first saw him, but I really got to advise him through Mr Cadbury. My father founded an organization called SPNR (the Society for the Protection of Nature Reserves), which was meant to protect valuable areas of wild flora and fauna in the UK. He selected 280 areas that should receive public recognition and protection as nature reserves. Mr Cadbury, the Chocolate King, was the director of this society, and I had served on their executive committee for about 30 years.

Mr Cadbury said that the Prince of Wales had made some enquiries about growing wild flowers, and Mr Cadbury told HRH that I knew more about it than the average person and he ought to ask me. Then Mr Cadbury was told to ask me, and that is how we started. The Prince is very enterprising with anything to do with farming or agriculture and he inspired me to add wild flowers to his garden. He had a very good lawn for wild flowers and we planted a selection of all the mixes that we thought were appropriate. The sides of the drive to his house was an ideal place for 'Farmers' Nightmare', so I put that seed in there. After that, his gardener gathered the seed each year, and was able to renew it. I think the gardens at Highgrove were always a great success, but that was due to the Prince of Wales' ability – nothing to do with me. For instance, bluebells are a great feature at Highgrove.

I have gone in for bluebells here from the start, because I knew from the history of the place that there had been a lot of bluebells growing here, but that they had been spoilt a lot by too much canopy from the trees. Bluebells like to have early light, so you mustn't have a dense canopy: you need to have a late leaf-growing tree. Tring Park, at the edge of the Chiltern Escarpment, had a marvellous bluebell wood because there were beech trees there. So I used to collect seed there and bring it to Ashton. At the height of bluebell time here, I always went out into the woods to see them because to me, the waves of bluebells were magical. One day I went up there with my farm manager and we were just walking through the oldest part of the wood when we saw an amazing sight.

A young lady had stripped, and was completely naked except for her Wellingtons, which she still had on, and she was diving head first into the bluebells – which were also full of brambles there! Both the farm manager and I stood rooted to the spot: we were so astonished. When she emerged from among the bluebells we asked her what on earth she was doing. She said, 'Oh! I always come up here and dive into the bluebells, because it is like the sea!' So we said, 'Oh, we quite understand!' and looked at each other in amazement. She was covered in scratches, but she seemed to ignore that completely. She was apparently just a trespasser, but I didn't mind a few careful trespassers – I rather liked it, because I thought they got keen on the wild flowers.

Animals seem very active in the bluebell wood, and now there is a mini-plague of

WHY WE GARDEN | Dame Miriam Rothschild

Miriam Rothschild and two of her dogs at home amongst the bluebells. Photograph *circa* 1995.

Muntjac deer there. This is a deer originally released by the Duke of Bedford. They are naughty little deer which breed like the proverbial rabbit and they are so tough that they can even eat bluebells, which are very toxic. I have seen Muntjacs amongst the bluebells with the flowers actually hanging out of their mouths where they have been tearing them up. But at the same time as I was watching the bluebells being destroyed by Muntjac, I saw the so-called 'Bluebell fly' which is a fly which looks like a bee, because it is fury, but it has an extremely long tongue, and it was *fertilizing* the bluebells. This reminded me that this parasitic fly is actually a very good thing to have in your wood, because at present there is a crisis among the lovers of bluebells. There has been crossing between the Spanish, garden-flower variety of the bluebell, which is a stronger variety than ours, and our own breed is threatened. It was an innocent mistake. The Spanish bluebell was introduced simply as a flower which was strong and easy to grow.

But nowadays, when fields are sprayed with chemical weed-killers, all the wild flowers are obliterated. That is one of the things that first turned me into a wild-flower gardener — another is the nostalgic but genuine delight I feel for wild flowers. Nowadays fields of wheat look like a snooker table! In the old days you got wild mustard, that beautiful yellow plant that looks like a wallflower, and weeds in the fields, like poppies. I wanted to save wild flowers for our children. I couldn't *bear* the sight of the whole country being turned over to dreary development — on the agricultural side as well as for living space. And setting fire to the stubble was one of the things which absolutely enraged me. The stubble not only provided a habitat for interesting plants, but food for countless birds in the winter when they had little else to eat. Now, thank goodness, this has been stopped.

I hope to restore people's interest in wild flowers, whether they are violets, bluebells, or daisies in the lawn. I love wild flowers, and any achievement I have had is in getting people to think along the same lines as myself. I have written some articles about the problem of how we can continue to expand as a nation, or even as counties, and at the same time preserve some of the wildlife. My father was one of the main people who saw the danger ahead. I am very backward in coming forward, but I want to see conservation flourish. Wild flowers are easy to grow if you give them the right conditions, but what you *really* want to do is to preserve the old habitats.

There is one other thing that I would really like to see. Here at Ashton, we have had one marvellously successful experiment. We have left 75 acres of fields alone. We harvested the crop and then said, 'finish'. It hasn't been touched for 54 years! We just let it *rip*. That area has just gone its own way and done what it liked. We didn't introduce anything there: just left it to nature. It is beside woodland, and it has been wonderful for wildlife. We have had 74 different species of birds in that reserve, and one grass new to the county and a wonderful show of wild orchids! There has also been a marvellous lot of insects. Then because of the insects we have had five species of bats there, and then tawny owls, which eat the bats. We have had foxes, badgers, hares and all sorts of animals. It has been such a pleasure. If ever there was a case for promoting a nature reserve, it is to get an ordinary strip of country and let it go and note what comes in there.

There may well come a time, a hundred years from now, when you could say, 'Enough is enough. This has just grown into part of the woodland – let's just enclose it with the rest of the wood.' But at the moment it is an intermediate type of reserve: beyond the grass but not yet the wood, and it has turned out to be most attractive to the rare species here. My one aim at this moment would be to see all the SPNR branches do something similar. You could lease the strips of land from the owners for 50 years; you wouldn't necessarily have to buy them. I look into the future with great hope now, that there will be more understanding between farmers and gardeners. I hope the beginnings of conservation will develop into a huge movement.

Buttercups at Ashton Wold, a simple but loved flower. When Miriam Rothschild started wild-flower gardening in 1970, no one else was doing it. Then as now, it seemed a wonderful alternative to herbaceous borders.

9

GORDON ROWLEY

PLANTSMAN AND SUCCULENT SPECIALIST

Gordon and his friendly prickly pear (*Opuntia robusta*). 'A reminder to learned academics who visit that we grow these plants for fun, not to be taken too seriously!'

'What wond'rous Life in this I lead'

When Gordon Rowley wrote me a letter addressed from his home, 'Cactusville', my interest was already aroused. The author of several books on succulents, and President of the British Cactus and Succulent Society, Gordon Rowley modestly stated, 'I have an undistinguished collection squeezed into a 24-foot glasshouse and no exhibition plants: I regard it as a workroom (or playpen) for botanising....' The letter was signed 'Cactophilously yours', giving me a foretaste of my visit to come.

To Gordon Rowley succulents are not a hobby, nor a source of income, but a way of life. Though his attractive garden does contain camellias, snowdrops, crocuses and many other plants, it is dominated by palms, outdoor succulents and a greenhouse full of more tender specimens. Succulents adorn his windowsills, and his sitting-room is illuminated with plastic flashing cacti. There are paintings, prints and embroideries of succulents on the walls; cushions in the form of cacti; and lampshades, a tray, cups and saucers all depicting these favourite plants. In his spare room is a fabulous Meccano merry-go-round for cacti, and at the end of my visit Gordon showed me an amazing animated film he had made of synchronized cacti whirling and dancing to the music of Tchaikovsky's *Polonaise*.

Yet succulents are not Gordon's only interest. His full but tidy house is a treasure trove of books, diaries and research material, collections of music, films, butterflies and fossils. Gordon Rowley, now in his 80s with few teeth but much vigour, is erudite and multi-talented. And he retains a childlike spirit and joyfulness; his conversation punctuated with peals of laughter. On the inside jacket of the book of which he is most proud, *A History of Succulents* (Strawberry Press, 1997), is a little interview instead of a biography. Asked 'What would you choose as your last meal?' Gordon answers, 'Chocolate éclairs garnished with marzipan and candied peel – nothing unusual.' This for me sums up Gordon Rowley's humour, imagination and playfulness – and I can just visualize the pastries: those too, shaped remarkably like exotic cacti.

In the early 1930s, when I was about 11, my mother, who was thoroughly doting and spoiled me, went to Woolworth's in Harrow and bought me a small potted cactus. Cacti are just one family of the plants called succulents, which have all developed ways of storing water. In those days all the cacti came from Holland and cost sixpence. It was a little Mammillaria, and I fell in love with it immediately and kept it on the windowsill – a tiny piece of desert. The cactus happened to be one which had hooked spines on it, and a few months later, I found a dead fly on the top and thought, 'Ah, this must be one of these insectivorous plants that traps flies that I have heard of.' So that was the first botanical mistake that I made!

What happened to the poor Mammillaria, I don't quite know; it didn't last very long, but from then on, I started haunting Woolworth's and everywhere I went with my long-suffering parents, I would say, 'Where's the nearest Woolworth's?' There was a wonderful big one in Oxford Street in London, with masses of succulents, and I still get a nostalgic flash remembering it if I visit a big nursery now. I remember the thrill of deciding which plant to buy and handing my pocket-money over.

We lived in north-west London and my parents used to take me to museums and gardens including Kew. Immediately one of the great highlights became the cactus house where I saw great big plants and where I really became interested in botany. Eventually I took a botany degree with chemistry as a subsidiary subject. It was just before the end of the war, and I had been allowed to finish off my degree during the war. At that time there was a great demand for soil analysis so I got a job at Reading University analysing soil and sewage and potting compost, and I did that until 1948.

After the war there were various grandiose ideas put forward by the government, and one of these was to found a series of plant collections potentially useful for plant breeding, and one of the collections was to be of roses. It was decided that the John Innes Horticultural Institute was the best place to have the roses, and they advertised for the job of keeper of this national rose collection in Hertford. I was lucky enough to get the job and had 13 glorious years there.

Of course I was paid to work with roses, and cacti were rather taboo, but I smuggled seed pans onto the windowsills. Also for two years, when they had some empty glasshouses, I did a whole series of composting experiments with succulents growing in John Innes compost and other mixtures. Then along came the director and said, 'What's all this rubbish filling up this glasshouse?' and I had to clear it out. But in any case, in 1961 John Innes moved to Norfolk to concentrate more on molecular research rather than flower breeding. Just then Professor Charles Singer, a well-known scientist, told me of a job back in Reading University in the Horticultural Department teaching taxonomy, or the classification of plants. I got the job, and again I was marvellously happy there.

I have never really worked all my life because I have always been paid for what I enjoy doing, which is why I am so cheerful. I feel very sorry for people who really have to work for their living because I have been so lucky all along. At the University, cacti were encouraged, and instead of keeping them on the quiet, I was able to mention them in my lectures and even supervise some student research projects with these, my favourite plants.

There are many reasons why I like cacti so much. First is the extraordinary sculptural look of the plants: the fact that they are condensed, with stark geometry, great symmetry and simple plain surfaces – triangles and circles and so forth. The texture of them, too, is unique. They are endlessly fascinating. The emphasis is not so much on the flowers (beautiful though they are in many cases, but many do not show flowers), but on the scent and the colour of the plants. You get bold washes of colour in the same way as when you go round a modern art exhibition. And I think there is a link there, because in my lifetime, succulents have become so much more fashionable and are grown equally by men and women, in conservatories, on patios, on windowsills, all over the place, and they fit in wonderfully with modern house décor. Cacti are the antithesis of the Victorian idea of gardens with fussy, finely divided foliage – I like them all, but those sorts of plants went well in the rather dark, damp, Victorian rooms.

Also I am an evolutionist and succulents are particularly interesting in that respect: they live at the very limits of plant survival in desert areas around the world. All plants need water but succulents have developed extraordinary means of enduring months and even years of drought and all this is related to their appearance: reduction of their leaves; small flowers or short flowering periods, and sometimes flowers which only open in the cool of the night, pollinated by moths and bats; and the development of protective spines and chemicals.

I have had the odd jab from a cactus, and if a dead carcass is lying on the ground and you step on a spine it can penetrate leather and go right through your shoe, but none of the spines are poisonous. If you get poisoned from a cactus prick it is because it gets infected afterwards. But euphorbias do have a white milky sap, which can be an irritant. Succulents are filled with water to survive, and if they were just there like that in the desert, they wouldn't last a day, because all the grazing animals would gobble them up. The only reason they can survive is by their heavy armour or because they are poisonous, with, for example distasteful alkaloids. To an evolutionist this is a constant stimulus.

Another reason why I love cacti is that they are collectable. I was born a collector. With everything in life, if I have one, I want to know what another one looks like, and then I go on and on. I have got a house-full, with *me* smeared all over it. I came to this house as a lodger in 1961, and it was marvellous because Reading University is just a short walk away. A dear old couple looked after me, and I would go home to Harrow at weekends. Then the husband died and the wife put the house up for sale and I thought, 'It is now or never' and as I had had about 13 different lodgings before, I didn't want another one, so I bought this house. I had to take out a mortgage, which horrified my mother, but it suited me perfectly. Some of the happiest years of my life have been here. People ask if I am lonely, but I have never been lonely even though I have lived by myself.

My interests were my passion and took over right from my earliest schooldays. I never really had time for anything else. I have had an all-consuming interest in natural things in particular; there is always something new. The deeper you probe, the deeper the problems are, and the more you discover, the more there is yet to be discovered. Downstairs I have got journals, abstracts, classified pictures of succulents and vintage prints. I also have a music library. Upstairs is another library of books, including very old herbals, my diaries going back to 1936, tapes, videos and films.

In the guest bedroom is a merry-go-round, which does go round, to music, and cacti sit on Meccano horses. I started at the age of seven with Meccano – I have got the original letter I put up the chimney to Santa Claus (my mother kept it) and I have been doing Meccano ever since. You see I have never grown up. My home help knitted little cacti people to go on the merry-go-round. It amuses my visitors. It amuses me, too. The guest room also contains my other schoolboy hobbies: fossils and minerals. We used to swap bits of quartz for white mice and guinea pigs. I wasn't so keen on the guinea pigs and white mice so I got all the fossils and crystals, sulphur, graphite, and things like Iceland's Fire which comes from a cave in Iceland and has double refraction.

My first schoolboy hobby was tropical butterflies, which I bought from a shop in London. Then I made my own collection of British ones, many that you rarely see now.

The fabulous Meccano merry-go-round built by Gordon. Knitted and plastic cacti spin on galloping horses to the sounds of music.

Gordon Rowley in his glasshouse amid 'some pet succulents'. He is holding *Pterocactus tuberosus* bought for 1s 6d (7½p) on 1 July, 1942 at a florist's shop opposite King's College in the Strand, London.

Nowadays, with conservation, you would collect them with a camera. I never throw anything away. I am a compulsive collector. I keep all Attenborough's programmes on video and I dote upon everything to do with early film. I have a huge library of my favourites: Disney, Chaplin, Laurel and Hardy. Since 1982 I have been collecting videos. I never have a dull evening now – life is never long enough. I have all the Marx Brothers films, the Sherlock Holmes ones, and all of Hitchcock's films – he is my favourite director: you are kept in suspense right from start to finish.

Another great hobby of mine during the 1960s was making films. I bought a 16-millimetre Bolex and started making amateur movies, like *Cactus Polonaise*. It cost about £12 to make, but it was great fun and it won an award in the Amateur Ten Best and has been shown on television a few times. I was inspired by Disney's Fantasia and I also belonged to a group called The Grasshopper Group in London who were the top amateur animators. The twirling cacti were all done with Meccano turntables covered with black paper. A lot of the effects were done in the camera, using double exposure or half exposure; others were created with mirrors or crinkly glass.

The main problem was the music because the amateur has no professional means of synchronizing sound. So I had to invent a means of doing it. Fortunately I had a projector which had a magnetic stripe on it and a clutch, and when you pull out the clutch the film stops in the gate. So I bought a 100-foot reel of clear striped leader and, by hand, numbered the frames from one to 4,000! Then I put the music on a sound-track and the film in the projector, and using the clutch I would stop and start the music and write the number of the frame down. I decided on the mood, imperious fanfare to start and so on, and then I found all the shots and just had enough film to make the whole thing.

My latest hobby, or collection, has been embroidered pictures of cacti. In 1968 I went to a lady's house in Colorado, and she had some really beautiful embroideries of cacti from Japan, which she had obtained through the president of the Japanese Cactus Society. They were done by a lady called Musako Sugiyama, who at that time spoke no English but who turned out to be an absolute angel. Now I have the largest collection of her work outside Japan. She sent me embroideries, based on her husband's collection, and then cushions, and we had an exchange system. I had a lot of second-hand books, which in Japan, were very valuable, and so I put a price on the books and she put a price on the embroideries, which in fact were a bargain for me. Then she sent origami and mobiles and she started to learn English and she sent me letters and photos of her family and I kept them all. I have one letter on the wall, where she ends, 'I am very glad to know you. What a happiness woman am I.' So since then she has been my Happiness Woman!

As with most things, with cacti you start off collecting on your own, but once you get contact with other people, mainly through societies, then you see plants available to trade or swap, and you can hear lectures and go on trips to specialist nurseries. When you start out, you think you can only get a few measly specimens from somewhere like Homebase, but actually there are vast nurseries which sell nothing but succulents, and it escalates. You are always on the lookout for new ones to fill the gaps and build your collection. You may specialize in one group, or, as I have tended to do, you have a bit of everything. There is a fairly good range of books on the most popular succulents, but there are whole groups on which there are no reference works, so I have always gone towards these sideline groups, with the result that I have produced a whole series of books, which are money-losers! And as I go from one group to another I have to dispose of some plants to make room for new collections.

To some people there is a monetary factor, but I don't think it applies with succulents. With orchids, of course, the plants are very expensive, but succulents are not comparable. I used to give everything away, but I realized that was a bit silly as one person would grab everything and not even say 'thank you'. But we all get spares; that is one of the joys of growing and propagating. I take my trays of spares to the local branch of the Cactus and Succulent Society and price them below the nursery price and all the profits from that go to the Conservation Fund which I set up in the 1980s.

At present, as always, I have a mixed collection. I've got Spanish moss all over the place, and elephant's foot (*Dioscorea elephantipes*), relative of the yam: the tubers grow above ground with a lovely woody surface. During the war they thought elephant's foot would be a useful source of cortisone and so a lot were grown. I've divided my greenhouse into three sections: a hot section for tropical plants, a medium section, which is just frost-free, and the end section which has no heating. There is a bit of everything because I like them all. A lot of my plants are surprisingly old; for instance I notice one label says 1942 on a *Pterocactus kuntzei* – a wartime baby. Another old plant is one of the few that you can actually pat; it is woolly rather than spiny, a *Mamillaria plumose*. A lot of people like my South African pebble plants; I tend to like minor plants that other people often to ignore, like my peperomias. A lot of succulents rest in the winter. We keep them dormant and dry, and then when the warm weather comes I water them again and clean them up.

I keep the centre of the greenhouse warm all year and have lots of seedlings growing in trays. There are also succulents from the Galapagos Islands, and one from Malaysia which has a hollow inside where ants nest, and then there is queen of the night (*Selenicereus grandiflorus*), which gets a flower spanning a foot across. I also keep Madagascan

Notocactus warasi. A popular cactus which occurs in Uruguay, Paraguay, Argentina and southern Brazil. It is fairly easy to grow and makes a good indoor plant.

endemics, which I propagate by grafting because they are very much endangered and I am very interested in conservation. Now there are two or three places in South Africa and South America where we have propagated plants and put them back into their environments and also cleared areas on site to encourage the plants to grow. We pinched these things from their habitat in the first place so I feel we should do our best to make sure they don't die out.

The central greenhouse is really my playground where I do all sorts of weird and wonderful Frankenstein-type things. You know humans and chimpanzees share about 99 per cent of their DNA? Well now botanists are looking at succulents and comparing their DNA because they are very difficult to classify, but the ones which have most DNA in common can be put together in the same genus group. So they are working out the family trees of these plants according to their shared DNA. I cottoned on to an idea from this by thinking that if two plants shared so much DNA, perhaps you could intercross them by grafting one on to another.

Even Aristotle knew you can graft an apple on to a pear, but you can't graft an apple to an oak tree. But I have tried doing some grafts with extraordinary results. I have used two plants which are from different botanical families which botanists would classify way apart, but in fact they will inter-graft and grow because they have shared DNA. I use published accounts of the DNA and have grafted five different plants all on one host plant, which probably tells us that they shouldn't be classified separately. No one else has done this particular aspect before. I have even grafted a cactus, a New World plant, on to an African portulaceae. If we can find plants with shared DNA, we can find new grafting stocks, for example, for fruit trees.

I get my stock from seed and cuttings and buying at nurseries. I have not been on too many expeditions abroad because I am the world's worst traveller. I get lost getting to the bus stop and I faint in the heat. If the temperature gets much above 70 degrees I start perspiring and can't see through my spectacles, and start to go weak at the knees, and of course all these cactus habitats are some of the hottest in the world. However, thanks to my friends, without whom I would not have got outside the front door, I did go on some trips, beginning in the 1960s.

We started with a marvellous Greyhound coach trip, which went all round the United States for nine weeks on one ticket! We were allowed unlimited travel and went through California and ended up in Florida. We started off in New York and had to learn the techniques of things. We got arrested twice for jaywalking. We must have looked a funny sight – two mad Englishmen in shorts, carrying rucksacks, bumming their way around the US, telling the Americans how to grow their native plants, because we also took lectures with us and talked to cactus societies.

In 1971 we did the same sort of thing in Africa, going all round the Cape. It opens one's perspective tremendously to see plants in the wild. Nowadays, everybody does that sort of thing, but then it was more unusual. Even at that time there were rules about what you could collect and we tried to be honest. In South Africa the land was privately owned, but in those days a lot of it wasn't fenced and you could just stop your car and wander off and see what was growing by the roadside. Nowadays it is much more fenced.

I went with a companion, a professor, and we always went with an authorized botanist. I corresponded with people over the years, so I had a lot of contacts who were only too pleased to take you around and show you things. Some people don't like doing that, and want to find their own plants, but you can go for hours and days in Africa without finding anything on your own. We either had collecting permits or we knocked at the door of the farm and asked if we could take something. Many of the plants I have now are collected from those expeditions – they may not look all that big – some cacti are incredibly slow-growing, but some, particularly the ones you see in nurseries, grow surprisingly fast.

Perhaps my most exciting day was when I saw one particular plant – Welwitschia – named after the German botanist Welwitsch, who discovered it in the early nineteenth century. It grows only in Namibia, in one of the most hostile deserts on earth. Now David Attenborough has filmed Welwitschia in some of his programmes on the lives of plants, but when we went I don't think anybody had filmed it. We drove out across a flat, featureless, burning hot, dry area with hardly any living plant in sight. It looked like Death Valley. We could just about see the track; if it had rained we would not have been able to, and we thought we would never see anything alive or get back alive ourselves!

Suddenly we saw these great green things looming up before us! We got out and touched them. They have just two great leathery leaves on either side. We had only one afternoon, but the weather was fine and fortunately there was a coastal breeze. It was wonderful. I was able to take a lot of still pictures and to make a short film, which has been shown on television. And it just happened that it was my fiftieth birthday, so what nicer birthday treat could you have than filming Welwitschia? Many people followed afterwards, but at that time, hardly any people had seen the plant. It is very difficult to grow. I did have it for 17 years, and then unfortunately I went away on holiday and the person who was meant to water the plants didn't do it and it died. It is one of those botanical curiosities – there is no other plant like it.

So that was one of my most joyous experiences. The thing, however, of which I am most proud is my book *A History of Succulents*, which I started in the 1940s. It finally came out in 1997 and was the one book over which I had a lot of control, with the result that it didn't have the usual mistakes in it. The only way I managed to do it was when I sold my parent's house in London and used the money. I took the photographs and thought of the design and it was really my *magnum opus*. I don't think I'll ever do anything as good as that again, although I am still writing more. There is so much that can be done: the future is bright. I'm 82 and live alone, so I can do as I like!

I have friends and visitors and I still go to the University and help on some student projects every two or three weeks. I am a fair-weather gardener, and then I generally allow myself to watch videos in the evenings. I think one of the secrets of life is to have plenty of laughter – so I like Laurel and Hardy and comic books. I don't do more than scan newspaper headlines, because they are so depressing. You could call me an escapist or a hedonist, but I try to cheer up other people. Mind you, you should see the botanists at each other's throats over names and classification. Some terrible enmities have developed, but I try not to let it get as serious as that. After all, why do we grow these plants anyway? We grow them for amusement and entertainment, as ornaments to enhance our lives. Many people just grow cacti on windowsills, but a lot of people like their greenhouses because they take them away from the hassles of everyday life. It is a sort of sanctum. In your own glasshouse, among your own plants, you are in your own little kingdom.

PART II
GARDENERS by Default

10

DAVE COOKE

TEMPERATE HOUSE MANAGER AT KEW

Dave amongst one of his favourite plants, *Rhododendron veitchianum*, which was grown in the Temperate House in Victorian times. Its native habitat is Burma, Thailand and Singapore.

'How vainly men themselves amaze To win the Palm, the Oke, or Bayes'

The elegant, airy Temperate House at the Royal Botanic Gardens, Kew is an enormous greenhouse, which in many ways is more impressive than the famous Palm House. The Temperate House is the largest ornamental glasshouse in the world, measuring 180 by 42 metres at its greatest length and breadth. To enhance ventilation it is designed as straight rather than curvilinear and is made up of a series of ornamented square and octagonal buildings with tiered triangular roofs. Designed by Decimus Burton, building began in 1860 and finished in 1898, with a full restoration programme between 1974 and 1980. Inside it is arranged geographically, and houses, amongst many other things, subtropical crop plants, fruit trees and the world's largest indoor plant, the Chilean wine-palm.

Gardening in a controlled environment is unusual, but it is Dave Cooke's midnight rescue missions at Kew, and plant-finding expeditions to places like Madagascar, which make his experiences unique. To find out more, I descended a wrought-iron spiral staircase in the south octagon of the Temperate House, and, skirting huge, winding white-painted pipes, made my way to Dave's office. There I found a man of indeterminate age – and coyly reluctant to reveal it – sitting at a desk surrounded by various charts, staff rosters, and photographs of motorbikes.

An incongruous view of the Temperate House with a palm outside covered in snow. The house was designed by Decimus Burton, and was built in stages from 1860 to 1899.

The Temperate House here at Kew is the largest display house we have and it covers a vast range of plant material in the temperate zone of the world. It is frost-free; we run a winter temperature of about eight degrees Celsius and then the heating goes off in the summer when it is ambient. The house is geographically arranged and has plants from temperate Asia at the north end, including a big collection of rare rhododendrons; plants from South Africa at the south end; and in the big central zone are the Australian plants and plants from the Americas. We also have plants from the Mediterranean area, through to New Zealand.

The Palm House is also geographically arranged, but their minimum winter temperature is around 19 degrees, so it is much, much hotter with about 80 per cent humidity. It gets extremely hot in the summer, when you can really only stay in there a few minutes before you want to get out. The Temperate House is much more spacious with a more pleasing atmosphere. I spent nine years in the Palm House. I landscaped it, met the Queen Mother, which was fun, and it was good. When people say, 'Kew Gardens' they immediately think of the Palm House, which is in the centre, near the public gate. A lot of people go there straight away, and it gets a lot of attention.

The Temperate House is slightly off the beaten track, which is nice, because if you are walking toward the south end of Kew Gardens, towards the lake and the pagoda, you suddenly come across this enormous glass conservatory, and you go, 'Oh wow! What's this?' and go in and enjoy the experience. Next door is the Evolution House, which is a one-directional house about plant evolution, which is fun and good for kids, with things like bubbling mud and a volcano. But what I like best about the Temperate House is the challenge. It is just so vast. Even to get from one end to the other, if you have forgotten some tools, is a long way. The whole of the Palm House would fit into the central part of this House. Another challenge in the Temperate House at the moment is to turn it back to what it was many years ago. It has lost its way a little bit, and our plan is to redesign and redevelop various beds throughout the House. It could be as much as a 20-year project, so that should keep me going!

Actually, to begin with, I didn't want to be a gardener, I wanted to be a chef. But I didn't get my qualifications at school, so I left school on a Friday and went into horticulture on the Monday. I didn't go to university or college although I did do a bit of day-release. First I worked for Richmond Council for nearly two years, as an assistant gardener. I went out on the construction gangs, did bedding and pruning in the terraced gardens at Richmond, learnt how to double dig a bed — it was like an apprenticeship scheme. Then a job vacancy came up at Kew in the local paper and I applied and got it, many moons ago — I'm not going to tell you how long, because it is pretty frightening. I started in the nursery, then moved to the Palm House, then worked in both Houses for a period, and then decided to stay in the Temperate House and develop it and bring it back to its former glory.

But I still thoroughly enjoy cooking, and have got the odd certificate in cookery that I have gained from night school. I think gardening and cooking go hand in hand. You grow vegetables at home and turn them into something to cook. In my spare time I also go off with a couple of lads from work and burn around a racetrack on a motorbike at about 140 miles an hour. I also have quite a large garden, but I don't do much gardening as a hobby. In fact I live on site. So when people say, 'How large is your garden?' I can say, 'Oh, it's 300 acres!' There are only about 12 of us who live here — one or two maintenance people, the curator, the director, the marine biologist. I live just near the Temperate House in case there is a problem with either of the two big public conservatories. One or two people occasionally wander into my garden by mistake, but generally it is quite private. It has a lot of fruit trees and is generally low-maintenance — except when I forget to mow

The Temperate House is the largest ornamental glasshouse in the world, so leaving a spade in the wrong place can give a gardener a long walk.

the lawn. I enjoy it to a degree but mainly I just relax in it – sit out and have a beer. I grow a few tomatoes, carrots and suchlike; no tropical plants!

Once, about six years ago, on a December night, I got called up by the marine biologist at about 11.30 p.m. and he said, 'You'd better come into the Palm House because it feels a bit cool in here.' The heating is controlled by a small computer, which shows a graph of the temperature, and I could see that it was dropping drastically. It was windy outside, which would draw some of the heat out of the glass, but I started panicking when it got down to about eight degrees when it should have been about 19 degrees. We called the engineer out, who had to come from Kingston, and when he arrived he informed us that three of the four boilers had stopped working.

The boiler house is quite near the Palm House and he started working in there, but it got down to about four degrees and the graph was still dropping. Eventually, well after midnight, he got one boiler started up, and in about another couple of hours he got the other ones going. But when the temperature drops in a tropical house, all the leaves on some of the plants drop off. Luckily we didn't lose anything, but it was a bit touch-and-go. We have got some emergency heaters which we can drag in, which would have been the last resort, but we were OK. The Temperate House is also controlled by a small computer and a very large boiler. We run off gas and just occasionally off oil as a back up.

So although gardening under glass in theory provides control, we are reliant on systems working. Also, the plants are actually a bit trickier to grow because of where they have come from. Tropical and sub-tropical plants take time to adjust to the light levels in London. And all three glasshouses collect rainwater off roofs into big tanks, and if the rain tanks run empty we have to rely on a backup system, which injects nitric acid into mains water to lower the PH level. Watering in all the glasshouses is done manually.

I organize staffing of the Temperate House over 365 days. This is another big difference from working in an ordinary garden. I do some weekend duties, and so do some of my staff and the odd student. Currently I have three other staff, and occasionally in the summer we have a few more students helping out. Each member of staff manages their own different areas: watering (we do have a small irrigation system which we put on in the summer), pruning, planting and carrying out biological pest control. Staff put out other bugs to control the pests, which teaches the public as well. Members of the public quite often ask what we are doing, and we can teach them about the green environment and looking after their own plants at home by, for example, using wasps to control whitefly.

I spend about 60 per cent of my time gardening. Like most managers, I could do without report-writing. We also rent the Temperate House out for private functions, and have fashion shoots inside sometimes, which takes time and energy but keeps us on our toes. The things I enjoy most are hands-on trouble-shooting, a bit of staff and student training, some teaching, and growing plants – that's what we are here for. At present we are undertaking a major restoration. We are starting with the south end, which will be predominantly South African Cape flora. I have been to South Africa and seen what it

Dave digging out geraniums in a bed at the south end of the house, where he will plant South African Cape flora.

looks like: the flora is absolutely incredible. So we have been experimenting with different soils and composts over the last few days to try and get the right acidity for the plants.

Sometimes we go out to the countries to collect the plant material but that takes a lot of time, and getting older plant material is now very difficult with plant conservation globally. But I have been to Madagascar and Africa and Asia a couple of times and I am very keen on the Americas. We also write to other botanical gardens that might supply us with seed. Seed is much easier to transport than live plants. We have two large nurseries, which grow most of the material that we want for a display, but my favourite plant, which unfortunately is no longer with us, was a palm that I was fortunate enough to collect in Madagascar in 1986, on an exceptional trip with John Dransfield, the palm botanist here at Kew.

We were in Madagascar for nine weeks, and my role was to climb palm trees ranging from five to twenty metres high, using climbing irons and a rope. One early morning we set off from the east coast in a canoe with two guides. We had a very small piece of material and photos of a unique palm that John had never seen before, and he chatted to some local village elders, who said they had seen it, only it was quite far away. Anyway we decided to try to find it, but the canoe was very small, so I couldn't take any change of clothing, just my climbing and collecting equipment and some food for a couple of nights. Actually I thought it would just be an hour or two round the cove, but after about eight or nine hours we got to a little inlet and pitched a rain shelter.

The two guides slept in a little hut, which was the only hut for miles around and was in fact a smoke house where a family would go out into the lagoon to collect fish and then smoke them in the hut to preserve them. I can smell it now. The family that lived there was sort of brown and smoked, like kippers too! Anyway we got up early the next day to try and find the palm. We walked for three-quarters of the day into the forest and up and down mountains and hills, through three deep rivers up to my chest, and eventually we came to a low wet valley. There we sat down to have our lunch of boiled rice and chocolate, and while John was really excited, I was quite tired and fed up, really.

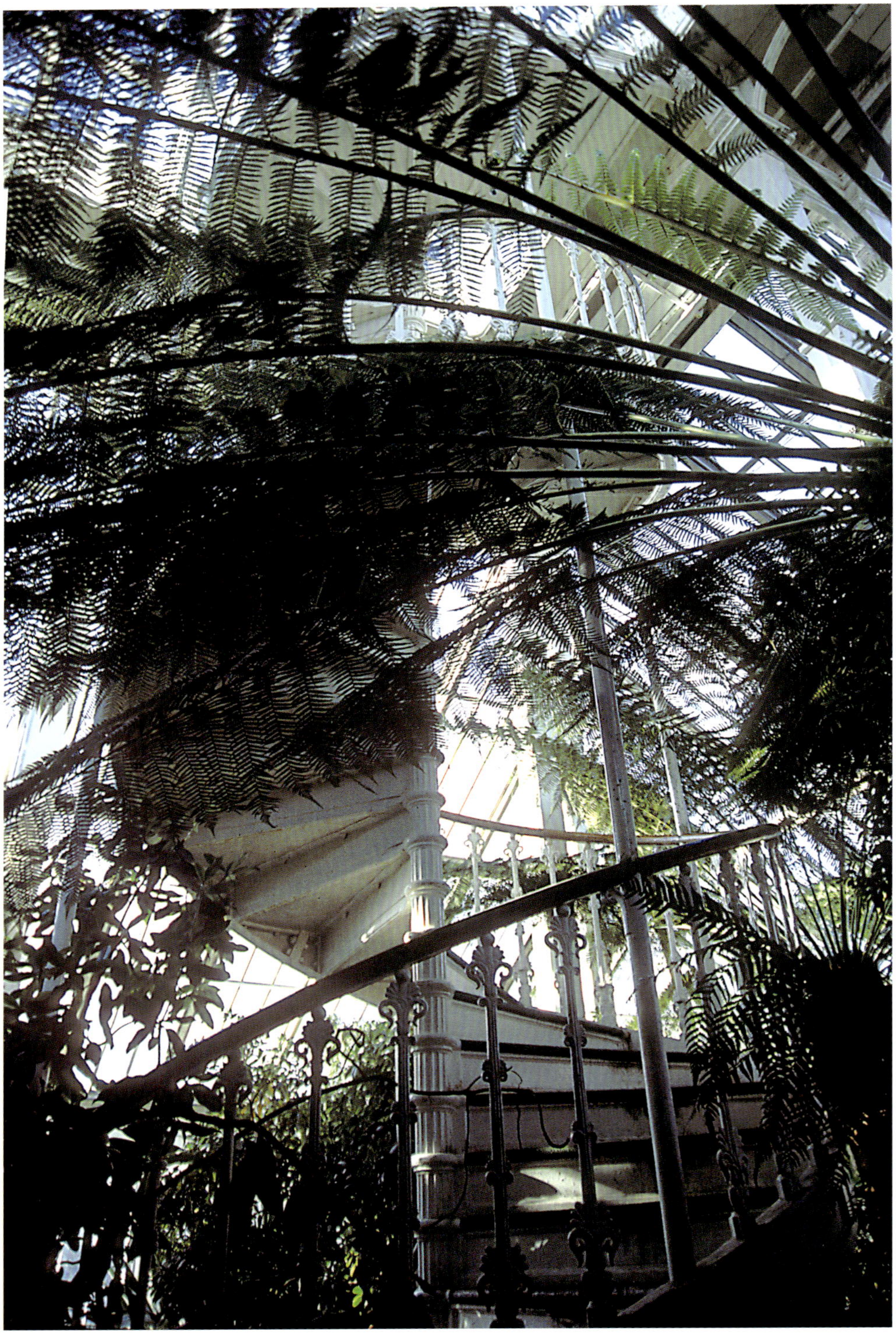

WHY WE GARDEN | Dave Cooke

One guide had run on ahead and suddenly he came back with some fruit of the palm! The funny thing was, the guide was called Narciss, as in narcissus or daffodil, but he was a really big hunky friendly guy and it made me laugh. John speaks excellent French whereas mine is abysmal, and so when John heard about the palm, he told me to get all my gear together and we found these two palms called the Forest Coconut. It looks like a regular coconut only the fruits are a bit like a large brazil nut. One tree was a bit smaller than the other, perhaps seven metres. I had only ever climbed a pine tree down in the conservation area here before, but a palm tree is completely different; it is like climbing up a concrete lamp post – the trunk is so hard. A couple of times I slipped 15 or 20 feet, and if you are four or five days away from a hospital, you do worry a little!

But I collected some herbarium material and some fruit. The herbarium material is dried and we press it and keep it at Kew Herbarium for plant identification. Kew Herbarium holds around seven million dried plants, so it is like a reference library. We also made duplicates for Madagascar and Missouri. I brought back about 20 seeds, which were distributed to other botanic gardens, such as the one in California and Florida. About three of our seeds germinated and we were really excited. The chromosome number was absolutely huge, so a lot of papers were written. Only one plant survived and it grew for about three years in the Palm House and then suddenly packed up and died. It probably knew I was leaving the Palm House and coming to the Temperate House!

The Temperate House is many things: part of our function is conservation, as well as acting as a museum and as an attractive space for adults and schoolchildren. Over the last six years we have gone off at a slight tangent and our aim now is to have more Victorian-type plantings, display work and flowers. Our new director is keen to get larger numbers of the public and schoolchildren into Kew, so the centre part of the house should be more attractive with floral material. For example, many years ago we had a big fuchsia collection, and I recently found a fuchsia society that specializes in old cultivars, so we have ordered some of those and will bring them back into the House. Part of my work is research, and in Victorian times the House was very lush with a lot of big material. But if you have too many really large plants it gets very dark, so we have to weigh it up quite carefully.

Another plant I want to increase, which did very well in Victorian times, is high-altitude, sub-tropical rhododendrons. They have incredible colours and flower sizes and shapes. I think they are far superior to the hardy rhododendrons that you can get to grow outside. They are very temperamental and need a lot of care and although one or two varieties could grow outside in a really sheltered position, they are better suited to some protection in the winter. But the public is able to see here, not only rainforests, but plants that they might possibly grow at home. One of the hardy bananas that we have here could be grown outside in someone's back garden.

We have got a large citrus collection, and people like that because many of them have

Opposite: The spiral staircases leading to a balcony high up in the Temperate House are a famous feature. They are still stunningly lovely, especially as here, seen through *Dicksonia atarctica*, an Australian tree fern.

grown an orange pip. I get one or two enquiries a year asking if an orange tree grown from a pip will ever fruit. The answer is maybe yes, maybe no, depending on the variety. We do have regular visitors who come to chat and talk about their gardens. I also have an odd person who writes to me on a regular basis, who highlights bits of his letters in different colours; I'd like to meet him one day.

When I worked in the nursery here, doing palm propagation, I was away from the public for a good number of years, so when I came up to manage the Palm House it was a shock. It was very busy and noisy with kids running everywhere but after a while you do get used to it and in fact we need to interact more with the public. We need to tell them not only where the toilets and café are, but ideally we need to tell them something extra as well. For instance we might advise them not to water their plants too much, or show them something in flower which they have never seen before, or the largest plant under glass in the world, which is the *Jubea chilensis*, about 16 metres tall in the middle of the Temperate House.

I have been fortunate at Kew. I landscaped the Temperate House many years ago, and landscaped the Palm House in the late '80s. If I had my time over I would do the landscaping completely differently; but it has been fun – really enjoyable. There is nowhere else in this country with the unmatched plant collection that we have here at Kew. We have got some incredibly rare plants. We also have really good staff, which counts for a lot as well. I have 24 beds in the Temperate House, and if I plan to do one bed a year, that is 24 years, and I think I might have retired by then. But I would like to go through from one end of the House to the other and replant, redesign, re-evaluate. That's my aim. And I'd like to be able to stay on my motorbike going round Brands Hatch! I'd like to travel a bit more, too. Meanwhile, I have had numerous job offers, but Kew is absolutely unique.

11

SELINA DIX HAMILTON
ROOF GARDENER

The cleverly designed roof garden can be seen from the modern, starker living room below.

'While all Flow'rs and all Trees do close
To wave the Garlands of repose'

Selina Dix Hamilton lives above her business – 'Eger Architects'. Walking through her modern, minimalist interior space, I was surprised to walk out into an old-fashioned, comfortable, overflowing roof garden. The hard structure is, admittedly, predominantly metal and glass, and a few plants are indeed architectural. Nevertheless the overall effect is one of softness and denseness, not dissimilar from a cottage garden in the sky.

I found it interesting that a modern architect did not have a matching stark garden. Similarly, virtually all garden designers I have spoken to who design hard landscaped minimalist gardens for others, do not themselves own one. Keen gardeners want a changing garden, not one that requires little maintenance and is 'finished'. And modern designers seem to require a haven of comfort and a degree of disorder and nostalgia. Selina is at ease in her garden and enjoys relaxing there. She likes tweaking rather than digging, yet she has managed to incorporate trees, shrubs, vines, climbers and herbaceous plants into her confined space, where she also has to contend with sun and wind problems. Her garden illustrates just how much can be achieved using containers on a roof or in a courtyard.

I am a roof gardener by default, because I only have a roof. Before that I had a town-sized garden, but when we moved here there was no open space, and so we put this top extension on about five years ago and made the garden a year later. I always wanted to live over my work, but I missed not having a garden. I have loved gardening for a long time, although not, I think, as a child. I am actually a landscape architect as well, although I don't do a lot of that. This garden is my trial patch in a way. I am always buying plants and everything is fighting for survival because I have put so many things in. But actually I don't like getting my hands dirty! I like doing clean gardening, so this roof garden suits me very well, because once you have planted the things, there is no nasty earth to dig or anything like that.

The amount of soil this garden needed was amazing. First I had a lorry-full, and my husband unloaded 100 large sacks and carried them on his back, up the equivalent of four floors (it is only three really, but the building used to be a factory, so two floors are very high). Then I said we needed another 50 sacks, and when they were up here they all disappeared, and we had to have another 100! Everything is planted in compost, which gave the plants a very good start, although they still need feeding all the time. The plants are all in containers, and they are all irrigated.

The irrigation proved to be the absolute salvation of the garden. At first we thought it all looked a bit manky because of the wind, but as soon as we got an irrigation system, everything perked up and was really good and survived the wind. We haven't had any losses except through drought, so now we water the garden for about an hour and a half a day.

Irrigation is vital, because even if there is a huge downpoor, very little of the water actually gets into the plants in the containers.

Another thing which of course we needed was a barrier to stop people falling over – which might seem a bit unnecessary now that there are so many plants, but at the beginning it was very important. We purposely made it a slatted fence, which is better for wind, because the wind seeps through it rather than building up and going over the top, but what has also happened is that plants go through it. It is rather like a garden wall where your best plants grow over the other side, into your neighbour's garden. But from outside, when you look up, there are a whole lot of completely different plants, like daisies, which you can't see in the garden, which is quite amusing.

I enjoy watching the plants grow and putting things next to each other to see if they work together. I love designing gardens for people, although I would obviously never design a garden like this, because it is just a riot. For someone else, I would have more discipline and simplicity. Here I have consciously put in as much texture as I could and I wanted it to be very green. I wanted it to feel quite enclosed, rather like a green box – a retreat away from the streets of Camberwell. It could have looked very beautiful with a single hedge all round the edge, but I love to have lots of plants and not to see any bare earth.

Every plant has to pay its way, so they are nearly all scented, too. Now I have got sweet peas, tobacco plants, lilies coming out, honeysuckle, wisteria, a *Trachelospermum jasminoides* on the wall, which smells glorious, and wintersweet, which smells lovely in the

Selina relaxes with a cup of coffee. On the arms of the chair is thyme, which she enjoys stroking. To the left are pelargoniums ('Sainsbury's variety!'), and sweet peas growing up the metal wavy poles that Selina likes. To the right the grass is *Miscanthus sinensis* 'Gracillimus', and behind a Lombardy cypress.

winter. Perhaps my favourite time is the middle of July, when all the lilies are out and the scent is absolutely amazing. But I always try to have something out. Recently I have bought a lot of plants from different sources on the Web, which has been very successful. They seem to arrive in much better condition than things I bought some years ago through mail-order catalogues.

The only annuals which I always have are tobacco plants, nasturtiums and pansies, because I love them so much. This year I also bought some little sweet pea plants, before I had decided where to put them. Then the only thing I could find that seemed suitable to grow them on were cane wigwams, which I thought were very ugly. Anyway we loaded the wigwams into the back of the car, with great trouble, when I suddenly saw these wavy bent wire things in the corner of the garden centre, which were much nicer. So I made my husband take the wigwams out of the car and change them for the wire supports! I am very pleased with these because they blend in and are not at all obtrusive.

Apart from the few annuals, most of the plants are perennial and I also have several herbs, because I like cooking with them, and I choose plants because they feel nice, too. I put them in places where you can touch them, like some thyme or a succulent in a pot on the arm of a chair. I think when you live in a city, to be able to touch something that is growing is rather soothing. You go out into the country in the summer and everything is so wonderful that you think, 'I should just move to the country.' But in a way, being in the city heightens your feeling of it being great to be somewhere green. And having such a small space makes you think very hard about what you want to achieve from it.

Here everything is very concentrated. The first things I planted were the architectural plants, like acanthus, and *Melianthus major*, which grows gigantic in the autumn and has a symbiosis with the crocosmia, with its scarlet flowers, which look lovely with the soft green. They are all in together, blending in a hotch-potch, almost like a tapestry. The other thing I love is things growing through each other, so I can have about four plants in one place. I have lots of different clematis (up here in the wind, I have discovered that the ones that originate from Poland do best – I thought that was

The roof garden leads straight out of the top floor sitting/dining area. Working chimneys keep a Chusan palm warm in winter, with *Crocosmia* 'Lucifer' to the side and nicotiana in pots on the right.

quite clever of me!) with things like *Jasminum beesianum*, which has small red flowers.

We also decided to plant a few trees, which I suppose is less usual in a roof garden. We've got a fig, and Italian cypresses in the corner, which have already doubled in size, so I have stopped giving them any fertilizer. We've also got a palm tree by the chimney, which is a working one, so the tree is kept warm in winter. And because we are not far from the river, we seldom get frost and I am able to have an oleander – a beautiful dark red one. We have got a rowan in the far corner, and yesterday I went to a garden where they had a morello cherry, and I am going to get one of those because I had forgotten how lovely they are.

I love the contrast of the lushness of the plants with what is quite minimal architecture and décor. You don't want everything too minimal. The flooring of the garden is decking and we have a wooden table and chairs. At first I had large plastic pots all round the edge, but I didn't like them because they were so visually intrusive and so I changed them all, and all the compost had to be changed to new containers. I wasn't very popular with my husband then, either! I felt very mean. You know, I talk about it as 'my garden' but he does all the horrid jobs. Now some containers are made from galvanized metal and others we made ourselves out of a roofing material. We have to keep everything quite lightweight, because we are on an existing building, so we need to have all of the load round the perimeter. That suits me very well, because it makes two little 'rooms' to sit in.

The garden is really an extension of the top room [a kitchen/dining-room]; you walk straight out through glass doors, which, when we have parties, and all summer, we have open. To the side is a spare bedroom, and that leads to the smaller part of the roof garden. We don't have a very traditional home. The door to the spare room was open once and one of my friends said, 'Oh, you sleep in the kitchen!' And I countered, 'No, we eat in the bedroom!' The big window goes down to the floor below, so you can see the garden from there; we are trying to make the most of what we have got here.

We put the garden at the back of the building, because it is the sunny side, but it gets very hot, so we put up a shade over the top made of a metal frame with timber rods, which run through in a slatted effect. It takes a little of the sun away, but the plan is to grow the vine and other climbers right over it, so it will be very shady in the summer, and then in the winter when the plants lose their leaves we will get the sunlight back again. It will be lovely. I can't wait for it; I think one of the most difficult things is not being able to hurry nature. I have been talking to the vine, telling it to 'hurry up!' The vine, *Vitus coignetiae*, goes bright red in autumn, an absolutely amazing colour. It only has tiny grapes, but I didn't really want real grapes because then there would be a lot of flies. We are trying to work with nature to modulate the environment.

I get loads of weeds, even though everything is in containers, and every sort of pest you can imagine – black, green and white fly, lily beetles, everything. I had a naïve idea at first that up here would be a little haven away from all the 'garden nasties' but we've got slugs and snails, even four floors up! Last year I fought the pests organically, but it wasn't terribly successful, I think because it is rather a stressed environment with the wind and so on, so the plants are particularly susceptible to pests. You need to be quite pro-active and catch things quickly.

In fact, the garden is more time-consuming than one might think, because it is a sort of scissors job, getting rid of any dead bits and constantly going round tweaking at everything. I guess if you have a large garden, you don't look after it with such manic obsession. I want it to be perfect, and if it isn't, I have to try and do something about it. I also want the things that I grow to survive, so I look after them very well. But if I don't like them, they get chucked out. I am not at all sentimental about plants which, say, come up the wrong colour. What I want is a haven on the roof.

The thing I like best is sitting in the garden with a drink! Also, I see this as a very social space. People come and we have meals out here. Most of the time, I am very busy working, so it is a place where we entertain, and where I relax. We like clean, uncluttered interior space, with no curtains or anything like that, so the garden is a complete contrast. I didn't particularly aim for a comfortable garden, but that is what it has become. It is a lovely place to sit in. We have got nice views of the floodlit church and Canary Wharf, so we are quite lucky with the roofscape. And although my husband does all the heavy work for me, he enjoys sitting here, too. I do let him out here to relax *sometimes*!

A view of St Giles' Church framed by purple verbena and the vine *Vitis coignetiae*. Several clematis and a wisteria also scramble up the pergola roof.

CAROLYN ELWES

GALANTHOPHILE

Galanthus plicatus 'Wendy's Gold'. A bright yellow-green ovary (the rounded organ above the outer segments) and large yellow marking on the inner segments ensure this snowdrop is always in demand, although it is difficult to obtain.

'Your sacred Plants'

Approaching the gates of Colesbourne Park in Gloucestershire, one cannot help but be impressed by the long, sweeping drive, the extensive woodland estate complete with church, ornamental temple, lake and river. Nearer the more modest house (the original 1850s mansion has been replaced) is a small, pretty, formal garden, and, in February, the ground almost everywhere in the Park abounds with snowdrops.

The snowdrop (or galanthus) is unique in many ways. Harbinger of spring, it is nowadays associated with hopefulness and joy although in ancient times it was connected with death. There are numerous varieties of snowdrops, and yet their differences are infinitesimal. They have a following of people known as Galanthophiles who, rather like train-spotters, are obsessive in the pursuit of their interest. Galanthophiles belong to snowdrop groups and have parties at which the flowers are minutely discussed. In February snowdrop-lovers can be seen reverentially kneeling before their object of adoration, assessing scent and gently pressing the bottom of the petals with the thumb to reveal the inner markings.

Carolyn Elwes, unassuming, attractive and 'tweedy', is a self-confessed 'snowdrop queen' and has an illustrious connection with the flower. Her great-grandfather-in-law was Henry Elwes, born at Colesbourne Park in 1847, a famed traveller who searched out new trees, plants and butterflies. He started the collection of snowdrops and introduced the outstanding *Galanthus elwesii* in 1874. Then the collection remained undisturbed for almost a century till Carolyn began to take an interest, which turned into zeal as she added more and more varieties. Now the collection is one of the most significant and comprehensive in the country.

Carolyn makes sure that the beds nearest the house are perfect just before her opening days. Here she tidies some *Galanthus* 'Galatea', which named after a shepherdess, is a long, nodding snowdrop.

In the beginning I don't think I even noticed snowdrops. I'm an 'Aga woman' so I very rarely left the house, and it was only when the late snowdrops came up during the 'March mating' – the Cheltenham Gold Cup – that I was forced out into the garden by 'the aunts', who knew there were snowdrops remaining here and were determined to save them in spite of me. So they forced me into finding clumps and they'd say, 'You've really got to split those up Carolyn! But I wouldn't, I'd just go back to the Aga and then they'd come again next year and say, 'We told you to split them, what *are* you doing? You promised!' And after a while you get worn down, and after I'd dug the first one, it was so much easier than I expected that I took it up, and got fascinated, and saw what was here and what *could* be here.

This is high Cotswold brush country and so it is really a spring garden. We get very late frost and a lot of dry arid conditions in the summer and, although I have a herbaceous border, it is a struggle to keep it alive. So I work solidly in the spring, getting the snowdrops ready to show when we open the garden to visitors for two weekends. Having put the garden to bed in October, I begin halfway through January, tidying all the time, and watching to see what is coming up, and getting very over-excited by one tiny nose coming through – this is a madness thing! You think, 'Oh my God, it's alive. Hooray!'

There is great pleasure in having something in the garden at that time of year – something that pulls you through the blues of January and February. You have got over the effort of Christmas, and suddenly there is nothing to get you into summer. But snowdrops light those little sparks. And suddenly they come in a flood, so you are clearing around them so they show themselves well, and marking them, and then the moment that part of the season is over you start digging and splitting or putting out a new variety if it has done well enough to start naturalizing. It is a very exciting time when a clump has become big enough to put in two places.

People like the idea of drifts of bulbs coming out from the roots of trees, which is very attractive, but unfortunately there is no food there, and it is very dry, and unless you can dig them really deep, they will soon die out. Snowdrops are actually not woodland plants, it is just that here, that is all that is left. If we were still living in the Middle Ages, they would be spreading down meadows. If you have sheep, the sharp little feet break up the bulbs; if you plough, they haven't a hope in hell, so the only places left are woodland. But if you plant them at the top of a bank, they soon naturally roll down.

Every year the little *nivalis* bulb increases and has a daughter bulb, and it will start to look like a mound of profiteroles! It probably won't seed, but it can put a root down and make another bulb and you can get sheets of flowers. But snowdrops don't really like wet soil or clay and they will reward you if you plant them three times the depth of the bulb, and if you fertilize them. Then when they get to a clump of about ten bulbs it is probably a good idea to dig them up and split them in your hands and spread them out. And goodness me, they do reward you if you do that! I'm amazed any survived here with 50 years of neglect. They are tough old things. They flop over in the frost and then stand up again in the sun. I have the greatest admiration for them, and they are *well* worth growing!

There is a very strong 'magpie element' in making a collection of snowdrops. I was very pleased this season to have another eight varieties and find one or two others to buy, so I have over 200 varieties now, so I think I am going to stop. Of course I won't! I say that every year, but then it is so agonizing when one of the 200 falls over and dies or doesn't come the next year. Then you have to frantically search and think who you gave one to, and see if they can spare you a bulb back. But

Bare earth, rather than grass, is more suitable for growing snowdrops. Dappled shade under deciduous shrubs is ideal, and fallen leaves make a perfect foil for the flowers. Snowdrops require lifting and dividing every two to three years after flowering.

200 varieties should be enough for anybody, even with a garden of this size, because you want to show them in their natural state, but also keep them well divided because they are so promiscuous. On the other hand if they weren't promiscuous you wouldn't get new ones. Few cultivars have been deliberately bred; most arrive by serendipity, and then are given or sold to other collectors. In fact the original collection here only had around 35 varieties.

The Elwes family has been here for just over 200 years. There was a well-known miser called Elwes, who inherited several fortunes and had two sons. The elder bought a house (now the WI College) in Berkshire, but only had a daughter. She ran away with the rector's son and although they were pursued, they managed to get to Gretna Green and get married before the outraged father caught up with them. Yet despite that, that line of Elwes died out. But the second son was bought Colesbourne by his father, and the family has continued to live here, building new houses on the site and moving about, but roughly in the area we now live in.

The estate must have been sold out of Llanthony Priory, and some of the houses in the village show very early Elizabethan guttering or lintels. It was a church-controlled estate which went through several improving owners, but it is still a village, which is nice. We all know each other and we all look after each other's business. It's great fun. We all get involved when the visitors come to the snowdrops. The pub does *frightfully* well and so does the filling station and practically everyone in the village helps to sell snowdrops or teas or something like that. So there is a community, amazing feel about it, which I hope will continue.

Henry John Elwes [1846-1922] was probably the first member of the family to live here most of the time, rather than in London. But then of course he spent little time here, too, because he was always abroad collecting things, amongst them the snowdrop species *elwesii* which now bears his name. He was a great authority on all bulbs and plants and his friend, Samuel Arnott, sent him a snowdrop to see what he thought of it. As it turned out, he thought it one of the best and named it *Galanthus* 'S. Arnott', and it is now here in profusion, although it was down to just one clump when I got here.

Henry John was a giant of a man in more ways than one; very tall and imposing, but his son, like so many sons of successful men, didn't continue with what he did but went off at a completely different angle. Then when *his* son, my husband's father, was killed in the last war, he rather gave up altogether. When my husband, Henry, inherited the estate it was very, very run down, and run by trustees until

Above: *Galanthus* 'S. Arnott'. I bought this plant from Carolyn. A large flower is borne on a stem 10 to 12 inches long (huge compared to the common snowdrop, *Galanthus nivalis*) and smells deliciously of honey.

he was 21, when they advised him to sell it. But he managed to cling on to it and make it viable again. He pulled down the Victorian house and built a new one and *then* began to look for a wife because he didn't want any interference about *that* sort of thing – and he and I have lived here ever since.

We met at a pony club dance, even though I am allergic to horses! In our day we had pony club dances all through the winter – you didn't have to hunt or actually ride. I was all right riding, it was just the stable work I couldn't do, which was very pleasurable for me, but less so for my friends! I gradually lost all my friends and had to give up the dances! First I was young, and then had children, and I didn't have any sort of gardening background – my mother was an artist and although she loved gardening, she was unable to inculcate it into me. My grandmother only allowed me to weed, because she could quite see that that was about as much as I was able to do. So when the aunts came and started nagging, I wasn't very promising material.

And my husband, Henry, did not really understand the snowdrops at that time either. He has always been interested in the arboretum, but when he realised that the snowdrops were a historical remnant as well he began to take a very close interest in what I was doing. In fact he was instrumental in helping me do the heavy work of moving the bulbs about. And there *were* still isolated clumps of exciting snowdrops at Colesbourne – some cross-fertilization and some mutations had occurred, and that is what partly began to raise the interest in snowdrops here again; particularly when I found what is now called the 'Carolyn Elwes' snowdrop. I showed the snowdrop to Matt Bishop and John Grimshaw (who have written a book on snowdrops since, and John has come to work for me). They said, 'Well, you'd better give it a name!' So I was thinking about that, and Henry said, 'You'd better call it after yourself, I suppose', so that is how it got its name.

'Carolyn Elwes' is a snowdrop that has lost its green pigment and the underlying green goes yellow in sunlight, like a form of sunburn. It is probably not a true yellow snowdrop like, say, the *plicatus* 'Wendy's Gold' or 'Primrose Warburg', because then it wouldn't change; it hasn't mutated that far, but a major part of its form is yellow, including the tips of its leaves. When I first saw it, in 1993, in a place where there were very few good snowdrops, it was large and yellow and I thought, 'Oh my goodness, it has got a virus; something awful has happened to it.' But it did seem quite healthy, so I dug it up and put it somewhere else, and it increased, and it is the first yellow *elwesii* species that has been seen since 1890. Ruby Baker, the snowdrop historian, confirmed this.

Then Daphne Chappell brought a group of snowdrop people round when she was beginning the Snowdrop Group, and I don't know whether it was one of them or not, but the clump was dug up and taken away! By that time I felt very possessive about this snowdrop and very cross, so I wrote to the RHS, and luckily I had a photograph of it (which Ruby Baker had taken), and I wrote to the bulb people in Holland to stop people in Holland registering it, because I knew it was the only one of its kind. It was like stealing a Mona Lisa! I have never found out who took it and I have never distributed it. But I still had a few left, and they started building up very slowly, and I hope that soon we will be able to distribute them. It is an interesting snowdrop, but not a great beauty: it is a bit of a bruiser really! But there was a great fuss about it in the snowdrop world, so in 1998 we decided that we should open Colesbourne for two weekends a year. We expected about 400 people and we had thousands. We couldn't control the traffic or anything, and it has gone on ever since, but we have got better organized.

People just seem to love to come and see the snowdrops – it is a disease really, but it only exhibits itself in early spring. It is terribly exciting because they are so enthusiastic. It is a wonderful opportunity for people to get out. Some people come back time and again and say, 'Oh, I see you've moved so-and-so', or 'That tree has finally fallen down; what did you do with the wood?' It is a great incentive because you have to keep thinking of something more interesting for them to look at next time. Because of the size of the garden area, I can show people snowdrops in drifts as well as in specialist groups. People who just think a snowdrop is a snowdrop, when I am taking them round, are not allowed to say that! I become very dictatorial. And if they are really persistent about it, I give them an exam at the end, and say, 'Well what do you think this one is?' and 'What's the difference between these two?' So they do go away feeling they have learnt something.

You get very 'Warburgish'. Primrose Warburg [1920-96] was a wonderful person. She used to have snowdrop parties, but she did like to make sure that everybody did things *her* way. If you didn't keep to the path when you were looking at her garden, you would get yelled at. She was very generous: she would give you almost anything in the garden if you asked for it, but you did have to ask for it.

Somebody said to her once, 'When do you take cuttings off something?' and she said, 'When they are offered!' She was very dry and amusing. She would have lunches where people would bring a group of snowdrops with them for identification or just to show off.

These occasions were quite riveting. You would walk round the garden in the morning, and when you were sufficiently cold that you couldn't feel your fingers or feet anymore and your nose had grown an icicle, you were then allowed into her house and given some hot soup and probably some sherry, which of course went straight to your head, so everyone became quite loquacious. And after lunch, when you had thawed out a bit, you would take your pot of snowdrops,

Above: *Galanthus plicatus* 'Primrose Warburg'. A rich yellow sinus mark (inverted 'v' on the inner segments) and bright yellow ovary make this a very distinctive snowdrop, sold at around £25 per bulb.

Opposite: The arboretum at Colesbourne Park makes a wonderful setting for sheets of snowdrops and an ideal hunting-ground for galanthophiles, described by journalist Ambra Edwards as 'having a fearsome reputation', with 'a competitive ferocity equalled only by the first day of Harvey Nichols sale. They are holders of an arcane and precious knowledge, and have an exquisitely exacting eye for detail.'

which you had brought with you, and ask what it was. I was doing a lot of that in those days. Then a terrible argument would break out as to whether it was just an ordinary hybrid, or a seedling or something special or new, or whether it was 'Neil Fraser' or 'Brenda Troyle' or 'Sam Arnott' – and I never could really tell the difference between those. 'Sam Arnott' does stand up very straight and has an absolutely wonderful honey scent.

You didn't have to be anyone special to be invited, just have some snowdrops of your own. I got in because I was married to an Elwes, even though I was unable to prove I was really that good. But there is something special about the friendship between snowdrop people. We all know each other very well for two months and then we don't see each other for another year and yet you don't really notice the passing of years except one feels just that bit creakier and they get a bit creakier. But there are new people coming into the snowdrop world all the time, just as sadly we lose the older ones. However it is a disease, like a rash breaking out in mid-January till the end of March, and we have very focused minds and only really talk about snowdrops.

Alan Street is one of the people with a passion for snowdrops. He found a double *nivalis* that looked up, not down, in his home village of Blewbury in Oxfordshire. It had a very green interior and so he took a few bulbs home and called it 'Blewbury Tart'. I think he called it that because it looked like an open-faced tart. But a number of people have come to me from Oxfordshire and said, 'Oh, I knew who it was!' in a very disapproving voice. So either Blewbury has a hidden reputation for ladies of easy virtue, or Alan was only thinking of his stomach – but we shall probably never know. And it would be so sad if there wasn't at least one lady in Blewbury who might have had a snowdrop named after her – even if it was a bit of a back-handed compliment!

Another person who used to be associated with the snowdrop lunches was dear Mr Herbert Ransom who grew some really special snowdrops and helped me identify mine and gave me a few of his. That is when I really began my magpie snowdrop collection. There is a kind of gossip column amongst snowdrop people. Someone will say, 'Have you heard, someone has found a new snowdrop in a wood in Northumberland, or in Poland?' or 'A whole new species has been discovered in Roumania.' And then your heart sinks because you think, 'Have I got room for it?' and at the same time, 'How am I going to get hold of it?'

Then you eventually get hold of the person who found it and you say, 'When you have got enough, would you like to swap it for so-and-so?' Equally, if you have only got a few, that is the right time to give them to friends, because something awful might happen in your garden, like fungal disease, or a mole, or someone sitting on it, and then you can always ask for one back. So you have to try not to be too miserly. I hate giving them away because you think only you can look after your own snowdrops properly. But now I know where each one of my snowdrops came from, and who gave them to me. It is like keeping an autograph book! I also draw each one as it is a better way to remember because you really have to look. That way I can recognize them the next year.

I don't do as much gardening as I used to because I have an outside job with the NHS and am chairman of an ambulance trust and various other things, and seem to have turned into one of those sorts of women, instead of the gardening woman, which is really what I would like to be. I employ a full-time gardener who has to do a bit of everything, including controlling the sheep if they get out and looking after the trees, but who has a special interest in snowdrops too. I keep on saying that when I retire, I will have more time for the garden, but I actually know in my heart of hearts that when I *do* retire my back will have gone, and I will only be able to crawl about in the beds and I won't ever be able to stand up again! But it will be worth it.

My children are boys, but one is married, and his wife is interested in the garden. So when I go to the great snowdrop heaven in the sky, I hope that she will have understood what I have been doing here and carry it on. I'm sure that they will. They'd *better*! I'll come and haunt them otherwise! I haven't done all this just to have it stamped on and mown down – no *way*! I'm a snowdrop queen! That is said about men and women in a kind of tone of voice to mean you are getting a bit above yourself – 'Oh, she's *such* a snowdrop queen!' But nonetheless I think we would all like to be snowdrop queens because it sounds as if we know what we are doing.

Actually, I am on the track of one last snowdrop. Well, one last snowdrop – who am I kidding? It is called *Galanthus peshmenii* and was discovered in Turkey and has a flower, which is almost the shape of a Turk's cap lily, with the most interesting profile. I have only seen pictures of it growing in pots, but I would love to have it here. I'll never stop. I always swore I would stop when I couldn't spot the differences: but the more you look, the better you become at noticing the differences, and the more your collection grows. So there is no hope really – you just have to go on and on!

13

ALISON GODING

COMPOSTER AND ESTATE GARDENER AT RHS HARLOW CARR

Domestic-size wooden compost bins full of vegetable waste by the kitchen garden. The correct balance of woody and green material is crucial, as is turning to encourage oxygen to stimulate bacteria, causing the compost to break down.

'Casting the Bodies Vest aside'

In 2001 the Royal Horticultural Society merged with the Northern Horticultural Society and acquired Harlow Carr, making it the most recent and most northerly garden in the RHS. The ten and a half hectares of gardens stand on what was once part of the Forest of Knaresborough, an ancient hunting ground, and later a spa – the bathhouse is now the Study Centre. Soil in the garden is very acid, due to the sulphur springs, and varies from sand to clay, although 'Carr' means 'bog'. One of the features of the garden is the humus-rich terraces built of peat, now being replaced by stone and leaf mould. This is just one area in which Alison Goding is involved, for she helps with the maintenance of the whole garden, although it was composting in particular that I chose to talk to her about.

A stereotypical composter would be a man: Alison is a slender female. But she loves her work despite the physical demands, because it combines all her interests: working outside, contact with the cycle of life, craft and creating things with her hands. Alison is kind and keen, and working in an RHS garden is ideal because it enables her to meet the public, do some teaching, and work in an eco-friendly environment – all of which she enjoys. There are three main composting areas at Harlow Carr: a huge concreted area known as the 'pad' where waste including bark, twigs and plants is brought in by tractor and trailer and then shredded; a large bin specifically for leaf mould; and domestic-scale slatted wooden boxes by the kitchen garden.

I became a professional gardener by chance. It was a complete career change because I had a degree in art and design and started working in textiles and fabrics, and then in the wardrobe department of a theatre. Then I was looking for another job and I worked for a kite-designer, which I enjoyed, only they went bankrupt. But I still fly kites! Anyway, I had always been interested in horticulture, even though I had very limited knowledge, and without a job I had spare time, so to occupy myself I decided to go to a college that a friend's mother recommended – Shipley in West Yorkshire.

My father worked in sales and we tended to move around the country quite a lot, so as a child we never had a garden for very long, but my brothers and I did always have a part of our own – I grew wild-flower seeds in my bit. But when I went to college I really started from scratch, quite late, and at that time didn't think it would be a career move. It was a two-year course and you had to do a work placement, and a situation came up here around six years ago, while it was still the Northern Horticultural Society, and I came here for about six months, one day a week. Then for the second part of the year I got a full-time scholarship here for six months.

For my second-year work placement, I went to Christopher Lloyd's garden at Great Dixter. I had visited the garden previously with my parents and thought, 'Wow, this is a fantastic place! I wonder if they let students work here?' So I asked the lady behind the counter in the shop, and she said, 'Go out and see the head gardener', and I thought, 'If you don't ask you don't get', so I went up to him and said, 'I would really like to come here. Do you take students?' He told me to write to

Alison crowned with autumn beech.

him with my details and he said he would see what he could do. So I really set up my own work placement at Great Dixter, and was there for a month, and thought it was wonderful. It was so different from Harlow Carr, with all the figs and peaches and grapes.

While I was still at Harlow Carr we had a staff visit to Wisley and the education officer there said to me, 'If you really want to get into horticulture you should come here!' So I applied for the Wisley two-year diploma, and was accepted to go there. Working at Wisley is a fairly unique experience. They have eight separate departments, and in your two years you spend between 12 and 16 weeks working in each department, so effectively it is like starting again, learning new skills with new people to gain a specialist knowledge in all areas. I wouldn't have got that anywhere else. For instance, at Kew they have academic blocks and practical blocks, but at Wisley it is predominantly practical, with the learning of theory in your own time, so it is quite intense, although I managed to win a prize – for best pest collection! You have to collect pests and diseases, and create a herbarium on a particular genus.

When I finished my diploma at Wisley I went back to Dixter for a couple of months and I am still really good friends with them. Then I applied for the job here at Harlow Carr and got it. Now I am part of the estate management team – there is one senior supervisor and three estate gardeners, responsible for managing the garden as a whole, rather than specific areas. I am the only female on the estate team here, and there is one at Wisley. Estate management is quite heavy work, so it is unusual for women to do it, particularly someone quite slim-built like me. But I am on a good team. And I am able to get into places where others can't!

The rest of the team are actually quite big blokes, and it sometimes takes someone smaller to get under trees and through bushes for bulb planting. Even treading over a bed to get to something is usually better if you are not in size 11 boots! It all balances out. But it is hard physical work, so I do usually go to bed very early. Three of us have been moving the National Rhubarb Collection (about 300 plants) for the past week and that has been seriously labour-intensive – really heavy. And composting is quite physical too. If I ever were awake enough to go to a dinner party, I wouldn't hide the fact that I had been turning compost during the day! It is like being a doctor – as soon as you go to a party or meet a new group of people you start getting questions fired at you.

Leaves are collected from all over Harlow Carr and then shredded. Here a tractor and trailer waits for its load by a beech tree. Beech leaves are actually slow to rot, as are oak, though the latter are said to be good for repelling slugs and cutworms, while pine-needle compost is said to be good for improving the flavour of strawberries!

We start work here at 8 a.m. People are often quite surprised that we work the same hours in the winter as the summer, but we are always busy and sometimes I feel it is like spinning plates to keep everything going. Traditionally people tend to do less in their own gardens in the winter, and the floral and ornamental team does wind down a little bit, but for us, on the estate team, it is really the start of everything. We have woodland management, lots of clearance, leaf raking and composting. Because we have 15 acres of woodland within the garden, we have an awful lot of leaves to deal with: some will go on to the big compost pad and some for leaf mould.

The garden here is split into two: floral ornamental, which is the island beds, the Mediterranean area, the scented garden and Alpines; and the part I am involved in, which is the streamside area, woodland and wild-flower meadow. We also have a role as caretakers or overseers of the whole grounds, doing arboriculture, turf issues, and composting. But most gardeners here also have a particular area to look after, and mine is the humus-rich terrace, which is undergoing renovation at the moment. It was created in the 1960s using peat blocks, at a time when the environmental consequences of peat extraction were not fully appreciated.

Now the use of peat is a very environmentally sensitive issue, and we are very keen for peat not to be used anymore. The peat blocks that were used to create the terrace, look a bit like loaves of bread and were actually taken from the bottom of a reservoir, so it wasn't moorland peat that was being stripped, it was residue that had been built up. But even so, it isn't something the RHS would want to encourage people to do. Now we are looking at alternative methods of putting the humus back into the soil and restoring the terrace by using stone or rock.

Part of the creation of the new leaf-mould bin that I am responsible for is so the leaf mould can take the place of the humus content in the soil. That way the acidity is retained and also the moisture gets into the

Above: Leaf mould is such good stuff that there is now an illegal trade in material removed from mature woodland. Luckily Harlow Carr has a plentiful supply of leaves. Here Alison stands on top of the leaf-mould bin to turn it. The centre of the bin is hot enough to cook a fillet of fish!

Opposite: Autumn leaves make leaf mould, used as a soil improver or mulch to grow more plants, and so the cycle continues.

WHY WE GARDEN | Alison Goding

clay to break up the soil and provide the requirements for the acid-loving, shade-loving plants that are growing there – plants that like their feet moist but well drained. These are mainly dwarf rhododendrons, meconopsis, erythroniums, and lots of primulas and hellebores. In the north, acid and shade form a common environment, but there are only a few gardens that have a whole collection of plants especially suited to this, like here.

At the moment we are clearing out the old plants because the area had been neglected for such a long time – you couldn't even see the terrace and it was just a mass of overgrown and dead shrubs, but next year it will look spectacular! I am preparing the leaf mould now so that next year when we are ready to plant, the mould will be ready and I can incorporate it. Leaf mould replicates the woodland floor, which would be the native habitat of many of these plants. The leaf-mould bin has been built up in layers of shredded leaves (which have gone through a lawn mower and a wood chipper) and larger pieces. So it has a really good texture, which I mix up, so that hopefully the top layer of fine bits of leaves will accelerate the decomposition of the larger leaves.

The 'pad' where most waste from the garden is brought and finally ends up as a crumbly brown mixture 'like chocolate cake'. Most organic matter can be used for compost. In medieval monasteries, monks were often buried in the orchards. Was it coincidence, or did they know that bonemeal is one of the best fertilizers for fruit trees?

Already the leaf mould has a faint tinge of white, which is the fungi starting to grow, so, unlike conventional compost, which relies on bacteria, it doesn't require much turning. The centre of the leaf-mould bin is amazingly warm and toasty, so when we do turn it, it is nice on a cold morning because all the steam rises and you end up really warm. I often used to think that if I got a fillet of fish, and wrapped it in tin foil, and put it in the middle of the leaf mould, it would probably cook. So last week I tried it! I brought a wrapped piece of smoked haddock in with me, and put it in the bin at 8.30 in the morning and it was ready by lunchtime. It cooked beautifully and tasted delicious.

There are two other areas we use for more general compost: some domestic-sized slatted wooden boxes by the kitchen garden act as a demonstration and educational tool, so we can run master classes for students on compost management; and two massive bays on the pad where we pile most of our annual weeds and prunings and clippings, provided they are not diseased. Diseased material goes on to a bonfire or occasionally a special skip. We hire in a commercial shredder about twice a year and the shredded material sits there and gets turned a few times. Then we get a screening machine in that has different grades of mesh on it, so you can determine what your finished size of particle will be. It screens out the stones and any hand tools which might have got in by mistake. So we end up with a lovely pile of compost and a pile of debris. I haven't ever seen anything really odd in the heap. Gloves are quite common, but we tend not to assume there is a person attached, so long as everyone is counted back at the end of the day. Occasionally a volunteer might forget to sign out and cause a certain amount of concern!

The compost will stand on the pad and be turned three to five times more, depending on the weather – if it is raining and cold we don't want the compost heap to cool down. Basically we are encouraging the oxygen to stimulate the bacteria which makes the compost break down, so the more air you get in it the hotter it becomes. Then you will get a nice crumby structure, which can be used throughout the gardens as a planting medium and soil conditioner and occasionally as a mulch. Potting compost is mainly bought in, but the nurseryman has access to our compost for adding in, and I am hoping he will be able to use the leaf mould too.

I feel that everyone should try to make their own compost if they have room in their garden. All you need is material, warmth, moisture and air. In summer compost will only take about 12 weeks to make, although it is slower in winter. The most important thing (which also avoids any unpleasant smells) is to have the correct balance of woody and green material, because you want a really good carbon-to-nitrogen mix. You can use most organic garden and domestic waste (such as leaves, twigs, weeds, non-glossy paper, straw, vegetable peelings) that will rot down eventually and return to the soil with the help of many tiny micro-organisms. If you have too much nitrogen, from, say, grass cuttings, it will make it wet and soggy and you will end up with a smelly, slimy mess. If you have too much carbon, from prunings, it will take ages to decompose, especially if it is not chipped very finely, so you would have a very dry pile that would take years to break down.

You shouldn't put any cooked food on a

compost heap because it can encourage vermin into the garden; nor things coated in oil or butter that will go sour and go to a mushy mess; nor animal or dog waste which can be very unhealthy; and perennial weed roots should be left out to die before being added to the heap. Ideally, you need to turn the pile quite frequently, about every four to six weeks, to get oxygen in and the heat building up. Heat kills weed seeds and also speeds up the process. The bins you can buy with slats allow air in and ones that rotate are probably good for older gardeners because they take some of the hard work out, but I have never used one myself.

    Finally, the heap should be moist but not wet, so you may need to add water in summer and protect it in the winter with a lid of newspaper, plastic or carpet. If you watch the basic guidelines you will end up with a lovely crumbly brown mixture at the end, which should be like chocolate cake! I like recycling materials. I love the allotment culture. I have an allotment where I grow soft fruits and the ingenuity and improvization of reusing materials is fantastic there. I have a compost bin but I am not there often enough to really use it properly, so if I need compost I sometimes nick a bit from the pad here! I also have a small garden, really just a raised bed around my house, which is tiny and not big enough to have compost.

    A lot of people assume that because I have a background in art and design, I am heading towards garden design at some stage, and while I would never rule that out, I think I have always been a very craft-based person, making things with my hands even as a very small child. I love being outdoors and the visual spectacle of colour, texture and form, but it is also the hands-on skill and craft elements of horticulture that I enjoy. My ambition would be to work in a garden abroad, even for a short time, just for the experience of a different climate and a different set of elements and plant species. One of the fantastic things about being in horticulture is that it is a transportable skill. Very basic things give me pleasure, such as tying in or training a plant in a particular fashion, or maintaining it to keep its form. I *really* like pruning. Creating something out of nothing, like the new compost bins, is also always really rewarding. And when you are getting a product virtually for free at the end, it is extra good. Horticulture is so varied.

    Someone in the office once asked at the end of a long day, 'Why do you do it?' And I thought to myself, there are so many things that I have seen this year in terms of wildlife and the weather that I would never see if I worked indoors. I don't have any problem getting up in the morning to go to work; I just really like my job. It is very hard physically sometimes and there are days when you just fall down in a heap when you get home, but I find it difficult to stay indoors now. This autumn, with all the colours and shapes has been absolutely fantastic, and seeing the virgin snow was amazing. So I love that aspect as well as all the fabulous flowers and scents, and also the *people*. Working in a public garden enables you to encounter people who maybe haven't seen gunnera before, and they come round the corner and gasp. Then the excitement of discovering something for the first time is infectious.

    Because we work in a public space we always need to be able to answer questions. Recently a lot of people tend to have opinions

WHY WE GARDEN | Alison Goding

Proud of her settee: Alison combined her two loves, art and horticulture, to make this sofa from sacks of compost covered in turf. Now a mouse, spiders and ants have a more comfortable home in the arboretum.

about television programmes. Everybody has something to express about a TV gardener who they either do or don't like, which is quite amusing. But they also ask for advice and the best way to do things. I think because it is the RHS they think we have some sort of secret recipe for success. Horticulture is sometimes clouded with mysticism, when in fact it is just good management which really achieves good results.

We are as environmentally friendly as we can be, although not totally organic in that we use some slug pellets in the vegetable trials area. We do a minimal amount of spraying and we really encourage biodiversity. We are blessed that we are in quite a rural location and have lots of birds, frogs and toads. Another thing we are excited about here is using by-products of the garden to incorporate biodiversity in wildlife. At Harlow Carr we use felled timber to create habitat piles, so that instead of composting everything we leave certain mounds of material *in situ* for it to degrade naturally back into the ground and provide a habitat for small mammals and invertebrates and birds.

In May this year we had a new twist on that, with a day when the garden staff came up with ideas for creating alternatives to habitat piles. Mark, another estate gardener, and I made some Hessian sacks and filled them with compost from the pad. We made a settee out of compost in sacks, and covered it with pieces of turf left over from another part of the garden. So we have a two-seater sofa out in the arboretum made of compost! We planted it up with wild flowers and before long there was a little mouse living in the side of it and also grasshoppers, spiders and ants. It is nice for children to see too, and marries together two subjects that are really close to my heart: art and horticulture.

Another thing I can get really interested in is pests, like moth larvae in the fruit garden, or beetles and wire worms which attack things like potatoes. Once you learn about pests' life cycles, and can impart that to students, it can be really exciting. Integrated pest management usually takes place under glass; it is much harder in a large garden. But what turns out to be bad in one case is good in another. If something isn't actually diseased but is spoilt by a pest, or if there is an excess of something, it can still be used for compost, so it isn't a waste. Some people are alarmed that we don't sell our rhubarb, but we compost it, so I see it going back into the garden. It is all part of the great scheme of things — taking away and giving back.

There is a certain sense of wildness at Harlow Carr — it is not a totally cultivated environment. Wisley is a demonstration garden and is very compartmentalized, but here you feel more that you are walking round one big garden and that you are sharing it with nature. There are always reminders that eventually everything will revert back to how it once was. To me that is positive: I think people are far too negative about death. I definitely feel that one day I will be compost too! What we do on a daily basis is all part of the cycle of life — and you see it here!

14

MIKE HANNA and JOSEPHINE MEWS

BELGRAVIA GARDENERS

Mike and Josephine take out dying plants and replace them with fresh ones in the window box of Claridges Hotel, Mayfair. One of their most beguiling qualities is that they don't take their work too seriously.

'And their uncessant Labours see Crown'd from some single Herb or Tree'

One day, walking passed the Connaught Hotel, I saw a small van with what looked like a coffin on the roof, bearing the intriguing name 'The Belgravia Gardener'. Next my eyes were drawn to Josephine: pretty, nicely made-up and wearing a fetching hat, her muddy hands seemed incongruous. But Josephine Mews and her work partner Mike Hanna (equally 'county' and poshly spoken) are contract container gardeners to the *créme de la créme*. Belgravia is one of the most exclusive districts of London. Along with neighbouring Mayfair, it has long been the home of many of the city's aristocrats and is the location of numerous embassies, hotels and restaurants. The architecture is typically in the grand Regency style with window boxes and flower containers in abundance.

The Belgravia Gardeners keep overheads low by operating from an archway in New Covent Garden, Vauxhall, where Mike's wife owns a florist's and party-arranging business. Josephine and Mike buy their plants from the vast wholesale market there, fill their van and the 'coffin' on top (made by a friend of Josephine's) and drive off to their wealthy private and professional clients. Mike and Josephine enjoy the freedom which their work allows them, and take pride in what they do, but they are refreshingly 'down-to-earth' in every sense; more practical than passionate. Josephine, young and single, is a dog-owner who likes flexibility. Mike, now in his 70s, used to be a jockey and polo player – they met by chance, through mutual friends. Individually, both gardeners feared an interview might lack interest. In this they were completely mistaken; however, they chose to discourse together.

We do the job for people who are rich enough and lazy enough to want us. We chose Belgravia because there is not much point in going to Hoxton really! Belgravia Gardeners originally started in 1981 with me [Mike] but it went through various names first. Then when the garden centre, 'The Chelsea Gardener', seemed to be making huge amounts of money, I thought, why not have 'The Belgravia Gardener'? So that is what we became, and six years ago, when I wanted to semi-retire, I sold half of the business to Josephine. But we are still essentially a man, a van and a watering can. That is our motto.

We do look after a few patios and some indoor plants in offices, but mainly we plant, water, feed, and maintain window boxes and containers. We used to do a few small gardens, where we had to mow lawns, but we decided it wasn't really our scene and we gave it up. We go to places about once a week and try to make them look really good. We have access to some of the nicer properties in London, and have keys, because they trust us not to trample their carpets in dirty boots. People like the fact that they will see the same person every time – not just another faceless Australian. A few of our clients, like Steiner's, we have had for about 15 years.

Because we are just a small company of two people, we try to be more like a personal gardener and take a lot of pride in what we do. We don't regard the Connaught Hotel as just a job: we like to think that it looks really good and *we* did it, and we take an interest in it, and have a certain loyalty to the people who run it. We have done all Gordon Ramsey's restaurants: his own in Hospital Road and then the one in St James's and Claridges, and we hope we will always do them. We like him.

Give him what he wants and he is a pussy cat; try and short-change him, or let stuff look dead or not properly looked after, and he will come after you, as he would anyone who doesn't give him the right thing. But we are not like him in having to produce something on a plate which has to be absolutely perfect.

Gordon Ramsey is quite specific in what he wants, although not everyone is as fussy. But when people really want something done well and are prepared to pay well for that, it is a pleasure to do it. It is less of a pleasure when people want the same for half the price. We are slightly up-market in that we don't deal with cheaper clients really. If someone said, 'Could you do a window box for me for £20?' We would say, 'No we couldn't possibly. We might be able to do it for £25 a foot!'

This is the only business I know, where people advertise on the front of their houses, whether they want you or not! You drive up a street and see boxes full of dead plants, and know the owners may be possible clients. We sometimes pop a card through the letterbox or knock on doors and ask people if they want us. Some people come up to us and ask, while we are up a ladder watering a window box, 'Do you do window boxes?' but what they *really* mean is 'Are you available to do mine?' The other thing they say, when it is pouring with rain is, 'You don't need to do that: it's raining!' Then we kick them in the head because of course window boxes always need watering. But we get our work mainly through word-of-mouth. We are not in the phone book and we don't advertise. We do one house and then the one next door wants us too.

At the moment we only look after one side of Claridges, Gordon Ramsey's restaurant side, and he pays for it. But we have just been asked if we would like to do the rest of Claridges. If that came off it would be something like £20,000 a year. It would be a bit more work, but not that much – say a couple of hours a week in the winter and double that in the summer. It is a job we would like because we could take pride in it. Other big companies work to a budget and exact numbers. We would rather not make quite as much money but have it looking super, than save ourselves a pound here and there on plants.

We have a contract with about 16 people who we do regularly, and then we do two or three one-off slightly bigger planting jobs, which give us a lump of cash. We prefer to try to cover about eight sites a day and have the next day off. Unlike cut flowers, which have to be done on specific days, we can be more flexible. We normally water on a Monday, but if we decided to go to the races on Monday instead, we could always do it on Tuesday. We don't make a fortune out of this job, but it allows us to do other things. It is not eight till five from Monday to Friday: one week you might work Saturday and Sunday instead of Monday, Tuesday and Wednesday.

The things we enjoy most are spending the money, and the independence! No one tells us what to do at each point in the day. And in our business, we can fire people just as much as we get fired by them! If someone is unbearable to work for, and rude and difficult, we just don't work for them. We are contract gardeners employed for a few hours a week, not old-fashioned gardeners who live on an estate and are expected to be there 24 hours a day. If there is a dead flower on a woman's magnolia, she can't ring us up and say, 'Come and pluck it off!' It is no longer tolerable to be

Josephine and Mike work on the planters in front of Claridges, at the entrance to Gordon Ramsey's restaurant, considered one of the best in London.

treated as 'the gardener' in that way. We like most of our clients, but it is really bizarre that when we go to a private house, you could count on one hand the number of times we have been offered a cup of tea.

On the other hand, we looked after a house in Chester Row, and one day I [Mike] was wearing a pair of Gucci shoes and I was swilling down the owner's little patio and she said, 'Oh my God, you should not be washing this down in those shoes! Have you no gum boots?' And I said, 'These are my only shoes.' Well her husband's wardrobe was full of hundreds of pairs of wonderful shoes, so she has kept me in shoes ever since! She also asked if I would like a drink and I said, 'Oh lovely, can I have a gin and tonic?' Then she sent for her housekeeper to get the drink, but she said to me, 'I have many gardeners — in my houses in Paris, in Virginia, in Portugal — and when I say, "Do you want a drink?" normally they have a cup of tea; you are the only one who wants a G & T!' She was all right really — I rather liked her — although she kept sacking us each time we went, and I would just go back regardless!

Housekeepers and butlers can be a pain in the ass, but they can be good, too, because they compete with each other. There is the housekeeper at number 45 wanting to have as nice a window box as the housekeeper at number 47. We like that. But then occasionally, the housekeeper at number 45 will tell the housekeeper at number 47 that she has got a very good, cheaper gardener! So jobs come and go. And although we are on duty all the time, we do much more in the summer than in the winter. Ideally we like a really hot summer where it pours with rain every night but never in the day.

Josephine loads daffodils bought at New Covent Garden Market into her van and into the coffin-like box on top.

We also do like the planting and standing back afterwards and saying, 'That looks good!' About 80 per cent of the decisions as to what plants we use are down to us, and it is really satisfying to drive down a road and see something you have done that looks nice, or to look down the side of a big hotel and see a whole sweep of colour. It is enjoyable when we are given leeway to spend a lot of money but to make it look spectacularly good. In London, it is not like real gardening. It is more like a form of interior decorating. If it is a garden, people want another room, only outside, to entertain, and it has to be instant. If it is a window box, it is ready-made decoration. It is strange to plant bulbs which are nearly over. You wouldn't normally plant a bulb already flowering, but would plant it the year before and watch its progress. It is all about creating an immediate impression and getting to know what the client wants.

We wouldn't put a whole load of chrysanthemums outside Gordon Ramsey's restaurant because his window box is like his shop window or his label. So we wouldn't plant anything very garish. We would use maybe only two colours. At the moment we have got 'Bridal Crown', which is a particularly nice-smelling, bold white narcissus, with yellow polyanthus. The 'Bridal Crown' is just beginning to go over, and it is too early to put in geraniums and lobelias, so we get something in a colour that we think he will like and use that. Actually he has his own colour, which is aubergine, so if we can find something on those lines we go towards that. He doesn't mind so long as it looks *elegant*.

We do have a few clients who want blowsy cottage-garden style with lots of colour, but mainly we go for plainer schemes. If we decide on something for, say, the Connaught, and they hate it, they will ring us up and we come and change it. But generally we veer towards the safe side; neither minimalist nor too gaudy. In a relatively small space in London it is more effective to be plain and simple. It doesn't work to go down the municipal bedding route of two plants of each colour standing in regimented rows. Banks of colour, structure, but not rigidity is what one wants.

During the summer most boxes are full of geraniums and trailing lobelia; in the autumn and winter we tend to use cyclamen. At the moment we are just coming out of a fashion for box – little topiary balls and hedges. In a container the ideal is to have some perennial plants, as a frame, such as an evergreen with some ivy hanging around the outside. That leaves you some space in which to put your seasonal plants. We use plants that will last a certain length of time and will appeal and look the part. Mostly we replace plants because we are tired of them rather than because the client necessarily is. And of course to make a living, the last thing we want is a plant that lasts the whole year! Mainly we do three plantings a year.

We haven't got anywhere to store the plants we take out, so we sometimes take them home or give them away. We don't have facilities to grow our own stock so we buy what we need, as we need it, from the flower market. When we get rid of the hydrangeas from the Connaught, someone can have those. People quite often walk past and say, 'What are you going to do with that? Can I have one?' and then it is nice to give it to them. We don't like waste. And we don't like to see dead plants.

Container plants need watering, clipping, feeding, deadheading. It is more detailed and fiddly than other sorts of gardening. Also, the soil needs frequent replenishing as well as feeding. We use processed horse muck, which is the best possible fertilizer, but if you are using it outside restaurants or even private houses, they prefer you not to put it on immediately before lunch! So there are a few jobs you do early on in the morning. Then in hot summers each premises will need a visit more than once a week because of the watering.

One of the things you don't want is the client who, when you offer him a maintenance contract, says, 'I've got a very good maid.' Because her idea of watering will be to pour a milk bottle of water over the top every few days. But it is the roots where you really want the water, so things have to be watered properly. On the other hand with the few office contracts that we have, the people who work there are inclined to water the indoor plants every day and they kill them. More indoor plants die of over-watering than not watering.

We didn't need any real training other than having a sense of colour and a sense of service. We can guarantee that someone can go and spend three or four weeks in Miami and come back and their window boxes will look as nice as when they left. If we wanted to make our business bigger, the market is there. We are both a bit lazy and unambitious so we both just want to retire in comfort somehow – by winning the lottery presumably – and if you could libel us a few times so that we could sue, it would be helpful!

15

JEAN HILL

CLIFF-TOP GARDENER

In Jean's steeply sloping garden, even mowing the lawns is a challenge. Steps lead to each level, here with Spanish broom in flower.

'Far other Worlds, and other Seas'

When I reached a remote Cornish fishing village set in Daphne du Maurier country and asked a local man for directions to Jean Hill's house, he replied, 'Keep straight up and when you get to the rocks, stop!' Jean's home is perched atop steep, craggy cliffs and her garden is a bane as well as a blessing. Rising over 100 feet and surrounded by the sea on three sides, her wind-swept, steeply sloping terrain used to be a stone quarry. The local slate is used to create winding paths, seats, steps, archways and walls that hold the many levels. Gardening here is a real challenge, but one which Jean has conquered over the last 30 years. Unlike many gardeners, she enjoys the ends rather than the means, and feels the garden is a demanding responsibility. Yet she has the same compulsion as the keenest of gardeners and feels unable to leave.

Her approach is practical and she uses plants able to withstand the salt-laden gales, which are the hazard of seaside gardens. Shrubs such as *Fuchsia magellanica*, *Olearia solandri*, and *Teucrium fruticans* give some wind-breaking shelter. But the mild climate also provides a home for succulents, gladioli, lampranthus, and dracaena palms. Throughout Jean has been careful not to obstruct her spectacular views, but to entice the eye outwards and downwards. At the bottom of a flight of 130 steps (descended and ascended daily by Jean who, at over 70, is remarkably fit), a gate opens on to a small sandy bay surrounded by rock pools. Here Jean indulges her other passion, swimming.

WHY WE GARDEN | Jean Hill

I was born in Sheffield, right in the middle of England, but the rest of my life has been spent near the coast. I started my married life on the Isle of Wight, and I lived in Plymouth before I came here. The sea has always been desperately important to me. I have got to be either on it, by it, or in it. The sea is my first passion and the garden my second; I am lucky I have got both here. I was an only child and my father died when I was nine. My mother was always very interested in gardens, and my father was too, I seem to remember, but when he died my mother used to say, 'Can you come and help me do this because I can't quite manage it.' So in my early teens we tended to rebuild rockeries together.

When I was young I trained as a gymnast, but I didn't teach for very long because I had elderly relatives to look after. I came here originally, about 30 years ago, so that I could look after my mother – this was going to be a holiday home where I could bring her and look after her and still swim. She loved the sea as well, but got to the age when she couldn't go away alone, and that is why we came. We spent a year and a half getting the house ready, but before we could come for a holiday, my mother fell and broke her leg and she never came out of hospital. But she knew the garden, and although she was elderly and frail,

Looking northwest across the Fowey Estuary to Ready Money Cove. Jean's plants have to survive the extreme conditions of sea gales. A living screen of plants provides a windbreak on the terraces.

my son carried her down to the bottom and up. She used to sit in the garden while we were working and say, 'Oh, it's so beautiful!' She had a lot of enjoyment from it.

There were three previous owners, and when I came the garden was very overgrown. My husband and I made it into what it is now, but my husband died on Good Friday 2003, and so now I have help twice a week with the mowing, the cutting of the back hedges and the heavy work, although I still do most of the weeding and the small planting. I spend about two full days a week gardening. What I enjoy most about it is getting it done! Anybody who gardens can't say that they really enjoy the work, but they don't like it not being done. A proper gardener will go into a garden intending to do something quite different and immediately start weeding or trimming back or doing something. They need to get it done.

I lead a busy life, which is good because I am not lonely, but I rarely sit in the garden. And although you see the garden from the house, as it falls away towards the water, you can't see it all. If it was reversed, and the house was at the bottom, you would actually have a better view of the garden. I go down to swim in the sea almost every day between May and October, and so I walk down and up through the garden. There again, I always stop and do some weeding on the way down or on the way up. I walk round the garden with people, I sit in it to watch the boats, and, in spring, on lovely mild Cornish days, which we sometimes get mixed in amongst the wet ones, I will go out and just sit and enjoy.

The main challenge of the garden is getting anything to grow; it is very, very windy. Because it is on a cliff you get a tremendous lot of turbulence. When you have a south-westerly wind, coming all the way across the Atlantic, it can go straight past the top of the cliff, but everything lower down hits the cliff, and the wind has got nowhere to go. The increase in the wind speed due to the turbulence is very considerable and plants just blow out of the ground. To an extent it is trial and error. I came here from a valley garden, which

Jean looks out southwest, at the bay where she swims. Punch's Cross on the rocks marks the outer limits of the harbour. The notebook in Jean's hand is her record of the plants in her garden.

was the opposite, and so I have had to learn. When we first came, my husband started working on the house, which was also very neglected, and I said, 'Could we have one day a week for the garden?' Well it never really worked liked that, and he spent most of his time doing the house while I did the garden, unless I needed some help with the heavy jobs.

When all the garden was cleared there was almost nothing there, so the difficulty was trying to establish the plants with no protection, and we learned quite a lot about that. For instance, once you get one thing going, it helps with the next thing. And you can't always decide where you want something, because there might be two feet of soil underneath or two inches, depending on the rock formation. I started off by planting more of what was here already. For example, we had a row of Monterey pines and *Cupressus macrocarpa* (a golden-coloured cypress) so we planted new ones, mainly from seed. Since we have been here we have lost four pine trees and one cypress. They blow over so the roots are up-ended, and one blew right over the cliff and landed on the beach. I also have some flowers (such as wallflowers, scabious, cistus and cyclamen), although if I had to choose between flowering plants and foliage, I would always choose foliage. I like trees, ferns and succulents, and love greens, yellow and greys, which are the best colours for the sea.

I haven't got many flowering trees. Things like honeysuckle will struggle and be quite good, and *Olearia solandi* from New Zealand will stand up to any amount of wind. Camellias are my favourite plant because they flower in the spring when it is gloomy and the foliage is always very lovely. It wasn't until we had been here some time that I discovered I could risk growing camellias — it is a question of finding somewhere to put them where they will not be too wind-blown. In the spring a lot of the trees, including the pines, go brown. They get burnt by the wind! If I had known at the beginning what I know now, it would have been a lot easier. I would advise anyone else with a cliff-top garden to go out when there is a gale and see what's happening. The other thing is that if you buy expensive plants, don't plant them straight away — repot them if necessary, and put the pot in the ground and see how they get on. If they show signs of windburn then at least you can move them to somewhere more kindly.

Planting the same thing as was already thriving was one idea, reading books about gardening was another, but it is pretty extreme here, so you haven't got much to help you. One useful thing is that when you do get plants established, and you plant quite close together, the plants hold each other up, and hold in the moisture. But if you try to water here, the water doesn't stay where you put it. It goes down to the rock, slides along and comes out at a completely different place! I know that if I water one lot of hydrangeas, the water comes out on the beach.

On the other hand, Cornwall is very fertile and mild and I can grow tender plants like *Agave americana*, a statuesque succulent, and lampranthus, which is a small succulent, but makes a mass of brilliant pink colour in late June and early July. It is very lovely and you can't really grow it unless you are in Cornwall, or possibly Bournemouth or somewhere on a south-facing sea slope. Another plant which grows in Cornwall is the echium, with its six-foot spikes of blue flowers. It needs some protection over winter, and if you get frost it dies, and it has to be more than two years old before it flowers.

I can't be a collector of plants here. If I can find plants that will survive, then that is a bonus. I was given a cotinus [smoke bush] and it is doing well, so I bought another one to put in nearby because it is a lovely colour. I have got two abutilons which I grew from seeds from a friend, and now I have bought another one which is a bit more showy, and I think to myself, 'I probably wasn't very sensible buying that because I don't know whether it is going to survive.' That is always the problem. In books plants are described as 'tender' but that means tender as regards temperature, not as regards wind.

Slate arches, walls and steps are a feature of Jean's garden. Here, looking up through 'the Monk's Cellar', seed heads of lampranthus are seen on the left. These are one of Jean's favourite plants, with their profusion of pink daisy-like flowers in late summer. Originally from South Africa, lampranthus is rarely seen in England but is suited to the mild Cornish climate.

The garden was developed in 1920 at the period when there was only a push mower or scythe for the grass. So originally they brought in soil and built up walls to make level terraces. It would have been a great deal better for us if it had not been done. The terraces have to be maintained and when you want to garden a top terrace from the one below, or weed a wall, you need to use a ladder! My favourite part is always the part I am creating or working on at the time. Then you get interested in that small part. But the advantage of having two people to work in a garden like this is that the mower has to be carried from one bit of grass to another; you can't wheel it and you can't use a wheelbarrow – everything has to be picked up and carried in sacks or a donkey (a big sheet with handles) or plastic buckets from place to place.

The walls have nearly all had to be rebuilt because they were starting to give way. They were built with soil in between, like a one-sided Cornish hedge, and the soil gradually washes out and the weight of the stones above makes the stones below *spit* out – in the way that you can put finger and thumb together and flick an orange pip. Then the wall has to be taken right down and rebuilt, using mortar at the back so it doesn't show, which is what my husband did, very beautifully over the years, and now my help, Peter, has a re-walling or re-paving job every winter. When we first came the walls fell down before we could build them up again. Now we can see the signs, and we take a wall down before it falls down, which makes life a lot easier. Then you take the stones out one by one instead of them all landing in a heap in a muddle.

In fact one of the most notable features of this garden is the masonry, and none of that is my work. But I did wash all the stones to get all the algae off so they could be reused. Nowadays you can do the same thing with a pressure hose, but at the start it was a question of a wheelbarrow of water and a scrubbing brush. The garden is a mixed pleasure, because it is a responsibility. The more of yourself you put into it, the more it is worth saving and the thought that it will not be as well cared-for in the future is not easy to face. But I have to think to myself, 'I will look after it as long as I can, better than someone who perhaps is less interested and just wants to come here for the view', because I have seen gardens in the village go *back*.

When we first came the garden was open to people from the village on the basis that you could come in and put some coins in a box. We couldn't keep this up because the garden could be thought to be dangerous, but it was difficult to close it and for everybody to know. We had not been here long when I came into the garden and found a village lass and her boyfriend making love down the bottom of the garden! Another time a party of young men came in early one Sunday morning when I was just leaving the house. I had by then perfected the phrase, 'Can I help you?' and they replied, 'No, it's all right, we are just going down to the beach.' When I said, 'It's private!' they retorted, 'Oh no it isn't. It is a right of way and we are going fishing.'

So we had to close the garden. But lots of people seemed a bit disappointed, and gradually my husband and I renovated it and decided to open it again, on a more formal basis, to raise money for charity. The first time was when we had a power-boat race here, because somebody suggested that we could raise money for the lifeboats that way. There was not all that much to see – because you just see vague lines right out to sea – but we did enjoy seeing the various power boats coming in and out, some of them upside down, and some in dire straights with the lifeboat dashing to and fro! Everyone enjoyed it, even though they leaned against one of the big stones in the garden and tipped it right

A sheer rock face covered with grey-green lichen forms part of this unique garden.

over, nearly to the ground, and we had quite a job to right it. I also found that it is useful that the garden is divided into lots of bits. When it is open I send nursing mothers to a little sheltered seat where they are private and have a nice view and not too far to walk!

Funny things happen when you open your garden to the public. We have a very splendid cat that lives a long way away and isn't ours at all, and very often people come up to me and say, 'That's a beautiful cat you've got!' because he *knows* when it is

WHY WE GARDEN | Jean Hill

Thursday afternoon and he comes up here, drapes himself on a suitable rock, and everybody admires him! I open the garden every Thursday from the first of May to the middle of September to raise money for charity, the lifeboats, a respite home for carers, and the coast watch. We have been doing it for about 23 years for the National Garden Scheme – they gave me a stainless steel trowel when it was 21 years, which was nice. There are many holiday houses near here so we get quite a lot of visitors, and sometimes I show groups from here or abroad on other days as well.

When we came to live down here, had anybody said, 'You will open the garden, serve cream teas and be very keen on gardening', I would have replied, 'Well let's go and live somewhere else!' But we came here and chose this: I did, mainly, for the swimming and the sailing and being close to it. There is no point in having a lovely beach for swimming if you have to get in the car to go to it or walk a long way. You might just as well go ten miles as half a mile. But here you can walk down to the water. I also keep a little boat down at the bottom, by the slipway, which was built up for my 70th birthday. You have to go down 130 steps, mind you! My knees are gradually giving out, unfortunately, but I am trying to keep them going as long as I can. We have got over 500 steps in the whole garden.

I have made up my mind that I can eventually not worry too much about the garden, and let it go, but still enjoy it, because, although I hope to be able to manage, I may not. If it is a question of saying, 'That has got to be done in the garden, and it is going to come to harm if it isn't', then I will struggle to do it. Then afterwards I will say to myself, 'What on earth did you do that for? That was *stupid*.' But the garden has given me a lot of pleasure, and I like to think that it gave my husband a lot of pleasure too. Latterly, when he was not doing gardening, he would get a meal, or cups of tea or coffee for *me* and the help that we had; so it was reversed roles. I spent all the time in the garden, and he would look after me when I came in.

I would miss the garden desperately if I didn't have it. I don't really feel I can go away in the summer at all, because of the garden,

Jean does not enjoy being photographed, but obliges patiently. She is sitting on one of the 500 steps in her garden!

but when I have been away at another time of year, the first thing I do when I come back is walk round the garden. I suppose I am locked into it really. There is the vegetable garden too, which my husband always looked after, but I can't let it go, because you can't leave land uncultivated and I can't turn it into a flower garden because it is all in terraces, so I have to pick and dispose of the produce. At the moment I am picking French beans and courgettes on a daily basis, and I have just finished picking raspberries. A lot of people come down here to retire and they do quite a lot of things. A number of people know me, but I don't really know them because I don't really get out into the village very much.

    First thing in the morning, summer and winter, I go into the garden and see what it is like, and I also walk into the garden last thing at night and wander around. It gives me tremendous pleasure to see how it is growing, and with a garden, if you make a mistake it is never irrevocable. The only thing you can't do anything about is time. But I planted, with hope, a little monkey puzzle tree. Whether it will ever grow into anything I don't know, but it gives me pleasure and I enjoy seeing it grow a little bit, even though it is still only about two feet high and very wind-battered. I am planting for the future I will never see.

16

BUDDHA MAITREYA
JAPANESE GARDENER

A Westernized Zen garden formed of chipped marble (rather than gravel) and rocks. The purple flowers are aubretia. A teahouse completes the scene.

'My Soul into the boughs does glide'

Mr Maitreya, a former Zen monk now living in Nottinghamshire, conducts courses in relaxation and meditation and follows a philosophy of awareness and being, rather than religion. He also writes Haiku poetry and maintains a Japanese-style garden which has become such an important part of his life that it is akin to a calling. With no formal training, Buddha Maitreya started creating the garden in 1980 out of a disused pig farm. It is now open to the public, and entering through what still appears to be the doorway to an old barn, one is met by the sound of wind chimes and flowing water, and the sight of bridges, lanterns and pagodas. There are plantings of bamboos, maples and cherry trees, alongside European tulips and mind your own business (*Soleirolia soleirolii*).

Buddha Maitreya's garden is a unique fusion of Eastern and Western tastes, like the herb and mango tea accompanied by scones and cream that he made for me. In fact both he and his garden are an enigmatic mixture. A man in middle age, his hands are youthful and smooth. This is especially surprising when you learn that he physically built much of his garden himself, mixing cement for stepping-stones and placing each rock in its position. Mr Maitreya dresses simply in blue cotton Asian-style tunic and trousers, but one cannot help noticing the harmoniously coordinated blue-tinted glasses. He stresses simplicity, yet his garden has many features. And Buddha Maitreya is not too modest to own that many people have told him that his garden is the most beautiful in Britain.

I left Japan because I experienced enlightenment. I was at university and I took a lay people's summer course in a Zen monastery in Yokohama, because I was desperately searching for truth. I was in a miserable, unhappy state, searching for liberation and so I dedicated my life to meditation. I sacrificed everything of the world and of myself. I was aiming at the final moment of achieving just sitting, just being, and finally I reached it. Then the voice in my mind said that to attain pure truth you have to get rid of everything – even just sitting. I had a revelation and everything disappeared: there was pure nothingness. The next moment there was pure brightness and everything was shining beauty. I found it. I was liberated from suffering. It was so happy, so free, so glorious. I saw the ultimate reality of the universe that is there within me and within all creation – I found it.

So I decided to become a monk and a teacher. But I was still a young man, and in such an old culture, I could not be accepted as a teacher and no one would listen to me, so I thought, 'I must go to America.' I was brought up in Handa, near Nagoya, after the war, and America was my dream country: the New World. There was always propaganda about America and the fact that it wanted to make Japan into an ideal country too, and so I always wanted to go there. But first I went to Thailand for a year, then to India for a year and a half, where the Buddha attained enlightenment. At that time I absolutely adored Buddha and it was in Mahatma Gandhi's ashram that I was first asked to teach, which made me very happy.

This was the time of the hippy movement when many people went to India to search for enlightenment, and so I taught many Westerners meditation. But my aim was still to go to America and so I left India. I was invited to go to Nepal and taught in Katmandu for some months, in the foothills of the Himalayan Mountains. It was beautiful there, but it was still not my place; I always thought I must go to the West. So I came to England, and I was invited by many universities and Buddhist societies and groups to lecture and teach meditation. They invited me because I was a Zen monk from Japan, and I was busy. It was while I was staying in Teversal in Nottingham that I thought, 'I must stay here for a while as there is plenty of work for me to do before I go to America.' So I asked someone to look for a place for me to stay, and they found this property for sale in North Clifton.

Buddha Maitreya meditates in a small pavilion on a hill with a cherry tree to the right.

General view of the main part of Buddha Maitreya's garden showing the carp pond with bamboo on the right, evergreen trees in the background and irises in front.

It was a deserted farm, with nothing there, but it had potential. At that time, we started with around ten people living a communal life here. We supported ourselves and had a little shop, but communal life is hectic and I could not handle it after two years. So I thought, 'Now is the time to go to America', and I tried to sell this place. But people who had come here for meditation said, 'Don't go to America. Don't desert us!' So I decided to stay. But I didn't know what to do with the two acres of land. A small part was cultivated for vegetables, but 99 per cent of the land was still wild. So, since I was staying and was going to make this purely a meditation centre, I thought I should use the place for something peaceful, and one day I thought, 'I will try to make a Japanese garden.'

I had no experience whatsoever, but I missed the hilly and mountainous scenery of Japan, and my interpretation of a Japanese garden is that it is mountainous and has streams and bridges and stepping-stones. In fact my concept is the natural landscape of Japan in miniature. But this land was all flat, so I asked someone with a JCB to move the earth to form a basic shape. It made a pond in the central part, and the soil which was dug out was piled up to make hills indicating mountainous terrain. All the rest I did with shovels and my hands.

The beautiful twisted trunks of the wisteria form a frame for the clipped leylandii behind.

I shaped each detail and brought in huge rocks from a quarry in Derby and placed lots of little stones collected from everywhere. This was 23 years ago, but after 10 years people said, 'This garden is beautiful', and after 12 years they said, 'You must open this garden to the public.' And so I did. That is how it happened.

I never designed the garden in detail; the basic idea was there, but every element emerged in a perfect form so that it is balanced, harmonious, meditative and natural. I had very little money, so I asked friends if they had any spare plants or suckers, and friends and local villagers gave me a lot. The majority of trees are ordinary English trees, such as forsythia, hazel and lilac, which are found in any garden. But once they started to grow, I began to shape them in the Japanese style as I felt was right, according to my memory and concept — maybe in my genes! So without any real plan, in some mysterious way everything is harmonious, as if it is in the right place. It is miraculous to me, because when I first came it was all so bare and empty, like the Gobi desert.

If I had been trained and ruled by tradition, I might have been too much constrained, and might not have achieved the free, spontaneous expression that exists in my garden. For instance, I have cut a lot of the tops of the trees off completely, or given them radical treatment to contain their size. Normally you would not do this, thinking you would kill the tree, but it has worked here. Each morning I spend about two hours working in the garden and each afternoon one or two hours. Some people think that a Japanese garden is fairly maintenance-free, but it is not like that. If I did not open it to the public, I could leave it a little more in a lazy way, but it is open every day except Monday.

Many people say the garden is the only place they have found peace and they really appreciate it. It also acts as a window to my meditation courses. People come to the garden, and then they decide to take a course. They are amazed by the garden and its quality of peace. Then they look at me and say, 'Did *you* really make this garden?' And I say, 'Well, I cannot believe it either!' This appreciation gives me great satisfaction. I work hard, morning and evening, but every time I finish work, I just enjoy. I sit and look at how beautiful the garden is, and know that I created it. This is my reward.

In a Japanese garden all the elements of fire, water, earth and air must exist harmoniously. If there is something missing or there is discord, then you do not feel peaceful. All the elements of nature must be in perfect balance,

Above: Buddha Maitreya on a stone bridge seen through waving bamboo.

Left: The carp pond with leylandii, wisteria, pine and holly in the background.

just like in all creation. But in the modern, competitive world – in the office, or street, or factory – there is no harmony. That is why there is so much stress and frustration in the world. In this garden the water is running in a stream: rocks are there, solid, for sitting and as symbols of earth. There is sunlight, oxygen, scent and colours: nature in miniature. Literally, mini-nature. That is the essence, and that is what gives the sense of peace.

So a Japanese garden has these elements and should also have some typical Japanese plants, like bamboo, pine, acer, camellia, azalea, wisteria. It can also have some stone lanterns or a little Buddha. But naturalness and simplicity are also very important. Some people who have been to this garden and then been to visit gardens in Japan come back and say, 'None of the Japanese gardens are as beautiful as your garden!' And when the BBC filmed *Songs of Praise* here, they said it was the most beautiful garden in Britain. It is a very good garden – one of the best. I know it. From April to June is the most glorious, happy time of the year. When I am in the garden I see the glory and preciousness of all life: the blessedness and miracle of all creation. Once I started to make this garden and to maintain it so that people trust that it is here in a peaceful condition, how could I go to America? Now this is my home. I am still very busy here, but one day I will just visit America, to teach.

I never thought I would make a garden, but now I am happy to share it with other people. It is what I created, with my idea of beauty and my love and energy put into it until it felt right. When it was completed I looked at it and felt great blissful joy. I realized that every bit of my garden is made with my love. It is like a manifestation of what I teach, that everyone can experience, and it is an extension of myself. It is a very different concept from the Western materialistic, greedy, selfish, rat-race world mentality. That only leads to more discontent, and many Western people are now searching for the original simplicity of nature, such as can be found here. Interestingly, many Japanese people are crazy about English gardens. I like them, too. But not as much as my Japanese garden.

Left: It was raining the day that Buddha Maitreya showed me around his garden. He feels the garden looks especially lovely in the rain.

Right: A cat rubs against the wooden rail of a hump-back bridge where a Japanese larch tree grows.

17

JANET OLDROYD HULME

FRUIT AND VEGETABLE GROWER AND RHUBARB SPECIALIST

The entrance to E. Oldroyd & Sons.

'Upon my Mouth do crush their Wine'

Rhubarb, a name covering the many different species of rheum, is a fascinating vegetable. It has an ancient history, originally growing in the mountains of China and Tibet, and now cultivated in much of Europe and the United States. Its oversized leaves at the end of thick succulent pink stems look almost prehistoric, and its uses are myriad. It can be eaten in crumbles, pies, jams, fools, chutneys, soups and sorbets, or drunk as juice and wine. Rhubarb is used medicinally; to clean burnt pots and pans; as hair colour; and as an insecticide. It has inspired art, music (a song by John Cleese) and limericks, and it still inspires Janet Oldroyd, a fourth-generation rhubarb-grower in West Yorkshire.

E. Oldroyd & Sons have been growing rhubarb for more than a century, and Janet is an expert. Happily, it is hard to stop her talking on her subject, in which she has an almost mystic belief. And visiting her forcing sheds in February to see the picking by candlelight, it is not hard to see why.

I would find growing vegetables a hard slog if it weren't for the rhubarb. We grow strawberries and most common vegetables, but forced and outdoor rhubarb make up about 65 per cent of our turnover now. As far back as we can trace, our family have been farmers, and my son is the fifth generation to be involved in rhubarb. Prior to rhubarb, the family were involved with strawberries and pigs – it was my great-grandfather who started the family in the rhubarb industry when he came up to Yorkshire in the early 1900s. He had been quite a wealthy farmer in the Wisbech area before the depression, during which he lost everything. He came to Yorkshire to start again. Then he became friends with a local farmer and taught him how to grow strawberries, and in return the farmer taught my great-grandfather how to produce rhubarb roots for forcing.

His son, my grandfather, was more interested in producing strawberries and vegetables than expanding rhubarb production, but the business continued, and my father still remembers to this day, being taken as a small child by his grandfather into a forcing shed for the first time. In that moment he knew that he had fallen in love with this crop. This was what he wanted to grow. When anyone walks in the sheds for the first time it is an unbelievable sight, and men, as well as women, gasp with delight and wonder. The colour, the darkness and the candlelight all combine to give a unique display, some say an almost religious experience.

My father, by now a skilled market gardener with a reputation for high quality produce, went into partnership with his brother-in-law. My father was determined to increase rhubarb production and he expanded the business significantly, going into debt buying farms at a time when other growers were leaving the industry, either by choice or necessity. He often tells me how after intensive bidding at auctions he was unable to sign the cheque for his hand trembling and had to ask my uncle to do it for him. He took a huge gamble, but he always said that rhubarb would again win people's hearts and better times would return.

Before the Second World War, there were more than 200 rhubarb growers in this area, which is known as the 'rhubarb triangle'; now there are just nine. The towns of Leeds, Wakefield and Bradford formed the boundaries of the triangle – the centre of the world's rhubarb production – which developed here for several reasons. Sheep reared on the Pennines gave rise to the wool industry in Leeds and Bradford. Even today we still use a by-product of that industry: waste from the carding and combing process of the fleece, known as 'shoddy'. The beauty of 'shoddy' is that it is organic and it is very high in nitrogen. The nitrogen is released slowly and is a key requirement for a forcing root, so 'shoddy' is ploughed into the ground prior to planting. Additionally, the massive Yorkshire coalfields provided cheap heating for the sheds. The heavy clay soil, high rainfall, early winters and the cold in this area are also perfect. Rhubarb is a native of the banks of the Volga in Siberia, so it loves moisture and cold.

But despite the favourable conditions, the industry went into major decline after the Second World War when refrigerated transport made imports of new tropical fruits available to a nation that was tired of rhubarb. One of the reasons that our family managed to survive this downturn was by growing other fruit and vegetables, as opposed to growers who purely grew rhubarb. My father decided that although he was passionate about his rhubarb, he would follow strict crop rotation methods to avoid disease, as with any other crop. Income from the other crops also helped, because it doesn't matter how much you love anything, if you are losing money, there is only one end for it all. He made the other crops subsidize the rhubarb, and today

Above: Janet Oldroyd holds a candle to inspect the rhubarb in her darkened shed, which is the biggest in the country. Some say that seeing the picking in the candle-lit forcing sheds is almost like a religious experience.

Opposite: In this shed the best of 'Timperley Early' has already been picked and the shed is being cleared out. Rhubarb must be harvested by holding the stalk near the bud at the base, pulling and twisting firmly. Cutting the stalk with a knife can introduce fungal infections.

rhubarb is what we are best known for and is the crop that gives me the greatest satisfaction.

I didn't join the family business until I had the first of my two sons. When I was young (I am 51), farmers generally did not want their daughters working out in the fields, lifting roots in the depth of winter. Throughout my early school years I intended to study business, but, after studying Human Biology, my ideas changed, and I eventually became a Medical Scientific Officer at St James's Hospital. Then when Lindsay was born it was easier for me to work at home, and I suppose my 'roots' took hold! Now my eldest son is totally smitten with rhubarb, and he will carry on the business controlling production, perhaps with James, my youngest, who is more interested in the business side of running the company: a perfect combination, avoiding brotherly conflict. Each family round here has slightly different methods of growing rhubarb, their own secrets and their own strains of roots.

In 1983 my brother, husband and I bought out my uncle and became directors. We increased the size of the market garden and the forced rhubarb output. Together we decide what and where each crop is grown. 'Quality Assurance' approval status is a must and requires much administration. My schedule demands that I go on horseback round the fields to cover as many crops in as little time as possible, and get in amongst the crop for a close look without causing damage. It's ideal!

If I have any spare time, I not only enjoy horse-riding but also driving horses. I love most outdoor pursuits, although I also enjoy researching into the history of rhubarb. But I am a modern farmer, so I don't get a lot of spare time, usually working 55 to 60 hours each week. More in winter, when the forced rhubarb season is upon us. Then I also give lectures to promote my beloved crop.

Sometimes when my mind and body are so physically tired, I begin to wonder, 'Why am I doing all this?' I begin mentally to leave the fold, but then in an instant I feel almost a blasphemous guilt and pull myself together. Just over-tired; I am no Judas.

One of the difficulties with forced rhubarb is that you cannot use a lot of machinery, and it is very labour-intensive. A lot of the work involves lifting the roots manually, and devising a schedule so that we do not have a gap in crop production.

Roots destined for the forcing process live outside for a minimum of two years. Whilst outside, you do not harvest any rhubarb

Above: A forcing root is sometimes so heavy it takes two men to lift it. The root is an energy store, so no earth is needed, only heat, which makes the stalks grow – up to an inch a day.

Opposite: Light damages forced rhubarb, so during harvesting the sheds are lit by candles. The forced stalks are succulent and mellow-flavoured, while the unwanted leaves are stunted and yellow – unlike the architectural rheum leaves sometimes used in the ornamental garden.

WHY WE GARDEN | Janet Oldroyd Hulme

that comes from those roots. This is for two reasons: first, you would deplete the energy store that you are building in the root; and secondly, when you pick the sticks, you would get lateral spurring from the main bud. We want big strong buds in a forcing shed – tiny buds produce second-quality sticks. There is one high-yielding variety, 'Queen Victoria', which can require three years' preparation. These are the largest and heaviest roots you can get. I love this dear old lady who in a forcing shed can be quite grumpy and demanding, but, given care and attention, could outclass the lot. At least that was until 'Stockbridge Arrow' was developed in the '70s at the Horticultural Research Centre in Yorkshire, where my father was an advisor for 12 years. 'Stockbridge Arrow' is my favourite.

Rhubarb is not a fruit: it is a vegetable. Most people think it is a fruit and that because a fruit swells as it develops and ripens, little thin sticks of rhubarb will too. But the thicker high quality sticks emerge from the root that way. Unfortunately, as the root gives up its energy into crop production, the strong buds weaken and finally send out class-two sticks. It is then time to call it a day with those particular roots and discard them to the compost heap. Roots that people have in their gardens might be 20 years old, and be big, but you could dig them up and throw them up in the air with one hand. A forcing root sometimes takes two men to lift and place in position in the forcing shed because it is so heavy!

When this root, or energy store, gets into the shed, it is heat initially which triggers the plant into growth, tricking it into believing it is spring. We are just replacing nature, not doing anything weird and wonderful. The first buds pop through and start looking for light.

But rhubarb is an amazing plant that can do without light because it pulls on the energy store in the root. This is why you end up with a product which is more succulent and less harshly flavoured, and also one that grows very quickly, because it is looking for the light all the time. It can grow up to an inch a day. Another difference with forced rhubarb is that the leaves are stunted, because nature doesn't need them, and yellow, because the chlorophyll is not working.

We have the largest forcing shed in the country, which enables us to allow visitors to share the experience at an annual festival. During those two weeks I give talks about the crop. As when harvesting, we cannot allow light to damage the crop, so the sheds are lit by candles. A concessionary, dim spotlight shines on to me as I talk in the shed, and the leaves can enlarge and go green in that brief time! Just having the door open at harvest time causes the sticks to turn and face the light – like plants on a windowsill. If you let light into a forcing shed, you would also allow in cold air. If you put artificial light in, it would slow the process down and make the sticks more fibrous.

The colour in the rhubarb stalks is not light-dependent; it depends on the variety, a bit like apples – some are more green or more red. Forced early varieties such as 'Timperley Early' are salmon-pink in colour; later varieties such as 'Stockbridge Arrow' are deep red. However, if you break open a stick of forced rhubarb it is white, like anything that has been blanched. Technically, forced rhubarb has to be lifted out of the ground, have heat applied, and be made to grow from its own energy. In a garden, if you put a dustbin over your plant but it is still in the soil, it is blanched rhubarb, not forced, although it tastes practically the same but is slightly more acidic and not quite as tender.

If you have rhubarb in your garden and have too much, you should pull it all away and let young sticks come up, which are in effect spring rhubarb, even though you might be getting it in September. It is while it is photosynthesizing that the fibres thicken, so you want to avoid it getting the chance to do that. Forced rhubarb takes about six to eight weeks from when you apply the heat to the point of first harvest. We then harvest for about a five- to six-week period only, because you have depleted the energy store. We have tried many times to get the roots back in production, but they just disintegrate, and now we just destroy the roots at the end of the process. That is the final thing which contributes to the massive production costs, because roots are fetching large sums of money now, especially the Yorkshire strains.

The loss of root is significant: you have two to three years when you have no crop. All stages of production are extremely labour-intensive: heating costs are now very high, and the forcing sheds are so low that you can't use them for anything else. The only way to try to make the shed more productive is to get two crops by using two sets of roots, initially planting 'Timperley Early', and once those roots are depleted, you empty the sheds and start the whole process again. This is impossible to do in sheds which have later varieties allocated to them.

Up until the early 1960s the 'rhubarb express' train would leave this area nightly, taking rhubarb to the old Covent Garden and other London markets. All the local growers would take their wares to the railway station. When the railways went into demise, they looked for alternative means of transportation, which required that the growers group together. My father's section initially brought all their rhubarb here, and lorries would take the rhubarb down to London. Now, as public interest in all things rhubarb is once again growing, plans are being considered to revive the train – but in reverse, bringing tourists in from the South to Wakefield.

In this area, too, when there were more growers, there used to be an annual rhubarb

Once graded the rhubarb is cleaned and packed and sent all over the country.

All the rhubarb is graded. Varieties such as 'Crimson Crown', 'Stockbridge Arrow' and 'Queen Victoria' (named after the rhubarb-loving monarch) have good flavour, high yield and huge red stalks.

show and dinner. It was a top-secret event, where you weren't allowed in anyone else's shed on the day of the show – very cloak and dagger! Passions ran high as people competed within the various categories for different varieties of rhubarb. There was also a cup for the best box of rhubarb in the show and the coveted title 'World Champion Rhubarb Grower' was awarded to whoever won the most points in each category – our family won that quite a few times.

The entries for the show would have to be in by 1 p.m. on a Saturday in February and judging took place all afternoon, while some growers retired to the bar to calm their nerves, got merry and had a few drinks too many. Later that evening the dinner and ball were held, which in its heyday, would be for around 500 people. After dinner there would be the usual speeches and prize-giving. Growers would talk together and air their disgruntlement about the state of the industry. Dinner was always made from local produce, with of course the obligatory rhubarb crumble. I remember one year a new chef caused quite a stir. Unbelievably, he peeled the rhubarb, and of course everyone there knew that that was completely wrong! It looked like celery pie!

During the forced rhubarb season I have it every morning for breakfast, and because I have to watch my weight, I usually cook it without sugar, in pure orange juice, which also enhances the flavour of the rhubarb. I have an under-active thyroid, so rhubarb is particularly good for me because it helps stimulate my metabolism. My family doesn't all eat rhubarb every day, but they eat a hell of a lot of it. My father likes more sugar in it than I do. Because rhubarb is a vegetable it has no natural sugar and is low in calories, so some people use it as a diet food now. The most popular way of cooking it is still probably rhubarb crumble. I have found it is the way to a man's heart! It's always the men who ask for it, and if you ask a man what his favourite pudding is, he will often say rhubarb crumble. Gooseberries also seem to appeal to men; it must be something to do with the sharp flavour.

Some people say that the acid in rhubarb aggravates their arthritis, although I haven't found that. Actually rhubarb has helped mankind throughout history, and it annoys me when people poke fun at it. Rhubarb has a massive history, and if we think of it in time-scale terms as the size of a book, the forcing process is just one sentence in that book. The earliest recorded use of rhubarb was 2700 BC. Then the root, kiln-dried, was used in China as medicinal drug. It was very expensive and commanded three times the price opium was fetching in this country. The rhubarb remedy detoxified and purged the system – in a similar way to the use of leeches. Rhubarb was also recommended as a cure for constipation (and in small quantities the prevention of diarrhoea), asthma, poisonous bites, diseases of the stomach and colon, venereal disease (which it was used for extensively), lung and liver problems, and the spitting of blood (TB).

This is a story I like: when Genghis Khan conquered part of north-west China and Tibet in 1220, his chief military strategist was given the choice of his pickings of the spoils of victory. He chose a large quantity of the drug made from rhubarb – much to the amusement of the other generals, who wanted women, horses and gold. But eventually it was the military strategist who got the last laugh. A few months later, all the men and the horses had a severe case of dysentery (they'd obviously drunk the same filthy water). This chap cured them within two weeks with his supply of rhubarb, and forthwith Genghis Khan decreed that all supplies of rhubarb had to be confiscated. Rhubarb was also involved in the wars between the British Empire and China. The Chinese believed that if they stopped the export of the rhubarb drug, the troops would be so ill here that they wouldn't be able to fight! Also, Henry VIII was administered large amounts of rhubarb on his deathbed. That is how highly regarded rhubarb was!

But apart from medicinal uses, in times of war, rhubarb has helped feed the nation. Children were even handed out sticks of it to dab in a small bag of sugar to replace sweets. Happy memories for many! Large amounts of rhubarb were grown purely for jam, which formed a large part of most people's staple diets. It helps to make the jams set, and if you get the concentrations right, it takes the flavour of the other fruits you put with it. It was perfect: it was very cheap, while fruits such as strawberries and raspberries were very expensive. Even now, we supply the specialist jam makers, Thursday's Cottage, with the forced rhubarb that goes into the jams that are sold in Harvey Nichols and Harrods. But they insist on forced rhubarb to get the flavour and colour of the jam, and even stipulate the variety 'Stockbridge Arrow', which we specialize in.

'Stockbridge Arrow' is an outstanding, new, main-crop cultivar, which I would recommend for most gardeners. If you don't pick for the first year after planting any variety, you will have plentiful supplies thereafter, although you should replace the plant every eight years and move its location in the garden to prevent disease. Another good variety is 'Cawood Delight', which is one of the best, but difficult for gardeners to grow. It is purely an outdoor variety, it doesn't force, and it has low yield, but it has good flavour, and is the only variety that keeps its red colour from one end of the stick to the other. In fact the colour goes up into the leaves, too, like fingers of red. My father looked upon 'Cawood Delight' as a specialist variety and insisted that we grow it here, so we still do. I am told that Saudi Arabia was one of the big purchasers of 'Cawood Delight', because they love rhubarb out there, but we mainly grow 'Cawood Delight' for root sales direct to the public.

I believe that rhubarb will come full circle. I don't think it is a fashion trend: now people know that if you want to live a long healthy life you have to eat things that are good for your body. Rhubarb fits that bill perfectly. But, in addition, people are doing research into rhubarb. A scientist who is studying rhubarb came here a few years ago, and he told me that research was underway into how rhubarb was able to cure disease, and they were at that time very close to unlocking the secret. Then in the spring of 2003, I noticed in the press that a new group of cancer-fighting drugs would soon be released, all rhubarb-based. Well, the Chinese regard the drug rhubarb as a cure for stomach cancer; perhaps, I don't know, is rhubarb going to be what people have been looking for all the time to cure cancer?

It could have been there all the time and we just could not see! One of the first ancient religions that only believed in one God as opposed to many, stated that upon the slaying of the Son of God by the forces of evil, his lifeblood spilled forth, and seeds were obtained. From these seeds, which were split into three, came man, woman, and what could have been the earliest form of rhubarb, the Rivas plant! It is such a similar story to Christianity, but in this version of the birth of mankind, was God trying to tell us something? Time will only tell. If that secret of the root is ever truly found, only then will we know.

I believe that the crop has a massive future, because prevention is better than cure. But roots will also be grown for use as a medicine. When I worked as a Medical Scientific Officer I was trying to cure disease; now I feel that I am helping trying to prevent disease by growing and educating people about rhubarb. Years ago, when I was working in the labs, sitting looking down a microscope, and the sun was shining in, I often found myself looking up at the sky and wondering what they were doing at home on the farm. So I suppose, really, I was always meant to be here. Was it destiny that got me back? I don't know about that, but I am here to stay.

ROWAN VUGLAR
COMMUNITY GARDENER

Winding paths, leading you to explore different areas, are a feature of the communal garden at Harleyford Road.

'Fair quiet, have I found thee here'

Visiting Harleyford Road Garden in an unprepossessing part of south London, one is aware of two things. First, it is not a typical London Square, where most of the garden can be seen at a glance; here there are winding paths seeming to entice you to hidden secret areas. Second, this garden, more than many others I visited, has soul. Somehow the fact that the garden is an oasis, made with devotion by local residents, for local residents, shows. Rowan Vuglar, originally from New Zealand, lives on the square in a flat full of his own large, bright decorative paintings, for he is an artist, as well as a self-taught gardener by profession. But he gives his free time to work voluntarily in Harleyford Road Garden.

In 1984 local people started to grow vegetables on a one and a half acre area of wasteland, which was the start of the present community garden. Apart from a few existing trees, the garden has been planted from scratch and now includes a wildlife area, pond and playground. There are times when it appears a bit desolate, for unlike Edwardes Square, where David Magson works (see chapter 6), Harleyford Road employs no paid gardener. Moreover no keys are required for entry: during the day, everyone is welcome. This gives rise to some typical inner-city problems, but it also means that the local inhabitants and those who work in the garden are able to use it to maintain a form of community watch. For in this garden, again in contrast to Edwardes Square, late-night intruders are likely to be tramps or addicts rather than dinner-jacketed partygoers.

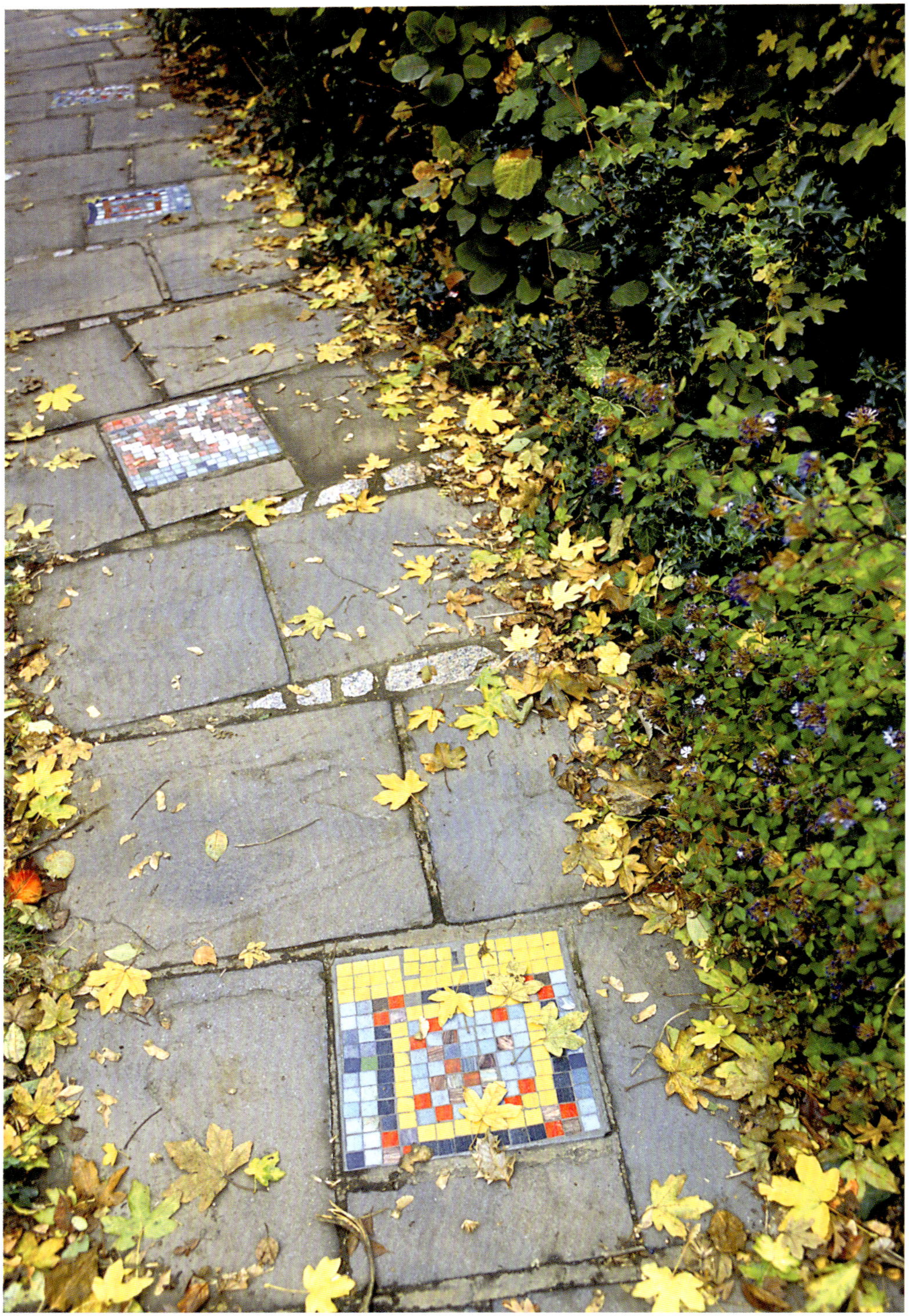

WHY WE GARDEN | Rowan Vuglar

One of my first jobs when I left school was with the local council in New Zealand, working in parks and gardens, and I got quite interested in horticulture then. I have been a fairly itinerant sort of person, travelling all through New Zealand and then Australia, moving a lot and having many jobs, which turned out to be gardening jobs. I am also a house painter and an artist – a Jack-of-all-trades. I came to London from Australia in 1986 and stayed round here with my cousin, who is a poet, for a while. This is actually an artists' community and there is either a poet, an artist or a musician living in most of the houses round here. I didn't know many people here at first and was quite shy, but a friend said, 'Come and help in the garden', and that is how I got involved. The garden had started about two years before, when a group of people decided to clear up the site.

During the war, bombs demolished all the houses that were where the square is now, and even when I came on to the scene, it was still very much a wasteland, with a bit of planting here and there. The land and housing around belongs to the council, and they just neglected it. So when the residents started to plant it we just kept 'shtum' and didn't dare tell anyone at the beginning. Eventually, it got the recognition it deserved, and at that point it was too late for the council to do anything about it, and it just became Harleyford Road Community Garden, and a group of ten or twelve people got together to do things.

One of the first jobs I helped with was putting in a pond with this friend of mine. When that was done he started sorting rubble, throwing good bricks over his left shoulder and bad bricks over his right shoulder and when he had a big pile of good bricks he made footpaths. A feature of the garden is the mosaics in the paths. A couple of local teachers arranged workshops and invited all the local kids from the square to come along. About 10 or 15 turned up and spent the day making mosaics, at that stage, sticking their patterns on to paper. Then when the paths were made the mosaics were added and set in concrete.

We have managed to get plenty of funding from the lottery, the local housing association and various other bodies, but we work in the garden voluntarily. The grants that we get from time to time go through the Committee and that was, for instance, how we got the railings to go round the outside. The planning of the garden evolved year by year. For example there was a patch of land about 30 metres long and about three metres wide, which was covered in nettles, and I decided to clear it up. Since I work as a self-employed gardener, every now and again I would be doing someone's garden and they would say, 'I don't like that bush. Can you take it away?' and I would say, '*Sure*, I'll take it away!' and I would dig it up, clear the nettles here, plant it, and make that space mine, if you like. Everyone has their own little patch in a sense, but it is not so strict that you can't just go and do a bit of weeding anywhere.

We always wanted a children's area with swings and things, and there has always been the idea that kids would be the main users of the garden. Of course it is a bit upsetting when you see them trampling over the planted areas, but generally the kids are pretty good. Sometimes, if you dig around in the under-

Opposite: Local children designed the distinctive mosaics that decorate the paths – a nice touch, making the garden unique.

growth you will find little tables and chairs where the children have made little cubby holes, which is rather sweet. People put out rubbish, like bits of wood or old chairs, and suddenly they are gone and they turn up in the garden, perhaps as a skateboarding ramp or as a little hideaway.

One year we decided to make a part of the garden into a small orchard with grass and some apple and plum trees, but an apple tree got pushed down by some kids and storms took care of the rest, so areas come and go. It all takes time and effort. One year I and another guy put in some big posts in a corner. They were old telephone poles, which we had to dig huge holes for, and then we planted roses to grow up them. I used to do most of the hard digging with a few others, but we are all getting to be around 50 now and a bit too old for it. But luckily most of the hard landscaping is done.

Some of the other volunteers have done gardening courses and are quite knowledgeable. I have no training or book knowledge but have got skill just by doing gardening. If you asked me the names of plants, I could never tell you, but I would know when to prune them and how to take care of them, and I have a good reputation for my work. But we all just get on and do what we feel like. Sometimes we have a big work day when we might all do something together. Like a couple of years ago we were getting a lot of traffic noise from Harleyford Road and decided to plant shrubs and climbers against the wall. So someone made food and we all dug trenches and did a big planting.

We tend to have meetings once a month, with a work day afterwards. I try to go to the meetings and then go out and do my bit. There are always arguments. For instance, this garden can be accessed from Bonnington Square, where there is another community garden, but they are run by two totally different groups of people. At one stage we tried to get them to amalgamate, but they were both so different in their outlook that it never happened. I find it hard to understand, but certain personalities won't be led by other people: they would rather lead themselves. Two friends of mine had an argument in the garden recently and ended up chasing each other with a hose!

Some weeks go by when I don't do anything in the garden, but usually within a month I would certainly do something. We have got three rubbish bins in the garden and they always fill up; hardly anything goes on the ground. I take it on myself to go and empty the bins, but it is so rewarding to see that people use them, and it is no big deal for me – I just grab an empty wheelie bin and fill it up. In the summer I mow the lawn once or twice a month, and I do pruning every now and

Above: Rowan is happy to give his time voluntarily to help in the garden – sweeping leaves or emptying rubbish – whatever needs to be done.

Opposite: The garden was always intended in particular as a place for children to play.

again, especially if there is an open day or something where we want everything to look nice. To some extent the garden maintains itself now, in that there is less digging and planting to do, although each autumn we get a whole load of bulbs and pop them in. There is one lady, Sandra, up the road who is out there most days tinkering around doing this and that. Then there is another lady, Amanda, who is out there most evenings with a hose. Everyone does their bit whenever they can.

Some people have aspirations to become community-minded, but if there is nothing for them to do, the idea slips and they just stay in and watch TV. This garden provides a community project that always needs attention. Every year we have an open festival in the square, which is really good and lots of fun. It is also a way of fund-raising so we can buy new plants. We held it last week and had a tombola, competitions, sales of tea and cakes, which all together raised about £400. From 1986 to 1996 we used to have an arts festival each year with paintings and music and sculptures round the square. Now, unfortunately, we are all getting a bit old and worn out to keep doing it each year. The core group of gardeners has always been the same, and getting kids involved is pretty difficult, but someone, hopefully, will take over.

I feel it is important because we live in not a very nice part of town, to be honest. Vauxhall is not the best area, and you either let it become a rubbish tip, or you try to do something about it. The middle part of the garden at Bonnington Square, only a few years ago, was just a pile of grass with dog shit everywhere and it was really revolting. So the residents who got that together just went in there and made it beautiful. It is a matter of saying, 'O.K., this is our home, so let's make it a really nice place to live.'

Many people use the garden to walk through. They might come from Bonnington Square and go out at Harleyford Road, and go on to Tesco's or whatever. If you count those people in with the garden users, there are hundreds. If you just count the people who go and sit or laze around in it, there are probably about 20 to 30 a day. A lot of office workers go out there in the summertime and at the weekend there are lots of people sunbathing. The local schools come and use it for their nature trails, and of course kids are out there after school too. The garden is open to all members of the public from about seven in the morning till dusk.

It is like a hidden treasure box in a sense. You can go to one part, and then you can leave that part and it is like being in another garden. Sometimes one area is in full flower, and a month later that is gone, but something else is happening. For instance the flag irises by the pond were lovely a few weeks ago, but now they are over, so you go to somewhere where there are nice roses. Seeing the garden come into life every spring is really rewarding. You see a load of sticks in the winter, and think, 'Oh, dear!' and then suddenly you can't see the other side because of the greenery.

Rowan stands proudly by the cherry tree which has his son's placenta buried beneath it.

When I shut the garden at night, there is jasmine by the gate, which puts out a scent at sunset, which just about knocks me over. That is one of my favourites at the moment.

What I enjoy about gardening is the aesthetics of it. I have been working in a garden today in Muswell Hill, which I have been maintaining for about 15 years. I go in and everything is untidy, and I come away and it looks like an art work. I like that. You can see what you have done and I really appreciate flowers and plants themselves. I am also very keen on organic gardening and never use sprays or anything like that. And most New Zealanders are keen on composting and we do composting in the community garden as well, so it is an integral part of the garden: things can be recycled.

Our own house doesn't have a garden. It backs on to the community garden, and has a back patio with about two feet of concrete and a clothes-line. Most of the houses here do have their own gardens, but not enough room for children to play. With the community garden, parents of young children worry unless the kids are in a group, because you never know if someone is out there intent on doing harm to children. When my son, Josh, who is 11, goes out there, we say, 'Make sure you are with someone.' They tend to run around with friends anyway. But as far as I know we have not had any trouble with anyone being nasty to children.

We have had trouble with the kids themselves sometimes, like in the last few months or so they have been spray-painting graffiti in the passageway between the houses as you come out of the garden. What happens is that it gets graffiti and then you fix it up and then it gets graffiti again the next night. I decided to paint it up since I also paint houses and always have a supply of paint handy. So I painted the whole thing really nicely and ever since then the graffiti has stopped. Everyone keeps an eye on the place and it is a nice feeling, actually. Kids do wrong, but then they learn from it – it is not a big deal. They play in the pond, and poke sticks into frogs, which you wish they wouldn't do, but I used to do that sort of thing when I was a kid.

There has been some vandalism in the centre garden at Bonnington Square, which is depressing. They had two wonderful tree ferns worth £200 or £300, which got stolen. That side of it is not so good, but you carry on. Recently we found a lot of needles in the garden from drug users, and they would confront me at dusk when I was closing the gate at Harleyford Road, and I was scared and I would have to call the local police. Eventually we had to shut the garden for about a month. Suddenly the whole square became aware that there were drug users in the area, and in fact they did stop coming here. Then the garden becomes a catalyst for public opinion as well as being a space for people to go.

About two years ago, some of the local kids used the garden to deal in cannabis. There were gangs, and some of the 13 and 14 year olds were getting beaten up. We thought, 'This is *not* what the garden is for', and so we shut it then too, and told people why, and it all stopped and the problem went away. The local kids know the garden is run by volunteers, and they know who we are, because we are their parents! Now people use the garden more sensibly. Although once, a while ago, I woke up in the morning and there was a huge hole in the brick wall. Someone had stolen a bus, and driven the bus through the wall! So we had to chase up the bus company, and the person who stole the bus wasn't insured, but eventually I think we got the money from the bus company.

Some other strange things happened a long time ago. It was the middle of winter and I noticed three children, all under the age of seven, walking about in the garden with no shoes on. Their parents were drinking in the pub over the road! My wife, Jane, let them in and gave them some food. In London, there are some pretty weird people floating round.

Another time, I went out in the morning to open the gates which I had shut the evening before, and found this woman who had been in the garden all night. It was cold, and she could have got out quite easily by just jumping over the wall, but she had kind of lost her mind, and was making little holes everywhere like a rabbit! I just about fell over with fright when I came out and saw her. We also have tramps living out there occasionally, but we don't encourage them.

People use the garden in various ways, really. A sad thing happened there once, ten or more years ago, when I went out and saw two women friends of mine standing round a hole and I said, 'Hi! What are you doing? Burying a cat or something?' And they *were*. I felt so bad, and slunk off, and actually as I went away I realized that one of them was in tears. The other interesting thing is that there are at least three placentas buried out there. My son's is, and a couple of other people who have had babies, either at home or in hospital, have taken the placenta home and planted a tree and put the placenta at the bottom. I think it is a New Zealand habit. There is a belief that the tree takes on the persona of the child and it is their tree.

My son's tree is about 50 feet high now. He was born in April, and when I came home, at about 4 a.m., I saw a cherry tree in the square and it had wonderful white blossom and there was a full moon so the blossom really stood out. So I thought, 'Right, a cherry tree is what it has got to be!' But it was April, which is the wrong time of year to plant trees. So we put the placenta in the freezer, and come autumn, we took it out, and bought a cherry tree and put the placenta in the ground with the tree.

Watching children running around playing in the garden is very rewarding. They have a great time with water pistols and everything. I get pleasure just knowing the garden is there, and that we have done it. It could have been a dog fouling area, or got built on with more back-to-back houses, which we don't really need. We are so near to the centre of town, but you come in here and suddenly it is all quiet, and kids can play off the street and it is an oasis, really.

PART III
LATE Deciders

19

JAMES CREBBIN-BAILEY
TOPIARY SPECIALIST

James uses long-handled shears for his first cut on a Buxus sempervirens 'Elegantissima'.

'Cut in these Trees their Mistress name'

Four years ago James was cutting hair, not topiary. Now he has swapped his scissors for shears, but his conversation is still peppered with references to hairdressing, and particularly to design, which is what he finds most satisfying in his job. He sells individual plants; exhibits at various shows; designs new, and maintains existing, topiary gardens. He is engaging, confident and proud of his work, eager to show his awards as well as his numerous drawings and sketches.

James lives in his mother-in-law's house in Twickenham where the garden displays little evidence of his profession. The front garden does boast a spiral conifer, but it is easily missed amongst the general untidiness. At first sight, the back garden, too, appears somewhat of a wilderness, and yet huddled at corners and edges of the lawn, and hiding ('from the mother-in-law') in a polytunnel by the side of the house, there are, in fact, young topiary plants developing.

The terrible thing about topiary is that it takes such a long time to achieve a result. You have to be very patient, and I am not, really, which is why I have so many drawings – to remind me how it is going to be eventually. It's like my pension fund! When I'm old and decrepit, those bits of topiary will help keep me in a reasonable manner. The sketches are work-in-progress, and people can look through and choose something, and I can say, 'It's not ready now, but it *will* be in two or three years' time.' But the time from a small plant to a finished large piece can take anything from eight to twenty years.

Sometimes I buy in ready-formed pieces from wholesale nurseries, which I might exhibit as part of a show. Shows are a good vehicle for getting known, and I sometimes get a landscape design job for someone's garden as a result. Originally, at say, RHS London shows, I worked on herbaceous principles, but I have found since then, that it is better not to have a raised stage and I have now also gone for much less symmetrical designs. At Hampton Court in 2002 I got awarded Best Newcomer, which was a bit special, and I got a lovely crystal trophy. I feel I am getting somewhere at long last.

When I left school I went to art school and did jewellery design, but I decided I didn't like it, and that in hairdressing I would still be using my art ability, so I did that for 35 years. I worked first in the West End, cutting men's and women's hair, and then had my own salon in Epsom. I enjoyed it, but at the same time I was getting more and more interested in gardening, especially when I bought my first house with a garden. Also, for the last 20-odd years, I have known Carol Klein – the lady who used to do quite a lot of broadcasting, who looks like she has been dragged through a hedge backwards! She's quite a character, and it was really she who got me started in gardening.

I originally met Carol at the RHS London shows in Vincent Square, and she was always short of help for Hampton Court and Chelsea Flower Shows and so I used to go along and help her. I loved helping Carol so much and got such a buzz out of the shows, that I wanted to do something like that myself. So I thought, 'What is the nearest thing to hairdressing in the garden?' and the answer was clearly topiary! William Robinson is quoted as saying, 'Topiary gardens are barbers' gardens', and he said it in a derogatory way, but I thought 'that's me!' I feel it is something that I have expertise in – I understand shape, balance and proportion – it is the same thing as hairdressing except that you have got a little bit more freedom than the limits of the hair you are cutting. It is also quite nice not to have someone tell you that you have taken too much off; plants don't talk back!

The imposing gates into the walled garden at Copped Hall in Epping. A burnt-out shell of a fine Georgian mansion overlooking its parkland is now owned by a trust. James helps with the restoration of the park and keeps his field stock of plants in part of the walled garden. Matting on the ground restricts weeds.

I don't feel I am at a disadvantage compared to someone who has had formal horticultural training; I figure that I have done my apprenticeship with Carol in the sense of learning how to put a display together. At first it was a bit scary on my own but it has evolved since then. Around the time I was thinking about going alone, I saw an advert at the back of the RHS magazine about a man who was selling up, and although he didn't have any topiary left, he was selling off plants that he was growing on into topiary. So I rushed down to Salisbury with my little trailer, and in several trips I bought his stock, and to my mother-in-law's disgust, brought the plants back here.

As it takes such a long time to grow topiary, I get most of my stock from people who have given up for one reason or another and I have ended up acquiring their small plants. Now I have a field stock area in Epping where I have about an acre of a four-acre walled garden and it is an ideal place to grow the plants on. The garden is on a slope right by the M25, but if the wind is in the right direction, all you hear is birdsong and you see a beautiful view and I think it is what I have longed for all my life.

At first I went to the walled garden for a fortnight and planted everything up and thought I wouldn't go again for months, but I go nearly every weekend. It is a constant joy. Topiary looks all very neat and tidy, but actually I am very sporadic in the garden. I will start one thing, and see something else, and end up with tools all over the place, and will have half-done everything. It is not being stuck behind a chair cutting hair. I used to love the people and cutting the hair, but it was being almost glued to the ground behind that chair that got you down after 35 years.

I am always learning now, too. Occasionally I have had problems with box blight, so now I only buy plants from reputable dealers. But actually I feel blight is far less of a problem than people think. If you have a plant that dies, it is easier to blame blight than the possibility that you didn't grow it properly! But one of the great things about box is that it is poisonous, so slugs and rabbits don't touch it. Up on my field stock area I get a lot of problems with rabbits gnawing the bark of the cedars, and they slaughtered some Portuguese laurel and they also love holly; but you learn to put a few sacrificial plants in, and see how they go!

What I didn't realize to start with is that in Italy, where a lot of these sorts of plants come from, they grow them in soil which contains no nutrients at all, so unless you feed and water the plant well, it will die. With an imported plant, you should either put it in the ground straight away or, if you want to keep it in a pot, take as much of the original soil away as possible and replace it with some decent John Innes or similar compost which retains water, otherwise the plant can't survive and will dry out very quickly. In Italy it will have been on a drip-feeding system that waters the plant three to four times a day and all the feed comes through that. But once you take that drip-feed lifeline away, the plant will die.

A pot is really an alien environment for most plants. With topiary, you are putting them under stress by cutting them anyway, so you also need a slow-release feed. Clipping little and often is also usually beneficial and will encourage the plant to bush out. Box, though, shouldn't be cut more than two or three times a year – from after the last frost till about a month before you think the first frost will happen. A conifer, on the other hand, grows relatively fast, and can be clipped more often. But box is the best. The society for topiary is actually called The European Boxwood and Topiary Society because boxwood is the best for topiary: it has a nice dense habit; there are a lot of varieties so if you want one for shade there is a good one, and the richness and the greenness of the leaves can't be beaten. Yew is a close second, and if you want height, yew is the best for that.

I think Churchill said, 'You pick up experience in the hedgerows of life', and that could very accurately be applied to me. I constantly look at new plants for topiary. For instance, for one of the London shows, I thought it would be nice to have a living cedar trellis, and although it didn't work terribly well when I used them, I am going to grow them for another couple of years so they are more mature and work better. I got that idea from seeing a solid dense cedar hedge at Wisely and thought it would look nice grown further apart and getting a trellis effect.

I have also got a Martian coming along! He is a very long, bow-legged Martian with rather a round body – rather an abstract concept. What you often do is to look at the plant first, and see if it suggests a shape to you, and with this I had two specimens that weren't good as single balls but which I thought would be fun as bow-legs. But it can work from both directions: you might have an idea and then think, 'Where have I got a plant that I could do that with?' Or, they can develop by default. My first piece of topiary is the one in the front garden. About 25 years ago, when I had my first house, I bought two balls on stems and had them out front looking very grand. Well, I managed to kill one, and the survivor defoliated on the ball, so I ended up with some bare stems, which became a spiral, and it is now turning into quite a nice organic piece of topiary.

If the plant is small and detailed, I use sheep shears to shape it. If it is big, I still prefer to use shears, but I use long-handled shears, whereas a lot of people would use electric clippers. That to me, is a bit too much like using clippers to cut hair, which is something I wouldn't do. But to get the shape, balance and proportion, I still use my eye. I run topiary workshop days, and I am always surprised that people can't see what I can see. I give the students a nice big bushy plant and let them pull it about to see the shape and then I let them hack it about, but the majority are too timid to do it. But I took a class of students who were doing a garden design class, and there was a huge difference –

Above: Concentration. The art of topiary can be traced back to the ancient Greeks and then the Romans. The Latin word for a gardener, *topiaries*, derives from the Greek root word *topia*, meaning 'landscapes'. *Topiarii* were gardener slaves of Greek origin who served the Imperial household and other wealthy Roman families.

Opposite: James retains an attractive sense of drama – I could imagine he was describing a fabulous haircut he was about to give me as he explained the process of topiary: 'Unlike sculpture, with topiary you wait for the plant to grow and then carve it out in an ongoing process which relies on judging and encouraging the plant's performance.'

one of them just slaughtered the plant down to nothing, almost. It is the ability to see shape, and have the confidence.

People often come and ask me how to turn a ball into a spiral. Well the answer is that you can, but it is not really advisable; what you really need is a single-stemmed plant. It is not until recently that I have managed to source a great quantity of single-stemmed plants, so now I am very happy because I can actually sell someone one if they want it. I found a wholesale nursery that grows plugs and had a bit of a downturn in their sales of box so they had three-year-old plug plants which had been grown in the polytunnel and had got very 'leggy' and hadn't been cut back, so now I have a great supply.

Another thing people usually ask is how to make a ball or a cone. A good guide to a circle is to use wire. You make up the size of circle you want out of the wire and bend two prongs in it to put in the ground, either over or next to the plant, to give you a guide for clipping. The best way to shape a cone is to stand directly above it and look down over it, so that you see the shape much better, and you shear downwards. Those two shapes are relatively easy, but a spiral is a bit more complicated; I keep trying to make a step-by-step guide.

Generally though, you can rectify mistakes. Like when I started to try spirals I might instead end up with a double helix, which I actually think is a nicer shape. I haven't had any real disasters. Somebody who was helping once cut the whole top of a plant off, but I never actually found out who did it – I just found the top of a plant on the floor. But fortunately it was a sales plant rather than a display one, so I wasn't too badly upset. Although every plant is special to some extent. In fact that is one of the reasons why I like doing design work. I can buy plants in for that, rather than selling my own plants. You spend so long growing your own plants that you start upping the price, hoping, in a way, that no one will buy them.

So making a living at it is not always easy. I had a client for whom I designed a front garden incorporating topiary and she wanted me to do the back garden as well. I was quite busy and she was in no rush, so I said, 'Let's leave it till the end of the summer', thinking that the job would keep me through the autumn. But then her marriage broke up and the whole thing fell through. I was very disappointed because, apart from losing about five thousand pounds, I had all these plans for the back garden. In fact I usually love working like that: I love for someone to say, 'Yes, do it, but go away and think about it for six months or so', because you are constantly coming up with new ideas.

The thing I really hate about the RHS is that they insist on you having your plans in for Chelsea and Hampton Court by the September of the year before. Since last year, I have totally altered what I want to do, but you really have to stick pretty much with the brief you gave them, which is a pain. Either you make the plans really vague, in which case they might not like it and say no or you risk changing your mind. This year at Chelsea I am having a mixture of traditional topiary with some unusual materials and structures using orange and black metal, and wavy flint paths: classical with a modern twist. Hampton Court, on the other hand, can be as outrageous as you can get it.

This year at Hampton Court I am using kind of Mohican shapes – going back to the hairdressing, isn't it? So there are oval, metal frames, with a kind of Mohican topiary on top. At the moment I am restricted to the plants which are ready now, so you can't be that outrageous with the shapes. The way to make it innovative is to come up with other ideas. Now I like to have asymmetric shapes, not matched pairs, and private people could take up this idea, too. Out of necessity, because I no longer work with a supplier at Chelsea, but on my own, I have evolved the asymmetrical style and actually done better. If I relate it to herbaceous stuff, it is perhaps like the 'meadowy' look that everyone is into now. The essence of it is to do something new. It exploits the ideas which are coming out of my head all the time.

I am always sketching and coming up with designs so it is a channel for my creativity. And it's fabulous to use my drawing skills again. Shapes I am working on for the future are, for instance, sensual curves and waves of undulating hedging. I am also working on sheep with copper faces, a broken heart, a scared cat, snails, a topiary poodle – but it is quite abstract, and only has two legs. Once a woman asked me for a topiary poodle and I showed her my sketch, and she said, 'Oh, no! I want four legs on my poodle.' And I said, 'Well, I'm sorry, but I tend to do stylized versions rather than the actuality', and she was very put out, asking, 'Why can't you do me a proper poodle?' and I repeated myself, but in the end I didn't do the work. It takes so long to grow these things that I would have had to look at her four-legged poodle for the next six years – so I'm sorry, but tough!

Mostly, though, I love all forms of topiary, and I love doing classic parterres, too. But I don't imagine I'll ever end up with a grand topiary garden of my own, because I don't think I'll ever retire! And while I am working, I can't have my own garden. How could I do other people's gardens if I had my own? When I had my own house and garden, holes and craters would appear because I would be doing things for other people and I'd think, 'Well, I can't get that, but I've got one in my garden, so I'll dig it up.'

Sometimes I maintain other people's designs, however, and that can be really interesting as well. One of the most unusual jobs I have worked on was for two guys who lived in a very modern house built into the wall of Highgate cemetery. Their topiary consists of tombstones and obelisks, which is great fun! You look over a parapet, because the garden is on two terraces, and there are these massive, oblong tombstones, surrounding a fairly conventional eating area with table and chairs.

From their garden you see the cemetery with the actual tombstones, and in the far distance, the tower of Alexandra Palace. The owners were having trouble with their compost as well as wanting the topiary clipped, so I went and sorted it out for them. It was when I went into the house and saw all the black satin and things related to death all round the house that it got a bit too spooky for me! But actually the garden, with its giant green tombstones, was very peaceful and tranquil – the ultimate, I suppose, in bringing the environment into your garden.

20

TERRY DAVIES

ALLOTMENT GARDENER AND BEEKEEPER

A honeycomb. Wax is cut off the frame and put in a spinner, which separates out the honey.

'And, as it works, th'industrious Bee Computes its time as well as we'

I used to think of allotment gardeners as serious and slightly old-fashioned: people who do not just tinker at gardening, but who grow plants or vegetables for a purpose and with knowledgeable vigour. To an extent this is true, but allotment gardeners also tend to be enthusiasts, experimenters and entertaining to talk to. This is certainly true of Terry Davies, who not only has an allotment, but also keeps bees. He is full of zeal and would encourage everyone to have a hive in their garden. He is also a jovial man, and rather bee-shaped in appearance.

Bees are emotive. They evoke feelings of fear in case of being stung; of balmy summer days with the distant, soothing sound of buzzing; and childhood memories of Winnie the Pooh. Bees are also important. Not only do they provide honey for their own and human consumption, but, in the process of collecting nectar, they pick up pollen which is then transferred to another flower, thus fertilizing the bloom so that fruit and seeds are formed and the plant can multiply.

Nectars vary considerably in flavour and sweetness: plum nectar has a sugar concentration of 15 per cent, white clover 40 per cent and marjoram 76 per cent. Most honey is a blend containing a mixture of flavours gathered in the working area round the hive. Clover honey is much sought after and heather honey is considered the thing for connoisseurs. But I can vouch for the fact that borage honey is also excellent – even if I did get stung twice watching it being made and was only saved by Terry's kind, good-natured wife!

WHY WE GARDEN | Terry Davies

With modern houses today, you don't have enough room at the back to have a real vegetable garden, so about nine years ago I got an allotment in Grantham, Lincolnshire. I began by growing potatoes and a few other vegetables, but I suffered a bit with my back, and then I got a rotavator, which got pinched, and I began to think, 'It is a bit silly just growing vegetables: I'll start growing fruit trees.' So I went on a trip to Gardeners' World Live in Birmingham, and, by chance, I came across a stand from the British Beekeepers' Association, promoting beekeeping. I had never thought about bees before, but they told me who my nearest county secretary was, and I got in contact with her. That was in 2000, and by that winter I had started off with a nucleus hive. I can only do it in my spare time – I fix computers for the county council in Cambridgeshire, working in schools, mainly, but already I have seven hives and may go to ten this year.

Initially, when I told the other allotment gardeners I was going to keep bees, they were a bit surprised, and a few were not too keen, but as I was down the bottom end, most didn't mind. The man next door to me, who grows lots of raspberries, did get stung once, but it was when we were trying to catch a swarm and he was wearing blue, which bees like, and we did tell him it might be best if he kept out of the way. But a lot of the allotment-holders welcomed the idea with open arms. They are not sure, but they think that since I have kept bees, it has improved the quality and the yield of their crops.

Last year there were four spare allotments, and I planted them with sunflower seeds and borage. I knew that they would grow well and that the bees would like them, and that it would make good honey. Pure sunflower honey is pumpkin-coloured. Borage is a good plant too, because it puts a lot of goodness back into the soil, and it is also used in medical research for women's HRT. But because it is not commercially viable, a lot of farmers don't grow it; they grow rapeseed because they get a subsidy for it. Rapeseed honey is all right, but a bit bland, so I like the borage and the sunflower better. And Grantham didn't just produce Margaret Thatcher, it produced lime trees, which the bees also like; it is almost like an intoxicant to them. So I have mixed borage and lime honey, too. I have stopped growing potatoes altogether now, and just concentrate on growing

A honey bee on a sunflower in Terry's allotment.

flowers for the bees. I have also got two hives down at 'Naturescape', Brian Scarborough's lovely wild flower farm and visitor centre at Langar.

We can't turn the clock back 50 years and expect farmers to have fields of clover, or cowslip meadows, which bees like, but we can have little pockets of wild flowers on farms or allotments, and try to encourage bees. One problem in this country is the short growing season. In Lincolnshire the majority of honey for sale is from rapeseed, but at the end of the year beekeepers might take their bees to the heather moors of Derbyshire or Yorkshire. They have to move their bees. Bees work a crop, and if there is no more food there they go back to the hive and eat the honey they've stored. So we're a bit like Blackpool – we try to extend the season!

We are also less blessed with good weather than people on the continent or in Australia or New Zealand, and in rainy weather bees stay in. Normally the bees go out and get the spring nectar and take it back to their hives. As each bee collects different nectar, the pollen is visible on its body in different colours, which denote the different flowers – like snowdrop, asparagus, yew – they all have different pollen colours. There are charts available identifying the pollen from these plants, which you could almost use to redecorate your house! However, if the bees are not out foraging, and they are hungry, they'll eat their stores of honey, so there won't be as much. At the end of the summer, we feed the bees for the winter. An average hive will take 30 pounds of sugar! That's for one queen and 40,000 or 50,000 workers. But they are quite happy. We feed them 'baker's fondant' which is like icing sugar.

People don't realize how important bees are to the environment and how tragic it is that so many have been wiped out with disease and with pesticides. So it is up to people like me to encourage new people to become beekeepers. For instance, they have found that when bees work a crop of beans, there is a 30 per cent increase. No need for any agro-chemicals. It might damage ICI's profits, but there is no need for it! So if we could become a nation of beekeepers, we would be better off. After all, there are very few places in the world that have any plants that don't need pollinating. The Falkland Islands haven't got any bees, because it is too windy for them, but I don't want to take my bees there, even though Margaret Thatcher came from Grantham!

We eat sugar because it is imported, but bees have been on the earth for millions of years and before we had sugar we just ate honey. Who was the most important person in an abbey centuries ago? The bee monk! He would have his skeps in holes in the wall, and he would provide not only honey, because there wasn't any sugar, but also the beeswax for candles, because we didn't have electricity either! Before hives there were skeps, which were wicker baskets, tapped off. In Grantham museum there is a picture of a skep in a lime tree from about 150 years ago. It is in the centre of Grantham, next to the Beehive Pub.

Years ago honey was used to heal wounds. It is a natural product, which has not been warmed or adulterated or mixed or blended. It is like pure whisky! But, although honey was thought to have healing properties, one of the first things that worried me about beekeeping was whether I would be allergic if I got stung, because I do suffer from allergies.

Now I have been stung a couple of times, and it hasn't been too bad, and I've found that keeping bees, and especially eating honey, I suffer less from hay fever! I think because I eat local honey, which has local pollen in it, my immunity builds up so that when I am in contact with airborne pollen, I don't get the runny nose and eyes.

Of course you can have accidents. I have opened up a hive, wearing my suit, feeling rather blasé, and left a little gap between my suit and my clothes and suddenly, while all the bees are buzzing around, two get inside the gap. You can't open your hood, or squash them, or get rid of them, and so you get stung. Some bees are attracted to women's perfume, and they are also attracted to the colour blue. Sometimes my wife has been on the allotment with me to pick the blackcurrants and next minute she'll say to me, 'You've set those bees on me deliberately!' but it is because they were attracted to her. Then as soon as you get stung, they put a barb into you which emits an ozone which is like a help-alarm to the rest of the colony, like, 'I'm being attacked, so send the squadron in.'

I would advise anyone who wants to start keeping bees to go on a beginner's course. Then, if you want to carry on, you will need a bit of equipment, such as a suit, gloves and a smoke gun. If you wanted to do anything, like become a racing driver, probably the first thing you would think about is, 'Can I handle it? Have I got the aptitude? What equipment do I need? How much will it cost?' Well, it is the same with bees. But it is not hard to learn, and you can buy some equipment second-hand. Some societies will even loan you a beehive to try out for a year. You normally start off with one or two colonies, or hives, containing one queen, a few males or drones and some female workers.

I buy my bees from auctions. In the same way that there are different kinds of cattle like, say, Herefords, there are different strains of bees, some more docile than others. There are Greek and Croatian bees, and at the moment I have Irish ones, which are gentle, and used to a climate similar to round here. Originally bees lived in rural places: in old trees, barns, lofts, near chimneys, and generally in warm places. If someone lit a fire, the bees would think it was a forest fire, and still today, they have the same reaction. When bees smell smoke, they fill themselves with food in case they can't get any for some time, and then, because they are full up, like humans after a meal, they don't feel aggressive; they feel relaxed. So when we want to calm bees down, we puff some smoke at them. Bees don't like feeling agitated. They know they have a job to do and a cycle to go through. They know their role in life!

Bees are a funny shape because they have too big a fuselage for their short wings, and at the end of the day, it is their wings wearing out which kills them. Workers, which are the females, only last 40-odd days from when they are hatched to when their wings wear out. They not only collect the nectar and pollen to make honey, they also feed and groom the male drones. There are just a few male bees in a hive, and all through the summer they live a life of luxury, doing no work at all. Their function is to mate with the queen.

It is like being in a small group in St Tropez with all these women around you, looking after you and supplying all your drinks, cocktails and parties. Fantastic! But come the end of the summer, the women go round the stores and they think to themselves, 'We haven't got enough room with all these males swanning around here,' so they kick them out!

Left: Before taking out the comb, Terry smokes the hive to make the bees docile.

Middle: Bees fly round Terry as he takes a frame from the hive. Behind him are James Greaves apples, which he grows on his allotment.

Right: Terry, fully armed in his protective clothing, examines a frame covered in bees and honey.

A queen bee will last five or six years, although a beekeeper will only keep them about two years because then they stop producing so many young. So when the old queen has gone and the new queen arrives, all she has to do is consecrate the marriage. A good queen will lay thousands of eggs.

In order for the bees to thrive we have to make sure they are clean, healthy, and free of disease. We check there is no moss and that no wasps, mice, kingfishers, or woodpeckers get into the hives. Mind you, I heard of someone recently in Skegness who closed up their hives every night and opened them up every morning, whereas normally you would only close the hives in the winter – he must have thought he was keeping chickens!

Eventually I would like to have 50 hives and be able to call myself a bee farmer. And I would like to produce what we call 'cut comb honey'. In the beekeeping days when there were skeps, the sealed honey storage comb was just cut out and sold. Then wooden frames were developed, and now the latest method of presentation is small pieces of natural comb packed in transparent topped plastic cases. The comb tastes like Sugar Puffs. You can't eat it all in one go it is so sweet and wonderful! It is like Cyprus honey Easter cake; like a honey-laced Crunchy bar, but all moist and soft. Oh, I *like* honey!

I'm a 54-year-old Welshman, and another thing I enjoy is singing in a massed voice choir. I have done one ultimate thing – I sang in the Albert Hall last year with 851 voices, including me! So *that* ambition is fulfilled, and the one which remains now is to increase the number of beekeepers. We never produce enough honey to satisfy demand in this country – we import 18,000 tons of honey every year! Why? Because city-dwellers think, 'We can't have bees.' But they're wrong. Eddy George, the Governor of the Bank of England, used to keep beehives on the roof of the Bank of England!

Everyone should keep bees, and if you look after them, they will look after you. Obviously if there is very little greenery around, you will get less honey – about 30 pounds' worth, perhaps, but in Lincolnshire, some people get about 150 pounds of honey, by moving the bees around. I know a bee farmer who has 180 hives and he averages two and a half tons of honey a year. There is a big market. Promote English honey, and we will all be happy.

21

JULIET LACEY
FLOATING GARDENER

Juliet picking lavender (which she dries to make scented bags) on the tree barge with the quince behind. White Russian vine scrambles over the skylit entrance to the barge. A starboard navigation light of the neighbouring barge is on the right, with Tower Bridge at the back.

'Mean while the Mind, from Pleasure less, Withdraws into its happiness'

One could easily be forgiven for wondering what on earth a floating garden or gardener is, and when I discovered it had to do with barges I was still not much the wiser. I imagined houseboats with some plant pots on top, but this is very far from the reality. At Reeds Wharf in central London, just downstream from Tower Bridge, four barges have been planted to support their own gardens in 30 centimetres of soil! There are box hedges, lavender, roses and even quince trees. They are roof gardens for the inhabitants, and at the same time, form a towpath or walkway. But while in some gardens one hears birdsong, rustling grasses or trickling water, here the sound is of creaking, as the barges rock and strain rhythmically on their moorings.

The moorings are owned by architect Nicholas Lacey who, with his playwright wife Juliet, has lived in a warehouse at Reeds Wharf overlooking the barges since the 1970s. Their flat is strangely familiar, having been used as the principal setting for the film *A Fish Called Wanda*. Moreover Reeds Wharf is right by an inlet where Fagin's warehouse in Dickens' *Oliver Twist* stood.

There have been moorings alongside Reeds Wharf since the eighteenth century, but creating a floating garden is an innovative inspiration. The gardens were planted and are maintained by Juliet, who is elfin and gentle but also animated. A theme of birth runs through the story of the gardens in that they started with a duck nesting on one of the barges; later a baby was born to the residents of another. Juliet herself nurtures the gardens like children and wants to create more – ones that will be her own 'babies'.

Yet running parallel to this aspect is the possibility of destruction and 'bereavement'. At the time of my interview, the moorings were under threat of an enforcement order served by Southwark Council to remove the barges because of lack of planning permission. This is the council that had to be taken to court to permit the building of Shakespeare's Globe Theatre on Bankside after claiming this was the only site where it could store municipal dustcarts. Apart from providing attractive, affordable homes to a community of more than 70 adults and children as well as being a habitat for wildlife, the moorings form the largest single collection of historic trading vessels on the Thames, including both sail and motor barges. Yet because local residents in luxury flats have complained of noise, all the barges are at risk. A petition, public outcry and an appeal have developed into an exciting drama which is yet to be resolved.

The Ancient Moorings, which my husband owns, have been here for centuries and some of the trading vessels are over 100 years old. We wanted to continue the tradition of having commercial barges here so we have about five or six Thames Lighters, which we used originally for storage. We have lived here 27 years, and moved in when it was still an industrial area with boats bringing grain up the creek to be milled in Mill Street. This block of flats was a Spillers dog food factory; we have seen a lot of changes. We gradually acquired the whole building, having a little bit at first and adding to it, and then my husband Nick built the penthouse where we live on top.

Nick got the idea of making a kind of business out of the moorings and leasing a mooring for a very small rent to people with their own boat, so it is a little company now. But the idea for the gardens developed when one of our Thames Lighters, which was empty, with its top open to the elements and its bottom full of sludge, gradually filled up with wonderful vegetation. Dormant seeds germinated and others blew in. A duck's nest appeared too, and all sorts of lovely things, like irises, for some reason grew in the hull, and we thought, 'Why don't we do this for real and make a proper garden!'

We started with one, and then each year, for four years, we added another. They are really roof gardens, and people live in the barges underneath. They are what is known as collar barges and are permanently fixed moorings, but some of the others, which are attached to the collar barges, are used as mobile homes and the residents take them across the channel for holidays. The gardens pre-dated the occupants' arrival so I had a pretty free hand, except for one which was rented by a landscape gardener who asked if she could design and plant her own garden. Unfortunately she left because her marriage broke up, and so the garden went a bit to rack

Overview of the floating gardens at Reeds Wharf.

Juliet on one of the barges, carrying her basket of gardening tools. On the left is lavender and a hebe bush. To the right is a weeping ash tree hung with lamps.

and ruin and it needs to be rescued. I designed the rest and planted and maintain them although I have no gardening background at all: my other work is as a freelance theatre director and writer. I am very empirical – I learn as I go, and am still learning everything.

I have always liked flowers but I never gardened as a child – we lived in flats abroad. Then I lived in a little cottage in Rutland and had scope to plant things, and I learnt a bit from my husband who is good on trees and vegetables, but mainly I have learnt from experience and from reading books and from one pruning course. I think gardening just takes off with a lot of people in middle age, when the children are gone and you want something to nurture; the garden becomes the answer and it is now a complete obsession. I think about the gardens most of the time, even at night. I wake up thinking, 'I'd better do that today. What a good idea!' And I rush out. It is a lovely, harmless obsession, which is beneficial to more than just oneself.

I do a lot of seed raising and propagation upstairs in the conservatory and I am starting to get very excited about layering – I might do a course in that; there are endless possibilities. I am also fortunate to have a little garden in Somerset now, where we grow mostly vegetables, and there are good nurseries there so I buy plants and also most of the trees from there. Now that the barge gardens are established it is more a matter of weeding, trimming, feeding and watering. I suppose I spend about 15 hours a week on the four floating gardens, and in the summer I have to spend at least two hours watering each evening as well. We do have an irrigation system but it doesn't work very well. I think the answer ideally would be little pumps, pumping up the river water, which would be more eco-friendly. Watering is the biggest challenge because the soil is shallow and exposed and so it dries up very quickly.

Another difficulty is the fact that the barges rock about and I get seasick very quickly! I have to pick the right moment when the tide is out. So although my husband once had his office on one of the barges, I couldn't bear it and have never spent an awful lot of time on one. Another problem with the gardens is the wind, which is unpredictable and different for each barge. I was also slightly thrown by the rampant success of everything! I find I want to control it a little, when some of my favourite shrubs get swamped by something else, and I think, 'I wish they would all slow down a bit. Maybe I should feed them less?' It is all rather new to me, but I am beginning to understand it now. Recently I have had someone to help me – a girl who comes once a week to water, but who is actually a professional gardener, so I am learning from her as well.

I get up very early every morning when the river is absolutely like glass and nobody is up and it seems wonderful to be in the middle of a city with these gardens. Sometimes in the evening it is the same. There is something very appealing about the whole idea of standing in the middle of the river growing plants. I also find it very satisfying that it attracts lots of insects and butterflies. I don't know that there is anything else quite like it. I imagine that in Holland, where people are so good at gardening, there must be something similar and I know that in the Southwark in Bloom competition someone got an award for a planted *boat*, but I don't know whether that was pots or an actual garden.

The four barges we have here have been described as a floating London square, but I don't really think of them like that. Someone else called them floating window boxes, which is quite a good description. On the other hand, the 'tree barge' has a lavender hedge leading to a square of quince trees surrounding a table and chairs so that people can sit out and have barbecues – there is oregano and borage planted conveniently nearby too! We would like to have chairs on each barge, so that the gardens are more than just a public amenity that you walk through to get ashore. You can of course see the gardens from inside the barges too, through the skylights in the roofs. One man has his skylight completely covered with plants, like a curtain, which he likes because it gets terribly hot.

All the people who have the gardens love them because it also gives them a source of flowers and herbs to pick. My husband and I chose the planting between us. He chose the bold things that I wouldn't have thought of, like the *Robinia* 'Frisia', quinces and apple trees, which are bearing fruit! I just planted the things that I love. I tried to plant annuals, but they weren't successful, and nor were vegetables, so it was trial and error. Hebe, for some reason, does very well, and silver-foliaged plants thrive in the dry conditions, so I have used opium poppies and senecio.

I also chose a lot of wonderfully aromatic plants – I can't really see the point of a plant that doesn't smell nice. So you get the most amazing kind of kinaesthetic experience after watering when you walk up and down. I think people do appreciate that. One bargee, a rather elderly lady, insisted on watering the new barge, although it is a huge job, because she loved the smell so much and found it tranquillizing. Each barge has a different atmosphere. One has periwinkle spilling over the hull; another has a weeping ash surrounded by herbs and Mediterranean plants; and one is planted up with divisions of box hedging, giving a more formal air.

The construction of a barge involves a kind of raised edge, which is perfect for adding soil. The soil is delivered to the foreshore and craned on board in huge white sacks. We got good topsoil with quite a lot of mushroom compost, which gave the plants a good start. Most of the soil is a spit's depth, which is the depth of a spade. In a few places where the roof is lower, the earth is two spits, and it is there that we have planted trees. First the roof of the barge is checked for leaks and sealed with anti-corrosive paint. Then it is set up with holes for drainage and the soil is added. We put wire netting on top to form a pathway down the middle, which is not slippery. There used to be river rats here, and they used the walkways as tunnels. We didn't dare tell anybody that they were actually walking on top of a rat motorway!

The rats have gone now, but there is other wildlife: lots of insects and birds. We have various pests, like ants, which have suddenly moved in, and snails. I try to control them ecologically by giving the snails to the birds. Every year ducks and greylag geese make their nests on one barge or another and lay their eggs. Then every year the crow devours the babies, so I am thinking quite seriously of asking if I can eliminate the crow, because no one is attacking his babies! Actually, talking of babies, since we have had the gardens and families have lived in the barges, four babies have been born. Two were not literally born on the barges, but two were, so we feel it is a fecund place that encourages nature and birth.

I am pleased that we have managed to do something that is a bit original and different, and also environmentally enhancing and a nice place for the growing children. None has fallen overboard yet! On the whole the people who live here are quite tough and nautically minded. My husband vets them and tries to make sure that they are not just people who have always lived in a flat before, so they understand about the tides and the conditions. But some very young people moved into one of the barges – city gents or whatever – and just after they arrived they threw a big party. Well, everyone walked outside and sat on all the plants! It was just before the 'open gardens' day and I was *terribly* cross. But they were so remorseful that they rushed out and bought lots of different plants to put in instead.

All sorts of people live here: we have architects, musicians, artists, solicitors and people with their own businesses in Southwark. But most of the people who live here are middle-class business people. You probably wouldn't expect that, but they are people like lawyers who go off to the city, and they all say that the moment they return and walk down the gangway in the evening, their worries drop away from them. They feel at peace here with the sound of the water. It does have a curative affect on stress, I think. I can feel it. I feel it more in the gardens than in my flat; something about the movement and the smells. Occasionally you get a nasty whiff, but that is the Thames. Mostly the smells are lovely: salty and woody – it's not surprising people want to live here.

The moorings *have* grown, so that some of the neighbours don't like it visually and they have complained of noise. There is no kind of precedent for anything like this; nobody knows what the law is exactly. The moorings have been here since Henry V's time, but suddenly Southwark Council has served an enforcement order to remove the barges. They say they are 'visually detrimental' and that they need planning permission, but through all history there has never been planning permission given to a boat. And nothing built before 1947 has planning permission, because that's when the Planning Act invented it.

We just wish we could all get together and talk about the problems rather than have legal action. We are going to appeal and ask people to sign a petition. There are 25 families here who are going to find themselves evicted. There are no moorings available in London for this number of boats, so many of the bargees could be made homeless. It is extremely unsettling for them. They are getting lots of legal and environmental advice, but they could end up having to go to Holland or somewhere and many of them have children in schools here. I am hoping that whatever happens I will be able to keep my gardens. I would feel bereft without them; it would be dreadful if they had to go, apart from all the time and work and money spent on them. I would be very sad. And what would happen to them? Is the council going to get a big tugboat and pull them all away?

The latest development is an attack on another front. The Port of London Authority has stuck notices on every single barge giving them three months to remove themselves. So

The wooden planks down the centre of this barge form a walkway, which is covered with wire netting to prevent slipping. Plants on the right include French lavender, honeysuckle, thyme, sage, mint and marjoram.

we have to take out an injunction against them. Meanwhile we won first prize in the community gardens class of the Southwark in Bloom competition! It is incredibly funny, really. With one hand we get prizes and with the other threats to go. We just have to wait for a public enquiry. It makes me feel rather aggressive. I desperately want to hang on to my gardens and lots of people are very supportive of them, so I feel very bullish about it. I think we should just carry on and go on planting and watering: that is the best approach. Let the law take its course, but come what may the gardens are not going to wither away because of an injunction! We just don't know what will happen next.

If we are allowed to continue we are planning a performance space for music, films and poetry readings, which people will be able to walk out to from the gardens. We have also got at least three more gardens to make. I would like to do one with a conservatory; a wild-flower barge with all British native flowers; and possibly one with a pool in it. I could do different colours, too. It is fun; like having a huge estate with all these different little gardens, each with its own character. I like the idea that each one is a separate island. One thing I would like to do is a wonderful garden from scratch that was totally my own. A different barge, which I would try to keep Nick out of. Nick likes to be involved and in a way it is good that we do the gardens together, but I would like it to be my *own* baby. One day, I hope.

22

JEKKA McVICAR

HERB FARMER

Borage, described in Jekka's catalogue as 'Annual, Ht. 50 cm. Attractive blue flowers in summer. Flowers can be used in drinks and salads. Young leaves used in salads.' It is also the name of one of her cats.

'How could such sweet and wholesome Hours Be reckon'd but with herbs and flow'rs'

Meeting Jekka McVicar, it is hard to imagine her early career in a rock band. Now her garden is her livelihood, she is softly spoken with an aura of calm, and she is totally committed to organic herb farming and to her family. Her son is studying oceanography and is 'scarily intelligent', while her artistic daughter designs the covers of Jekka's extremely informative mail-order catalogues (the farm is not normally open to visitors).

Jekka's farm consists of a series of polytunnels used for the different stages of growing herbs, from propagation to specimen plants; a shed housing a potting machine, for Jekka fulfils large orders; some pre-fabricated buildings in which she and her family used to live but which are now offices; and her first potting-shed, sentimentally moved from a previous garden 'because I couldn't be without it'.

Jekka sells culinary, aromatic, decorative and medicinal herbs: there are around 500 varieties of these, all known intimately to her. She talks to her plants and calls them 'my babies', treating them fondly as she does her pets, including cats Borage and Chelsea – Jekka is an eight-times Gold Medallist at Chelsea Flower Show, in addition to being a successful writer and lecturer.

I was baptized Jessica, but my family called me Jekka and when I went to work in London, there was another Jessica in the department and they said, 'What are you called at home?' and I said, 'Jekka' and that was it, it stuck; from that day on, I was always Jekka.

When I first left school I went to art college and, after my foundation year, I met the members of a rock group, and I joined them. We made two LPs and played at all the big festivals: Hamburg, Glastonbury and the Isle of Wight. I was a flautist, saxophonist and clarinetist — and then one day I decided to go straight. I decided I had had enough of being on the road and all the hassle of being a female in a pop group in the '70s — all the rest of the group were male — and then we got a manager who put a lot of pressure on me, and I thought, 'Oh, sod this!'

So I walked into the BBC one day and asked for a job. I sat there all day in Television Centre until they interviewed me, and I got a job. To begin with I was a dogsbody in drama and serials but I worked my way up and then I left and went into community TV and then moved to do that in Bristol. Later I worked for Bristol City Council training unemployed school-leavers as my crew. I taught them how to use cameras and write scripts and make programmes on matters arising in the council. Then the police force discovered me and asked me to come and build them a studio and run their video unit. I was the first civilian in the Bristol area to go on scenes of crime. I hung out of helicopters and filmed traffic flow and got strapped to a motorbike backwards so I could film road camber and had great fun, but I became pregnant so I had to stop.

In between these jobs, in 1976, I worked on a herb farm, called Tumblers Bottom Herb Farm, doing potting. I come from a family of horticulturists, so I knew about potting, and I knew about herbs because Mum was a good cook. So when I was suddenly at home, with two children under two and my husband away working, I sat in the kitchen and wrote a list of things I might be able to do from home. I had been a musician, I could cook... and suddenly a girlfriend of mine called Ruth came in the door and said, 'Can I go into your garden and pick some tarragon?' I remember this as though it was now, although it was 21 years ago. At that time you couldn't buy herbs in shops and she needed some for a particular recipe and I said, 'Yes, help yourself.' And then I thought, 'I wonder if I could actually do this from home?'

So I converted the wardrobes into cold frames and started growing herbs. I would put the children to bed and lecture in the evening about how to use herbs in cooking. My audience once was one person, but I refused to give in and gave her the whole lecture. Another lecture I had two people — one knitting, the other asleep — so I learnt my trade, like the old comics on the boards. Now of course I lecture to large audiences, which is great fun. Anyway, then my darling husband came back from South America to build space satellites in Bristol, and he looked at our house. I had plants everywhere: on the windowsill in the loo — there was not a surface that didn't have plants — and he said, 'Either you stop, or we move.'

By then I was also supplying shops. I used to line the orders up from the front door to the back door in old boxes, and would stick the children in the car and the plants in the back, and go off delivering. So we started to look for somewhere else to live and I found somewhere down the road here, near Alveston, and the owners said, 'Go ahead and put a tunnel up' and I started putting the plants in, but once the tunnel was finished, they said, 'Oh we don't like tunnels. You will have to go!' This was 18 years ago, and I was driving up the lane and saw this little cottage, two up, two down, with a barn attached. It was totally derelict, but it was on the market with an acre of land. It was a sealed-envelope bid, just before Christmas, and at Christmas we heard that they had accepted our offer. It was fantastic.

I will never forget the day we moved. My darling little children aged three and four walked into this totally derelict house, with me saying, 'Isn't this fun!' and thinking, 'What have I done to my family?' Eventually we got a small mobile home put up, which is now the offices. My husband was still flying around Europe a lot, but we all managed. I built up the nursery, doing wholesale only then, supplying garden centres and shops. So I worked during the day, but I never missed any event at school and was always here in the evening, which was really important to me.

Sometimes the farm went through difficult phases. There was one summer, 11 years ago, when I wasn't selling because it was hot and people weren't gardening and I had a lot of stock left. A friend with a nursery nearby suggested that I take my herbs to the Vincent Square show in London, because there was no one on the RHS show circuit with herbs. I said, 'I can't go *there*!' But I did. I borrowed a horsebox and put all the plants in, and I got a silver medal at my first go. Then the person running Chelsea Flower Show asked if I would apply for that, and I got in that year, which was difficult because the children were seven and eight and I was totally green, but I got a silver gilt medal at my first Chelsea, which was absolutely tremendous. Now I have done 11 Chelsea shows and we have had eight gold medals.

But the part I like best is growing the plants. I think about the herbs, 'Is it ill, is it well, what's up? Why is the soil loose on the top; does it have vine weevil?' It is always nurturing and also totally inspiring. I grow

This is where Jekka propagates her herbs. Once grown, she sells them by mail order and at many shows, including Chelsea, and she has recently supplied the new herb garden at RHS Wisley. Her organic herb farm also holds several open days and herb workshops.

Jekka pruning a Chilean myrtle, *Luma apiculata* 'Glanleam Gold'.

herbs which have been around for thousands of years, and I may be around for 80 if I am lucky. If you take coriander, or dill, there are records dating back to 2000 BC! That is incredible in itself. The same dill plant that was used by Tutankhamun, we are growing today, unchanged. Other ancient plants, not herbs, have been found in the wild, but there are no records of them having been *used* as part of the diet, as medicine and to stop pain. I am growing something which has a history, which is beneficial to man: it is not just an adornment. I could not just grow flowers.

You can enjoy herbs as flowers, but I like the fact that you can use them to the benefit of your family. For instance dill – if you have a child who has an upset stomach or is suffering from gripe, you can make a tea out of the seed, which takes away the griping. If you use the leaves in cooking, you help people to digest the food. I think that is wonderful – the fact that a plant which can look so beautiful can be so beneficial. The other thing I love doing is talking to people about it and opening their eyes to the fact that a certain plant may look fantastic when it is in flower, but it is actually the roots that have drawn all the nutrients out of the ground, which are so good for you. I feel that as we are so hi-tech now, my herbs have actually come into their own.

When I did my first business plan, 20-odd years ago, I thought I would peak in ten years and I would have to find other things to grow because herbs would be on the wane. For instance, alpines used to be tremendously popular, but they have been overtaken by grasses now. But the demand for herbs is growing all the time. My collection has gone from 30 herbs, when I first started, to 475. As the world gets smaller, more plants arrive here; it is very exciting. And although I have not done much travelling myself, I am fascinated by the way people use the same herb in different countries. I use herbs in every meal and I have herb teas. Rosemary is one I really like – it is a very good tonic and clears the head. And I like to eat flowers, and started a fad for salad rocket some years ago.

About five years ago I had to make a big decision whether to do even more wholesale and drop all the shows. Because we are organic and have Soil Association Certification, Waitrose approached us, and I realized after talking to them that I would have to cut my range down to 20 plants and turn the farm over to all-year production with lights and automation to keep the costs down. Yes, I might have made some money for once, but I wouldn't have been a happy bunny.

Being commercial might be easier but also you wouldn't have the love in the plants. If you go to a commercial nursery it is much more clinical and they don't actually know what they are growing. I can tell you what everything is, how it is used, where it comes from. It is much nicer like this. And also why throw away all those plants? And who else would look after them? There are lots of small herb farms but they don't have the range, and they supplement herbs with herbaceous. I have been *very* dogmatic that there are only herbs here, so we are one of the few growers of just herbs. And I can't throw anything away – I like them too much.

As with animals or children, you don't have a favourite, but you have one that you are particularly fond of because it is awkward, or smells wonderful, or because when it flowers, it takes your breath away. I adore lemon verbena; just to rub the leaf is fantastic. I love some of the little weird ones that I grow, which some people may even walk by – I think creeping savory, when in full flower, is just breathtaking. I like things like shisos, which are really difficult to grow, and some years you get them and some years you don't. But I have grown plants which I think are beautiful, and no one has wanted to buy and I can't think why. But if I see, say, an angelica, which I haven't got, I *must* have it. It is just like collecting stamps.

I have only been growing herbs for 20-odd years but I have already managed to conserve one. It is wonderful. I am the only

Jekka and her dog in front of the potting shed that she became so attached to that she had it transported from her previous garden.

grower left in England growing *Calomeria amaranthoides*, the incense plant. It used to be in all the big posh houses. It has delicate tiny coral flower bracts in late summer and the whole plant has this incredible incense scent, but it can cause irritation to touch and burn people. Just to know that you are the custodian of this plant for the next generation is amazing. Who knows, it might be the cure-all forever!

Being organic is also very important to me. You can't sell a plant to someone to take medicinally and not be organic. Also, when I first started, with just culinary herbs, I had a one-year-old and a two-year-old crawling around my feet and the last thing I wanted was to turn my back and for them to eat something by mistake. So we were always organic, before it was trendy. I give my plants Bach Flower Remedies, which is a little worrying, in case it is like 'mad cow' because I am giving flowers to flowers! But the Rescue Remedy seems to help if my large plants have gone into shock at shows – they come from really nice cosseting to somewhere much too hot with no good ventilation in tents.

I enjoy the shows, and my first book came because I was asked so many questions by the public at the shows. I managed to buy more land with the royalties from the book, which was tremendous. The other writings came because I needed the money to keep the farm going, rather than diversifying into other lines, like, say, bulbs. I only really sell plants from 1 March to 1 July – that is the season when people garden. So I lecture and write and things are evolving again which is very exciting. A number of garden designers have honoured me by asking me to do their planting plans. So I choose the plants, and how far apart they should be in the beds, because I know how the plants grow.

I am also lecturing abroad, taking trips to Europe and South Africa, which is mind-boggling because I have never done it before. I have once taken people round the Botanic Gardens in the Caribbean and I have travelled with the children to Sardinia, where we saw myrtle growing wild, but I have not inflicted the garden on my children. Now I can go and look at gardens without boring them – because I used to be totally bored when my parents looked round gardens! My children won't want to take over this farm, but my daughter has my flute, and my son has my clarinet and sax.

And I think my family will always use herbs. If I had to give one piece of advice about herbs to gardeners, it would be to start with the plants they are going to use so that they physically handle them. Whether it is chives, oregano, or thyme, you will keep picking and handling them and grow to love them. And you will use them in your cooking which will inspire you to be healthier. Then build up to the ones you are just going to look at. Herbs by their nature are wild plants that we have tamed. They have been around for thousands of years and are usually *officinalis* or *vulgaris*, which means they are not hybrids. Because they have survived so long, they will probably survive whatever you do to them, which is inspiring for someone starting to garden. At shows, I used to worry what medals I got, but now I feel that if I have inspired just six people there to garden, especially in today's society when everything is in such a hurry, then that is wonderful, because they will slow down and look.

23

RORA PAGLIERI

CREATOR OF A HIGHLAND GARDEN

Rora's garden is huge. As you turn a corner a whole new aspect comes into view. Here the clipped hedges and topiary are softened with lavender and rhododendrons.

'This delicious Solitude'

Rora Paglieri, an Italian widow trained in architecture, has created a garden from scratch from reclaimed wasteland in the Highlands of Scotland. The garden still bears the signs of infancy and has yet to establish and gain comfortable maturity. Yet it already boasts many of the features found in a traditional garden, such as the one at Cawdor Castle. It includes a manicured courtyard garden with parterres, a yew maze, a laburnum avenue, ponds, a vegetable garden, and planting all around the house.

Rora is sprightly, animated, and looks younger than her years. She is not obviously wealthy in appearance, yet her four-sided house built around a courtyard and the garden are vast. Somewhat of a recluse, her indoor pool is 25 metres long but only one lane wide, for she lives alone, apart from her staff, filling her days in Scotland with her passion, gardening. Rora invited my husband and me to have lunch with her; we ate in the pretty conservatory overlooking the garden, the three courses served by a demure manservant wearing white gloves.

Someone recently described my garden as 'a historic garden in the making' and I thought that was fantastic, because that is exactly what it is. Nowadays, you either have an old, historic garden, or a small, new one – nobody has tried an ambitious project to make a garden which spans history, and that is what I am trying to do.

I was always in love with plants and flowers, since I was a very little child. It was magic: I even looked at the grass. For me, nature is at its best when it creates plants. I have always felt that. But I was a town girl in Piedmont in Italy, with only a terrace with a few pot plants and no garden. I trained as an architect in Italy, although I never took the degree. I got married before the end of the course and went to live in Kenya and had a coffee farm – I had always had it in my mind that I wanted to live in Africa. There I did have a garden, and learnt a bit about plants and flowers. However, soon after I moved to Africa my husband died, and so I stayed on, on my own. I lived there 23 years.

I loved Kenya to start with, but by the end it had become too crowded and was not my free country, as I used to think of it. I happened to come to Scotland to visit some friends in 1987, and I saw this ruin and was fascinated by the square shape of it. I feel the square gives the idea of strength. It was for sale for peanuts, and first I thought I would buy it as a holiday home and come here in August when everywhere else in the world is crowded. Very soon I forgot the holiday home idea, and after two years of work on the house, I moved here.

What is now my house was ruined stables. I left the shape exactly as it was, and kept all the same windows and doors. On one side there were cattle, on another horses, and there was a granary. There were no roofs or floors and it took busloads of workmen every day to complete it. I kept as much as possible of the original barns, because I liked them so much. I designed it all myself using a lot of wood inside, as well as antique furnishings. The main living area has a wooden balcony all the way round, because I imagined having a big feast with Scottish pipers for the millennium. And I did: in the year 2000, I had a big party here.

When I bought the house there was no garden, and I had no overall plan for it; it is too big and was covered in weeds. It was an enormous job as it was, doing it bit by bit, but

Most people would assume the belt worn by Rora at all times contains money. Actually it houses her secateurs (and cigarettes)!

Rora's house (in which she lives alone) is on all four sides of this formal courtyard garden. Box hedges form parterres in the shapes of Celtic symbols and topiary sheep. Green is a favourite colour.

you would have had to be an ultra-millionaire to tackle the whole thing from the start. Also, it is only when you have lived in a place that you see what is needed, and what kind of soil you have, and what will work well. Usually I am a very silent person: I don't talk at all. But give me the subject of my garden, and I am known to talk! The first thing I finished outside was the walled courtyard garden. It is formal with box hedges forming parterres in the shapes of Celtic symbols. In the centre is a statue basking in the sun, looking towards the winter sunset. I made topiary shapes of, for instance, sheep by designing scale drawings, which a gardener converted to wire frames.

Now the garden has expanded all around the house, on different levels. Weeds are abundant here, so in various areas I have gravel and slate and bark chippings covering the earth. At the back of the house is a lawn and the maze. In 2002 I added an indoor swimming pool to the back of the house: it is 25 metres long, and I do 40 lengths each morning! On the roof of the pool outside, I planted lavender, which is magnificent. You don't see such terrific lavender even in France, because here it gets the warmth from the pool underneath.

I also planted a *Magnolia grandiflora* against the back wall of the house, which is said not to be able to grow in the Highlands. Now, the moment I hear something like that, I have to experiment and try it. I also have a lemon tree, which has already survived two winters outside in Scotland! And I have a vegetable garden and only eat my own vegetables. Most Scottish people don't have fantasies and only grow 'tatties', leeks, carrots and parsnips – but you can grow everything here: asparagus, artichokes, whatever. I try to tackle an important project in the garden each year, which I have done up till now. I have recently planted a wild-flower meadow, and last year I planted a four-tiered hedge beside the drive leading to the house – all of different colours: red, dark and mid-green, and grey.

This year I am starting a scree garden.

My ambition is to make my garden live long after I am dead. It is my creation, you see, and I would love it to be here forever – something beautiful. For instance, the maze at the moment looks like nothing, but when it has grown up, it will be wonderful. I designed it in the form of a Celtic Iron Age carnyx, which was discovered around 1816, less than a mile from here! A carnyx was a very long trumpet [known throughout Europe from about 2000 BC to AD 200. It was held vertically so that the sound travelled]. They were made out of bronze, in the shape of a wild boar's head. They were used in battle and had a wooden tongue which moved, making a loud noise.

I drew a plan and planted the little yew trees to form the shape. I planted it four years ago, and it was a disaster, and it had to be replanted two years ago. Scotland is the best place in the world for most plants, because they love it here. The climate is very good, but we have two enemies: first the wind, which can be terrible – I have been blown over three times, and I am a sturdy woman, not a little flower; second is the clay soil, which contains good nourishment, but it holds water. The yew shrubs all died at first because of lack of drainage, so I had to improve the soil.

When I arrived here, I didn't know the names of any plants, or how to grow them, or anything – it was a white sheet. I worked in the garden during the day, and went to bed with the encyclopaedia! I first came here with two African gardeners that I had in Kenya. They knew even less than me, but at least they could dig holes and do watering. Then they left because it was not their country and they were not happy, and so I have always hired gardeners. I have done a lot myself, but I could not do it all. One of the things I enjoy most is cutting the grass on my sit-on mower. In doing that, I tour the garden, and I always have my secateurs with me. I notice everything, but also I just enjoy the ride!

I want to make a garden where I feel comfortable and where I can take a lot of pleasure and have things to look at all year round. But actually, I use the garden to work in! I work in it about 14 hours per day! I am a director of an Italian company which makes toiletries, and I have to go there once a month for four days, but I am always pleased when I come back. I feel free here. The space is so wide and there are so few people. You hear all the birds singing – it's a dream. There are a lot of animals in this garden. At the bottom, where it is wild, I let a farmer keep his sheep, because I like to see them. I have visiting mallards on the pond, plenty of pheasants and other birds. When birds from the sky choose your place to live, it means I have created a good place; they are not something I bought and put in the garden.

Once a mother and young deer came to my front door and ate my roses at 4 a.m. – here it is light at 3 a.m. in the summer. I rushed upstairs and took dozens of photos, and then I realized there was no film in the camera! I was so upset, although it was funny. I didn't mind the deer eating the roses; it was wonderful that they were there. There were lots of foxes originally, but now the garden is too groomed. Unfortunately, the only things remaining are the rabbits – and I would gladly be rid of all of those.

My favourite colours in the garden are greens. I like a few colours here and there, but nothing garish. A large part of the garden to the front and side of the house is given over to a stream and ponds – my loch. On the original map of some 30 years ago, there was a little blue line, so I enquired about it and found that there was a stream that used to feed the mill. I tried my luck and got a digger and found the water, and also dug another pond and planted things like irises and gunnera. To the right I have a magnificent 'Constance Spry' rose – I have a photograph of myself and my grandchildren by that rose – and further on is the laburnum walk-to-be. Everything is 'to-be' in this garden.

I am very good at visualizing things that are not yet there. I propagate a lot of the common plants myself, but if I want some fantastic tree, nowadays I use the Internet, which is very easy. Before you had to go through the RHS Plant Finder, and it was much harder. Also, when I first started the garden, I had spent all my money on the house, and I am not the sort of person who borrows from the bank. At that time, I went to a nursery and saw a beautiful mimosa tree. It was extremely expensive, but I saw that they also sold seeds, so I bought a packet of 12 seeds and planted them. Half of them came up, and I potted them up. By the second winter only two had survived, and one was much stronger than the other. So I planted it in my conservatory and it grew and grew so

The pond, complete with visiting birds and ducks, and what Rora describes as 'the laburnum walk-to-be'.

that for the past four years I have had to chop and chop it so that it doesn't go through the roof! The tree is nine years old now, and over four metres high, and in the winter the perfume is fabulous – just when you need it.

I love the nine months from February until October. I hate November, December and January because of the short days. I wake up very early in the morning and live with the light. In the summer I get up at 3 a.m. I go to bed at around 10 p.m. but the last hour I spend sleeping in front of the TV! Almost all of the rest of the time, I spend in the garden, and at night, I still think about it. I don't change a lot of things once they are done, but I am always producing new schemes. I don't really have time to entertain guests. The garden has taken the place of people in my life. It is my passion.

You need to get a lot of joy out of gardening, or not do it, because it can be very frustrating. I am 65, and to feel love at my age is fantastic, and I am in love with this garden. It is the luckiest thing that can happen.

The conservatory where we were served lunch contains an enormous mimosa tree which Rora grew from seed.

24

HANNAH PESCHAR

GARDEN SCULPTURE SPECIALIST

'I love heads. The sculptures don't damage in the ground.' Here *Industrial Legacy* (mild steel) by Rick Kirby is framed by fading rhododendrons.

'The Mind, that Ocean where each kind Does streight its own resemblance find'

    Hannah Peschar is feisty, sharp and intelligent. Both a businesswoman and an aesthete, she has gained a reputation as one of Britain's foremost experts on using outdoor sculpture creatively. She lives in a fifteenth-century cottage tucked away off a leafy, winding, narrow road in Surrey. 'We bought the house in 1977 for £44,000,' she told me, 'And every tree came free!' Surrounding the house are ten acres of garden, designed by her husband, Anthony Paul. Over the past 20 years Hannah has used the garden, with its streams, ponds, bridges, large trees and architectural plants, as a sculpture gallery.

    Walking around, it is difficult to imagine that each work of art was not made especially for its particular position in the garden – and indeed, some were, but many were not; for it is Hannah's particular talent to place outdoor sculpture perfectly. Amongst the many things she takes into account are space, height, light, form, shape, colour, and the element of surprise. The sculptures, framed and enhanced by their setting, are mainly by young British artists and are mostly for sale.

I am Dutch, and I met my husband, Anthony, in a pub in London — in a real pick-up place in King's Road, but I didn't know it was a pick-up place! We fell in love with each other, and I decided after a while to stop living in Holland, and move in with him. It was simple, and a long time ago. When we bought this place, the garden was very neglected. It had not been tended for 27 years, so there were high nettles, dead elm trees, and a 200-year old walnut tree, fallen down, which might have been rescued but no one bothered. The stream burst its banks after heavy rain and the whole garden got flooded. We are on heavy clay and the ponds were all silted up. My husband is a landscape designer, and he set to work on the garden, but I played my part too, mainly saying, 'No, you can't do that!' So we had very, very heated discussions about what could and could not be done.

At that time I was working as a foreign correspondent. I did that for ten years, and then, a little over 20 years ago, I lost one of my jobs, for a radio station. There was a lot of politics involved, and I wasn't at all interested in politics, and so I didn't do a very good job. I was much better at writing interviews with writers, sculptors, painters, actors and that sort of thing, which I kept on doing for a while. But I was depressed about losing the job, and I had time on my hands, and thought to myself, 'Why don't I do something with this garden?' So I decided not to be an intellectual any longer, but to do something very tactile.

I am someone who always gets ticked off in museums because I touch everything, and I have always been a sucker for contemporary art. I have a friend in Holland who has a gallery in the country, in a huge, old barn. I met her in London, and she told me what she was doing and I visited her when she had an exhibition of sculpture in her barn, but the sculptor brought so much work that she couldn't place it all and she put one or two pieces outside. That is really how I got the idea.

I knew a lot of artists in Holland, but not in England, so I went to some of the major art colleges and started talking to the heads of sculpture departments, and told them of my plans, and what I wanted, and my ambitions, and they thought I was mad, because nobody had done that. I got a lot of raised eyebrows and people asked, 'What on earth do you want a garden with sculpture for?' And they scoffed, 'Nobody wants sculpture in their garden. It is just a waste of time.' Even my husband said, 'You will never make any money out of it', to which I replied, 'Maybe making money out of it is not my first priority. I am looking for something spiritual to do, and I am going to do it. Nobody else is doing it, so I am going to be the first, and I like to be the *first* in anything I do.'

So I had a few grumpy years with him, but then more and more people came, and then Prince Charles came to open an exhibition, and then I started to sell and get wonderful publicity in the press, and now lots of people come. I was the first, although there are many now. They have all been here, to have a look at how I do it! So I am desperate to keep a step ahead. I am an art dealer who specializes in finding and commissioning sculpture, displaying it and organizing exhibitions of art that can be placed outdoors. There is a lot to it, other than it looking good outside: the sculpture must weather all right, and survive frost and every element that falls on your head or blows past your face in a garden.

All the sculpture is on loan, and if it doesn't sell it goes back to the sculptor. There are, however, a few pieces in the garden that I secretly hope that maybe the sculptor forgot about, and that nobody buys. That is a very strong feeling. I have one client at present who is trying to buy a piece that I don't want to sell, so I tell him that it is impossible to move! Often I have an idea where I will place a sculpture in the garden here before I get it, and I also like to involve the sculptor in finding a place. So we do it together, and we never have arguments, because it always seems to work. Then if someone buys the piece, and they would like me to help them place it in their garden, I do.

There is a gentleman in Bedfordshire who bought three pieces a few weeks ago. They were the first pieces of sculpture he had ever bought, but he was able to afford some really nice work. I went to have a look the day before they were placed in his garden, because some work is so heavy that you can't just pick it up and put it somewhere else. We walked around the garden, and he showed me where he wanted it, but he asked my advice. One piece was just not well placed. It could be much *better* placed, and I suggested putting it near the house on the terrace, so they could see it in the winter from indoors. Sometimes you want to see something from the kitchen or the sitting-room. And this particular terrace was huge, and needed breaking up. Anyway

Above: Hannah's placement of sculpture relies on connecting shape as well as light and dark to mirror and reflect the garden so that both trees and sculpture are seen anew. *Luna* (glass and burnt iron) by Sunny van Zijst.

Opposite: 'There must be interaction... otherwise, why put a work of art in the garden?' Here the link between the giant hogweed and the sculpture is transparent. *Cocoons of Light* (glass and stainless steel) by Keiko Mukade.

they did it, and they rang me the next day and said, 'We are so glad we listened and took your advice, because it looks absolutely splendid.'

You have to be diplomatic about it, because when someone buys a sculpture for the first time, to go outdoors, placing it is a very exciting moment. I know, because I find placing sculpture so exciting myself. I am quite a good photographer, and that is about composition, and I do the same with sculpture, only it is three-dimensional. So you have to explain how the light plays with a three-dimensional piece of art, and the surrounding landscape. I try to find a place in the garden where there is a supporting element, or something that will enhance the art and where the art will enhance the surrounding nature. There must be an interaction. For me that is vital; otherwise, why put a work of art in the garden?

When I started collecting sculptures to display 20 years ago, many sculptors wanted a place in the middle of the lawn, in full sun, because that was similar to when they showed their work in a gallery or museum, and they had space, white walls and static light. I wanted to challenge this idea and place work amongst foliage or under trees – amidst growing things, which changed, as did the light, and where the work was not necessarily viewed instantly upon entry. The element of surprise is also very important, and is another thing I love, and which most people enjoy. Sculptors have changed their work over the last 20 years as they have become aware of changing light, rain, snow, and reflections, which make a sculpture always look different – much more than in a gallery.

It does not matter if the sculpture is figurative or abstract, but I have a lot of experience of visiting the Summer Exhibitions at the Royal Academy, and in the first years of me showing work here I saw the most horrible figurative work, because it was 'all skin, no bones'. By that, I mean that with someone like Henry Moore, who had a classical training, you can feel a force from inside the piece, and it shows. I saw a lot of work that was pretty and smooth, but hollow. It has changed a lot these days, but I try to avoid work like that. I also like to promote abstract work or work that is semi-abstract or semi-figurative. Above all, sculpture must be stirring and thought-provoking, otherwise after a while, I am bored stiff with it. I have some work in the garden, such as a pyramid shape made of flat pieces of Welsh slate, which is very simple, but because of that, I don't get bored with it, even though I have had it for years. I have to walk through the garden to see it, and the effort is always worthwhile.

This garden is lush, dramatic and sensuous. We have leafy tunnels, nooks and crannies, as well as vistas and open spaces. The plants are very important, often adding an element of surprise when pieces are half hidden. Mainly the plants are architectural, such as the massive gunnera. If you look at how the plant is structured, how the enormous leaf is held up like a roof, you see that quite a few contemporary architects get their inspiration from nature. Stansted Airport, designed by Norman Foster, is an example, where the roof structure is very like a gunnera. If you look at a hosta leaf the skeleton is structured in a completely different way.

A lot of people don't *see* that, because they only expect pretty flowers in a garden, and there is *so* much more to plants than just pretty colours. We have many different greens, greys, as well as some wild and cultivated flowers of other colours. And we have a lot of white, in the giant hogweed, which comes from the Caucasus and grows enormous within a few months. I love gardens where the plants show energy. Some people find it scary. I don't; I find it fascinating. Children love it here because it looks like a rainforest. It is *not* a cottage garden! This is not a place for faint-hearted people but for people who are young at heart, as I suppose I am!

The thing I enjoy most about what I do is *placing* new work. The whole mini environment around it *changes* dramatically. I visualize a place and it is a gut feeling. It has to move my senses. The sculpture draws you to different places in the garden, enabling you to become aware of your surroundings. I look for form and shape which links with the sculpture. These may be circles and spirals that echo patterns in bark or buds, or that contrast with the long verticals of the trees. On the whole I prefer to put pieces straight on the ground; plinths are a bit dated, but occasionally you can't avoid them. Heads, for instance, are sometimes better on plinths. I love heads.

Above left: In the sun, *Ghost* (wire mesh, galvanized and copper painted), by David Begbie, is mysteriously seen.

Above right: *Ghost*, equally effective but quite different in the shade. 'The light plays with a three-dimensional piece of art and the surrounding landscape.'

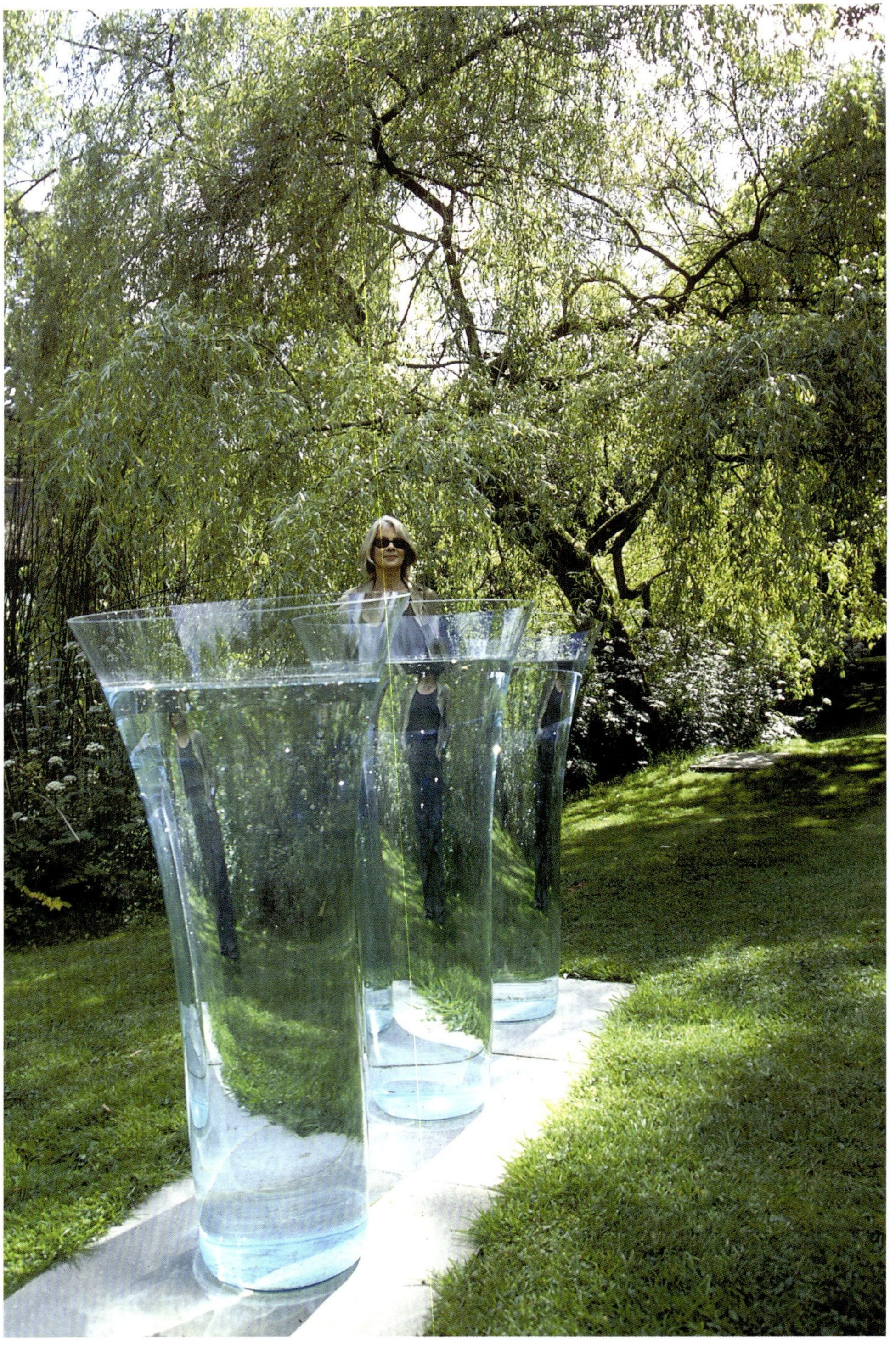

WHY WE GARDEN | Hannah Peschar

The sculptures don't get damaged in the ground, which is soft – they just need to survive the weather. Fired clay, oak and bronze are particularly suitable for outdoor sculpture.

At present we have an exhibition called 'Density and Light' which is of work in fired clay and glass. Each exhibition runs from May till the end of October, so I try to change a lot of the work in April. My clients are very varied. At the beginning, they were mainly foreigners – either living here or abroad, or sometimes a couple, one of whom was from abroad. Now, that is no longer so. Most of my big clients are British, although they are the kind of people who travel and have seen a lot and are well educated. They have learnt to open their minds.

Above left: In this revamped water garden by landscape designer Anthony Paul (Hannah's husband) large plants and trees support, frame and enhance the collection of contemporary sculpture – here *Damsel Flies* (steel and plastics) by Paul Amey.

Above right: *Shoal* (aluminium and stainless steel) by Paul Amey at home in a natural sweep of a stream.

Opposite: When I asked Hannah where she would like to be photographed she chose *Leaning-Straight-Leaning* (glass and water) by the well-known Dutch sculptor Bert Frijns. Hannah likes it because it is simple and looks easy to make but is really very difficult.

Not everyone comes here to buy sculpture – it is a wonderful partnership with my husband. Some people come here because they want their garden to be done by him, or they have had their garden landscaped by him and want a sculpture. Perfect harmony. Occasionally, and very secretly, I change something in the garden so that it goes with the sculpture better. Usually it is when my husband is not there, and it is mainly pruning – and he doesn't notice because he is too busy. We have a private part of the garden that we use to sit in, but most people have gone by 5 p.m. so in the evenings in the summer, we have the place to ourselves. My favourite time is early summer when everything is growing up so big. Gardeners get annoyed with me because I always touch plants and flowers. I never break them, I am *very* careful, but I like to see them from all sides – like sculpture. That is what I do.

I am proud that I have been a pioneer in showing contemporary art in gardens and that subsequently journalists and garden writers started to write about it and open the public's eye. Because of that, I gave artists the opportunity to create work which they could sell outside a gallery. I am also proud that I have sold sculpture to a lot of people who had never bought a piece of sculpture before. That fills me with warmth. A garden is less intimidating than a white-walled gallery in Cork Street. People can walk with friends here and bring a picnic or a glass of wine, and it mellows them and they become more receptive to the idea.

I used to get the occasional nasty remark from my very traditionally minded, stockbroker-belt neighbours, who complained, 'Your garden is full of rude pieces!' That was because I had genitals, tits and bums in the garden, although now the neighbours have loosened up a bit. You would be surprised how many people from around here have started to buy! Or you might get comments if an abstract sculpture is made out of steel, which rusts: 'It looks like the remains of a car crash', or 'It looks like scrap metal' – all *terribly* predictable. But the positive remarks enable you to laugh at the negative ones.

We have had a few small pieces stolen – two very small bronze birds – but never any vandalism. We once had a big group of school children from London in the garden. It was their day out and it was a mixed group of boys and girls, and the girls were all in beautiful dresses – there were a lot of ethnic minority children, and they didn't have to wear their uniform on a day out. I said they were allowed to touch the sculptures, and feel the textures with the tips of their fingers. One boy was feeling a piece of glass sculpture and a boy behind him whacked him, pushing him into the sculpture. The boy was not injured, but the glass broke, and I am afraid I was furious and sent the whole coach-load back to school. But the boy who had pushed got almost lynched in the coach by the other kids! It is a sad story. People have fallen in the water – but that is fun. Everyone just laughs.

Tomorrow we are having a special fundraising event for a charity I am involved with called 'Kids for Kids' which gives goats to children in a remote area of the Sudan. I grew up on the Beatles, and today I wrote a speech for Ringo Starr, who will be saying a few words – a memorable moment! I just hope to go from strength to strength, probably staying here, although I would rather like to help advise an entrepreneur who wanted to start his or her own art collection. I am already helping a client who wants to start his own private sculpture garden which will not be open to the public. I like doing that kind of thing.

I try to encourage people to trust their own senses when they look at the shape instead of killing their brains trying to understand what it means. So many middle-aged people are so conditioned, but when you get children of about four to ten in the garden, art gives them a sense of freedom. And sculptors are not con artists – most of the people whose work I show here have had a training of five or six years, just like a doctor or a lawyer. They demand a lot of respect. I am also always impressed to see how artists with families thrive on their creativity and their imagination, and for them it is a lot easier to endure life without having a vast amount of money, and that is a gift.

So I love working with artists, and I love placing their work. By placing a sculpture in a garden you create either a place for reflection and meditation, or a place of worship. That is rather a heavy word – I do not mean the worship of a god, but of whatever you want to worship at that moment. By just placing a work of art between some plants, that is what it really boils down to.

25

RICHARD PIM

WATER GARDENER

The mill wheel with red campions in front.

'Here at the Fountains sliding foot'

Richard Pim has owned his two-and-a-half acre site at Westonbury Mill, Herefordshire, for 35 years, but it is only relatively recently that he has lived in the watermill and single-handedly created a garden around the old millpond. In fact Richard uses the garden to some extent as a vehicle for his love of making things. Virtually everything in the garden has been made by him, sometimes employing feats of great ingenuity, such as his gargoyle-spouting water tower powered entirely by a water wheel. Richard is untrained in horticulture, and most of his working life has been concerned with underground water, in contrast with his present life which revolves around water above ground.

Versatile and gracious, Richard now opens his garden to the public, and indeed there is much for them to see and admire. The garden, with wonderful views of meadows and hills, is almost entirely dedicated to water- and moisture-loving plants. There is a tangle of streams and ponds surrounded by waterside plantings; a bog garden; a willow tunnel; a rope bridge and a wooden one; a summerhouse and a water tower. And Richard is still full of plans and ideas for creating more. I loved the natural look of much of his garden, and hope that the future will not bring too many follies and bizarre inventions, but I suspect that some, at least, are on the cards.

I like water! I bought the mill in 1968, and then for the next 30 years, I was working overseas as a hydro-geologist – work involved with underground water. When I bought the mill it was falling down and the land was completely infested with brambles. We did a lot of work on the house to make it habitable and it became a weekend cottage while my wife and children lived mainly in Shrewsbury. I used to come back here and loved the place and the idea of making a garden, but I didn't manage to get on with it because I was always away.

But I did dig most of the big pond about 15 years ago. It has an island in the middle with a tree on it where I built a tree house and I put up the rope bridge as a children's plaything. I also planted gunnera and some of the big irises as well as a load of other stuff, but most of that just disappeared without trace, because immediately I went overseas again and the jungle came back. So for 25 years it stayed chaotic here, and then six years ago I separated from my wife and came to live in the mill and decided to make this a garden.

I do everything myself. I am obsessed with DIY, so I hired a digger and a dump truck and extended the big pond in three days. But I'd hired the digger for a week, so I was left with four days of digging time, and a piece of land about 50 metres by 30 that was just wasteland, so I dug channels and shaped the ground as the mood took me, entirely, without any thought of prior design at all. Basically I took a lot of soil out and put it on to raised paths around and also developed three boringly featureless mounds that were there. In the middle one I now have a kind of cairn with a water fountain surrounded by a pond.

Then I found I had a lot of awkward large pieces of tree to dispose of, so I piled them up with the earth and it gave a shape to the island on the right. I also made a bog garden at the front, which was probably part of the old millpond, and at the end of the garden, behind the large pond, is a walkway with a steel pergola over the top.

I have had no horticultural training and don't even read books on garden design – it seems to me that when you look at those books it appears as though everyone started off from the same manual. I would rather just get out there and do my own thing: what I feel like that day. I have never had a garden of any kind before this and I just wanted to do it *my* way.

I love making things, and that is one thing I *did* know about. I am quite a good carpenter so I liked making the hump-backed bridge, mainly because I was curious to know how you could make an arch out of wood. I did it by getting lots of planks one inch thick. Of course you can bend a single plank, so I jammed them in the garage so that I had the curvature I wanted and then just added more planks, gluing and screwing them together to build up a big beam of ten planks, which looks like a single beam. I made the steel pergola by hiring a welding machine for the day and bending some reinforcing rod. Anybody can weld; you just need to get out and try.

The planting was more experimental. I got two postal catalogues from water gardens and I bought one of everything in the two catalogues! It was an outrageous thing to do. They must have been furious when they had to write all the labels and put a single tiny sprig into all these separate plastic bags. Apart from the gunnera, which I had already got going, I didn't know anything about the rest of the plants – I had spent my life working in the desert so I hadn't even visited gardens. I love the wet and the green here, but deserts are *not* boring – there are extraordinary varieties of colours and textures to the land. They are two extremes; desert and here. Anyway, I ended up with 242 different plants and a hell of a mess because of the digger and the dump truck, so the place looked like a construction site and all the ground was compacted.

When you dig, it is impossible to keep the topsoil separate from the subsoil, so I put a lot of clay on the surface and it was all a terrible mess and all these plants arrived the day before I went off to Nigeria on a work trip. So I stuffed them all in a long line into the clay and came back about three months later. Remarkably, most of the plants survived, but they were grid-locked in the clay and miserable, so then I began to learn about the whole business of soil preparation, which is

Left: Richard standing on the rope bridge, which connects to an island in the pond.

Opposite: Richard looks out on his garden from the 'Monet' bridge he made himself.

just *everything*. It seems that one of the most important things about gardening is getting the soil right before you put the plants in and so I really went for that.

I got massive amounts of sand from a quarry just down the road – I am lucky that I don't have to buy little diddy bags from a garden centre, I can buy about two tons a time in a big trailer. I also got lots of compost and manure and started mixing and spreading and digging and rotavating on a pretty huge scale – I suppose I am good at that – hard, physical work. I enjoy it, and also the satisfaction of getting something right with the planting. For instance, at the end of the channel near the house, for two or three years I had some *Ligularia przewalskii*, and I thought that on the edge of the water in alluvial soil they would be totally happy. But they just didn't thrive. Last year I dug them up and took them further along the edge of the same channel but rotavated a lot of sand and a little manure into the soil, and they just shot up and now they look *magnificent*. A little breakthrough like that is very satisfying.

Also, only two years ago, the back of the garden was a very boring orchard with lines of hopeless cider apple trees which were terribly

The restored mill pond at Westonbury, with candelabra primula in the foreground: *Primula beesiana* (mauve-pink) and *Primula florindae* (yellow). Further back are the white spray-like flowers of *Rodgersia tabularis*.

The water-spouting tower with hand-carved gargoyles against the darkening Herefordshire landscape.

dull and disappointing, but there didn't seem to be any watery connection or potential there. There was, however, a very small stream, a trickle really, in a ditch that ran along the boundary between my orchard and the next field. I always liked the view through into the field – in spring it is absolutely beautiful with all the buttercups, and there are usually stallions there which gallop around with their tails flying. Anyway my nephew and I decided one day that we would bring that into the garden.

We hired a digger the next day and cut down all the orchard trees and diverted the little trickle from the ditch diagonally across the orchard, and used all the soil that we dug out of the ditch to make a bank, and managed to align the new stream with the Monet bridge and the view through into the field. That is probably the best thought-out plan in the garden – even if it was only thought out one afternoon and done the next day! I am very lucky here that I don't have to worry about liners and all the artifices that most people need to create their own ponds. But I would say to other people, get some plants and have a go; don't be scared. Don't get bogged down in the bog!

I feel that this has got to be my life's work now – to make this into a remarkable garden. Last year I opened the garden to the public for about six weekends. This year I am opening five days a week. I am hoping that I can get it going sufficiently well that it can be my job and my income. I have lots of other ideas I want to incorporate into it, which I can't discuss yet, but which I will try out and see what happens. I love making follies and features. For instance, the tower was entirely my concept, although I had a lot of help as well. Most of the stonework was done by a mason friend, but I carved the gargoyles from Forest of Dean sandstone – they are not cement!

I have had a whole lifetime of making things, and once you know how to, and are used to the idea of being able to make things, you just do it. The idea of the tower was to use the water wheel and a belt-bucket system, which would take water up to the top to fill the tank, and when the tank is full, it flushes, like a gigantic loo, and the water comes out of the mouths of the gargoyles. I have just perfected it and it gives a good big jet of water about every ten minutes, which is rather fun! Then the middle part is a pigeon loft where I hope to have fan-tailed doves coming to roost amongst the spouting gargoyles. The fantasies I have are almost unlimited!

26

SARAH RAVEN
CUTTING GARDENER

The flowerbeds at Perch Hill overflow with colour, but the occasional use of gold feathered grasses complements the intensity of the flowers stunningly.

'Into my hands themselves do reach'

Sarah Raven grows flowers and vegetables specifically for cutting. She also keeps pigs and chickens; runs a mail-order business; runs courses and lectures on gardening and flower arranging; writes books and articles; is a TV presenter on *Gardeners' World*; and is a wife and mother. Bearing her commercial enterprises in mind, the first thing that struck me about her garden is that it is relatively small, but also beautiful. It is situated around a series of buildings (including her house, an oast-house used for dispatch and a school for the courses she runs) in the middle of the Kent countryside. Sarah's character spills into the garden: her tendency towards untidiness, love of colour, and exuberance are all evident.

Immediately in front of the house is a dahlia garden filled, at the time I visited, with lovely soft greens and deep velvety reds. To one side is a polytunnel for propagating; on the other side is a herb and vegetable garden, cottagey in style and endearingly disorganized. Behind the house is an oast garden with bold splashes of deep greens, purples and oranges. But most striking of all is the allotment-style garden across the little road, bang opposite the house. One tends to think of traditional cutting gardens as functional rather than attractive – tucked away out of sight at the side of a house, where the strict rows of flowers are not viewed. Sarah's garden is filled with tall, waving jewels of flowers, strung like precious necklaces, with grasses at the corners like ornate gold clasps. Dominating the display were glowing white foxgloves, royal blue cornflowers and anchuzas, double black poppies, mauve alliums and multi-coloured sweet peas.

I talked with Sarah in her house, which she admits is totally unsuited to her needs, with far too few bedrooms. Her kitchen, however, is huge, painted in cool colours with bright china bowls, cushions and curtains. Children and staff wander in and out and there is a strangely mixed atmosphere of relaxation and hectic activity. Sarah herself is warm, modest and busy. She never mentioned her television appearances until asked, wore no make-up, gesticulated in conversation, and stopped every now and then to ask others, 'Could you bear to feed the pigs now?' 'Is someone doing the school run?' 'Will they finish the building work on the gardening school in time?' 'Are you hungry? We'll just go round the garden and then I'll make supper.'

Opposite: Sarah, immersed in huge flowers, is cutting the main leader of *Digitalis purpurea* 'Alba' which, amazingly, will then branch lower down to form new flowers.

In a strict sense a cutting garden is a place where you harvest cut flowers. I am more of a productive gardener in that I also cut vegetables, herbs and salads – bringing the whole garden into the house. I grow plants that are 'cut-and-come-again' so I can go into the garden tonight and pick every bud and flower and in three or four days' time they will all be back again, as opposed to, say, peonies, which, once you pick them, there won't be any more. So I am a specialist, I suppose, in experimenting with plants and finding an increasing number that are cut-and-come-again. Whether they are very good salads, such as Japanese mizuna, which looks lovely in a winter salad bowl with its sharply serrated, bright green, slightly spicy leaves, or really fantastic unusual annuals, like the exotic flower salpiglossus, which is also cut-and-come-again – I try to find new plants all the time which give you an ever-filling cup!

My interest in gardening started quite early on. My dad was a botanist and collected a lot of plants in the wild, which was allowed then, although it isn't now. He travelled around Europe with my mother and found quite a lot of euphorbia, hellebores, weird irises and orchids. So I was brought up in a plantsman's garden in Cambridgeshire and *loved* finding plants in the wild with my father, particularly in Europe where it is more luscious than the rather reduced flora in Britain. I am not a 'stamp collector' [an accumulator of rarities] – I like beautiful plants everywhere, so places like Greece and Italy are very exciting to me.

When I was younger I was a doctor, but my relaxation was always gardening. I had a garden in London that I was obsessed with as a turn-off from the hospital. Then I had a child and took 18 months off, since I could no longer really do junior doctors' hours. But because I wasn't very good at doing nothing, I set up a florist's in London. Then I went back to medicine for a year and a half and then decided that I would prefer to do gardening rather than medicine. The two sort of dove-tailed – I had already written *The Cutting Garden* [Specialist Garden Book of the Year, 1996] but I was mainly buying commercial cut flowers, and one of the reasons I wanted to move to the country was that I realized there were many plants being sold quite expensively, which were actually annuals, and very simple to grow — you could just shove them in your backyard and didn't need to go to the florist and pay a fiver: you went out with your scissors and it took five minutes!

I love cut flowers and wanted to find things that actually loved being picked, unlike the flowers in my parents' garden. There, when I picked a lily, which had been collected in Rhodes on top of a mountain, not surprisingly they were not very happy. It is wonderful that all the staff here can go and pick flowers and take them home and it doesn't make a dent in what is going on. My parents' passion for gardening drove my own passion, but their type of plant didn't suit my temperament, which was for abundance. I wanted huge quantities rather than very rare species.

So that is how I discovered my own way of doing it, and actually no one else was doing this. Cutting gardens were very much a Victorian thing — Victoria and Albert had an amazing cutting garden at Osborne House on the Isle of Wight, and of course other people had them too. But with both wars, and the lack of labour, from five gardeners in a walled garden of a grand country house, you went down to none. Because of this, that way of annual gardening, whether it was vegetables on a large

Brilliant flowers take centre stage against the backdrop of fields. White digitalis, black double poppies and blue cornflowers.

scale or cut flowers, just went.

I had already grown things like unusual sunflowers in London, but in the country I was able to experiment and grow them on a bigger scale, and it was easy. Once I cottoned on to that, I started writing about it, and then everyone else wanted to do it, and so I started teaching, which I do four days a week now. Sometimes I teach propagation and germination, but I also do a lot of floristry – so it is kind of from seed to marquee! I am not a formal florist – I never use oasis, it is all pretty relaxed. I also sell seeds and anything that I use and that isn't widely available (like rootrainers, waterproof tissue and felt ribbon). But the thing I like best is gardening. One of the tragedies of my life, which I am trying to sort out, is that I do not garden enough at the moment.

I love gardening for the complete *combination* of things it gives me. There is intellectual stimulation, which I get from working out why something works and why it doesn't, so it engages the intellectual side of my head. Then the visual aspect is terribly important to me – with annuals particularly, because twice a year you are creating a completely different look in the garden. There is also the physical part, which I also enjoy enormously; getting down and doing a bit of digging. And it is productive. I really love the side of gardening where you can go out and pick your supper: a feast for the body and the eye. Teaching and writing about gardening, too, certainly both engage the side of my mind that wants to be challenged. Finally, there is the spiritual aspect, although not in the conventional sense, but going out and training tomatoes at five this morning was very peaceful and hugely calming.

For me, the rest of life is very manic, running the business – which is the bit of what I do that I enjoy least. I don't like having a lot of responsibility for a lot of people – whether it is just day to day, finding them enough, but not too much, to do, and the whole thing that goes with employing lots of people: I employ about 15 to 20 people according to seasons. The business has grown so much that it has completely taken over family life. My husband [Adam Nicholson] and I used to have an office and spare room, but now it is the mail-order department – we are surrounded by the business. So if I can get to garden, it gives a sense of reality. Gardening is the only thing I can find that engages with all those things that I think are important for happy life.

When I choose plants to grow, colour is perhaps the most important thing. I like very strong colour. Having started in flower arranging and moved into gardening, rather than the other way round, I had already started to use very bold colour combinations. It was temporary, because cut flowers don't live very long, so in a way you can afford to be much braver and push the boundaries much further. Then I found that once I had mixed magenta and orange or crimson and orange in a flower arrangement, I wanted to plant the garden in the same way, because that is what stimulated me.

I grow biennials, which you sow one year and they flower the next, and annuals, which you sow each year, although some self-sow, but most perennials are not cut-and-come-again, so I don't grow many, except euphorbias and some delphiniums. Annuals and biennials are far less bother than people think, and give a varied, dazzling, glamorous display in the garden and in the house. My favourites change. For a long time I have been keen on a fantastic biennial Iceland poppy called 'Meadow pastels' which is scented [rather like narcissus, but it has very large flowers in whites, creams, yellows, apricots and orange].

I love lupins and particularly a florist's lupin which we have got at the moment called 'Blue Spear', which is incredibly elegant and looks like a peacock's feather. Also it doesn't have too many flowers. A lot of lupins are too dense, but this is quite sparsely covered. I love things where you only need a single stem, rather than a whole arrangement, or you just have floating flowers. I like very simple things, really. I also adore scent, particularly in bedrooms and upstairs, so lots of sweet peas, and night-scented stocks.

I use the garden mainly for experimenting with plant combinations and individual plants. We do lots of trials here every year, partly because that is what goes in the catalogue as seeds to sell, and partly because I enjoy it – not everything is commercial. It is a kind of romantic concept mixed with commercialism in that people might come here to learn how to arrange flowers for a wedding or a party and they will pick in the garden and then I will teach them. And they can see that from one packet of seed you can get huge abundance, so it is *not* expensive. That is another thing I love about this sort of gardening: it is in *no* way exclusive. You don't need to spend thousands of pounds landscaping your garden. You need to spend £25 on a few packets of seed that will fill your entire garden.

For people who are frightened of seeds, as most of us are to start with, it is very much a case of someone showing you once and then you are away. Then it is an addictive thing which will just snowball. I certainly got a friend to show me first, and I didn't realize how easy it was, but the seeds came up three or four days later and then I did a few more. It is a science and, if you have five or six tips up your sleeve, you cannot fail to succeed, because the seeds want to come up. The two techniques for growing seed directly into the soil, or under cover, are slightly different.

With direct sowing it is the six Ts. Timing – you want to sow when the soil is warm and moist, so from the middle of April till the middle of June, or later if you water with a sprinkler. If it is too hot and dry a lot of annuals don't germinate, nor if it is too cold. Here we do spring sowing from mid-April till mid-May and autumn sowing from mid-August to mid-September. The next T is tilth. Having a fine soil consistency is very important. You only have to have that where the seed is going, not throughout the whole garden. The third is thin sowing so they don't come up competing with very close brothers. The fourth is thinning. That is the infanticide bit where you have to leave spaces of about three inches when the plants are about an inch tall and you have to chuck out the babies in between. The fifth is transplanting. Once the plants are about two and a half by two and a half inches, you need to dig them up and put them somewhere else, planting them 12 to 18 inches apart, depending on the plant. Lastly is tying up. It is crucial to stake cutting flowers or you get very twisty stems.

In a greenhouse or polytunnel, we use a system of coir or heat-based pellets, called Jiffy 7's, which cut the amount of time involved in propagating by three quarters, because there is no pricking out and no potting on. You basically put two seeds into the dimple at the top of the pellet and one or other germinates; if both do, you take one out. Once the roots have filled the net, you remove them and plant them out. It is very simple – my children do it – and it costs the same or less than multi-purpose potting compost. The two commonest mistakes are growing things too dark and too hot. You want to grow things at about plus five – pretty cold, ideally outside under a cloche, or in a cold frame or greenhouse if you are lucky enough to have one. Then you have all-round light, whereas in a room inside you get a tall thin plant drawn towards a light source. So ideally as cold as you dare and as much light as possible and bottom heat if any at all, rather than air heat.

Of course vegetables are grown from seed too. I am very interested in unusually coloured, but very tasty vegetables. You can't have something that is just weird: it has got to taste good, too, so we experiment quite a lot. At the moment we have got crimson broad beans [Red Epicure], orange beetroot [Golden Beetroot] and Purple-podded peas. You have the normal vegetables, and just a scattering of an unusual one, which is visually exciting and tastes good. I also adore using vegetables and flowers mixed together in decorative arrangements: the whole idea of nothing being set in its place. I like everything being fluid.

I used to be a bit of a 'stamp collector' in terms of unusual vegetables, but we have reduced them a lot and now grow things we like eating. These are beans, whether broad or French – not so much runner beans and a lot of peas, because I am very fond of pea tips and I like eating peas at different stages, raw as well as cooked. We also grow lots of carrots, new potatoes, salads, courgettes, pumpkins, squashes, tomatoes, aubergines and chillies. I don't really bother with the brassicas, other than purple-sprouting broccoli, because we don't eat them much. I grow a lot of herbs, too, because I use loads in cooking.

When I did *Gardeners' World* [in 2002, with Alan Titchmarsh], it was all shot here, at Perch Hill. It was enjoyable, but I just had a seven-minute slot, which is really very short and made me realize that I would like to do a whole half hour myself. So I am working on

Sarah in her polytunnel with her seedlings. She is an ardent believer in growing annuals. 'It actually takes less effort to make the most dazzling annual garden than it does to give a dinner party.' And hardy annuals are 'adaptable, glamorous, easy, cheap and productive'.

that idea now. I would like to continue to encourage people not to be snobby about plants. Here I tend to teach quite well-heeled people, who often have very set ideas about what they like, and those ideas are *very* safe — they like the colours pink, grey, mauve, blue and green. The thing that I enjoy most, and hope that I have done a bit, is to get them to accept that that isn't the law, and that actually orange is an *incredibly* effective colour, particularly inside.

You can dare not to be Nancy Reagan, or even someone like Rosemary Verey, who was a brilliant gardener, but, in my view, she is remembered for creating fantastic romantic gardens full of beautiful pink roses. What I like is gardens which perhaps give you less of a show in June, but give you more from March till December, which we can do here. And gardens which give you a strong, jungley, Rousseau-type pallet and feel, which are not very manicured, but there is more chaos and abundance. That is what I hope I am encouraging people to do.

Yesterday I taught a group of very conventional people in Somerset, and sometimes it gets me down, but sometimes I can see that just a few of them have, in a way, been given permission to go a little bit wilder than they would before. I am saying that you haven't failed socially if you grow an orange plant! And there is this weird snobbery and conservatism that they worry that their friends will come and say 'Ugh! That's ghastly, darling. *So* vulgar.' Tied into that is also encouraging people to grow dahlias, gladioli and chrysanthemums. Dahlias were a great campaign of mine, and other people's. I have moved on to gladioli, because I think some of them are absolutely *fantastic* and now I am petitioning for the chrysanthemum — simply because, again, I have found five or six varieties that are totally superb. I hate chrysanths that are ugly, like everybody does, but you just have to know the right ones.

Sometimes when teaching you make awful blunders. Like I have talked about tulips, and there is one called 'Maureen', which is an incredibly good, late, ivory white tulip, and I have said something like, 'It has got a hideous name but a beautiful flower' and then I find there is someone in the audience called Maureen. I am quite blunt in my teaching: some people like that and some don't.

At the end of my very first course, Adam, my husband, who had a regular column in the Telegraph entitled 'Perch Hill', wrote all about the course, and all the ladies, and he referred to their clothes, and to their cars, which are pretty flash motors that he called 'cheques on wheels', and that emptied the school for about four months! We are quite expensive, and people come who perhaps don't have enough else to do. [Adam, grandson of Vita Sackville-West and Harold Nicholson, who was very kind while I was waiting to talk with Sarah and made me a cup of tea, popped in again at this point. Now he pipes up, 'You can't *possibly* say that! You attract a very high-class clientele. But I must say it was so nice, looking out and seeing these cheques on wheels driving up!' They both laugh, then Sarah continues:]

Opposite: Walking back to the house, Sarah turns in her 'dahlia garden' (where actually, in early summer, black, clove-scented dianthus are in flower), and looks fondly at the bunch of flowers she has just picked. 'You can fill your house with flowers, herbs, salad and veg one day and, in four or five days, the whole lot is back to be picked or admired again.'

WHY WE GARDEN | Sarah Raven

Probably about a quarter of the people who come on the courses are allotment growers or normal suburban or urban gardeners. About a quarter are interested locals, and the rest are people who are well-off, who sometimes bring their gardeners with them. On the vegetable courses, men often attend, but they very rarely come on the flower-arranging ones. A guy turned up on the bridal course the other day, and my eyes popped out on stalks, but it turned out he was a husband who sat in the car park all day! His wife couldn't drive, so he drove her from Norfolk and then back again. Incredible! Not like Adam. Adam does nothing to help me in the garden. He once only got the rotavator out, and then wrote an article about how he loves rotavating and how he is so brilliant at it!

It is quite messy here, and the interface between domestic life and well-heeled ladies can sometimes be quite funny. Everybody thinks we live an idyllic lifestyle. But I am a very, very chaotic person. I am 'Mrs Untidy' and everything is scattered all over the place, and I work incredibly hard and am a mother and a wife, and so everything is very shambolic. Yet everybody thinks I am 'Mrs Perfect' and I am so not Mrs Perfect [Adam: 'Oh, you *are*!'] So we get lots of slightly wry smiles, when they see, not quite dirty nappies, but the general mess.

We are building a new school, which starts this week. It is a very exciting building, designed by quite radical architects. I was very influenced by a restaurant in Amsterdam called the De Kas, where they grow all their own vegetables. The De Kas is a bit worthy, and I don't think growing your own vegetables has to be like that — it is really good fun, delicious and a huge life-enhancer. So you don't have to be a spiritual, earnest, worthy person to do it. I hope people will seriously learn but they will also have a good time.

We are doing food and flowers and, luckily, because it is quite an exciting project, we have got really great people coming to talk, both in gardening and in food. The whole idea is that everything is seasonal so they can't cheat like Nigella Lawson or Jamie Oliver and go to the supermarket; they have to genuinely engage with growing. Other than that, it just has to be good fun, tasty and simple, not elaborate. It is *not* spending 45 minutes making a flower arrangement or a dinner — it is five or ten minutes spent chucking stuff together. I am very excited about it. I will teach a bit, but also get other people in, so that I will be able to listen to them, cook for the lunches, which I love doing, and garden more.

I have lived here nine years, and for possibly the first time, when I walked round the garden this morning, I thought, 'It is really rather nice here!' It is very hard work keeping it all going, but we are beginning to get there now. We just haven't had enough money to do what a lot of people do, and sort everything straight away. We have recently got some pigs, which are incredibly sweet and incredibly funny, and the chickens were in with the pigs this morning, on their backs, and the garden was looking very beautiful in the light. Then I went to the polytunnel and saw all the tomatoes, and it felt good. It is a business that takes a lot of labour, but I couldn't do it if I didn't love it. *One* day, we will sit in the garden, but I have to say we don't now, ever!

27

KIM WHATMORE

URBAN GARDENER AND DESIGNER

Kim is articulate and thoughtful in conversation.

'Short and narrow verged Shade'

Kim Whatmore is a professional garden designer who also has her own small, charming town garden.

Approaching her terraced 1860s house in west London, I thought the front garden and the bright orange door unprepossessing, so that walking through the house to the tranquil, lush, oasis at the back, was an unexpected delight. And meeting Kim Whatmore was an unusual pleasure too.

She is emotional and passionate, but also frank and honest, voicing many gardeners' anxieties. She admits that designing gardens for others is easier than for herself, and that whereas she hopes other people use their gardens as places for social interaction, her own is a visual garden enjoyed primarily as a place looked at from inside. She loves creating beauty, but is nervous when change is needed, and frightened by the prospect of plants dying. And her candid account of the problems arising from the dynamics of being a woman designer are very revealing.

My garden is a combination of the exotic and the traditional, which is quite important to me. I've got the Englishness of foxgloves and camellias, in combination with tree ferns – all shade-tolerant, because there isn't a huge amount of sun. Also, the garden is quite small – eleven metres by four metres – and has both planted areas and lots of plants in terracotta pots. The space is divided into three interconnected parts: timber decking by the house opens to a circular area of paving, bordered by planting and a curved timber path, which continues to the back arbour.

I have lived here seven years, and when I came the garden consisted of concrete paving slabs all the way through, with very narrow borders on either side. There was an enormous shed at the end and another near the house. The guy who lived here was a plumber, but he also made some sort of alcoholic beverage out of damsons, and the sheds were part of that process. Also, although I think he was extremely fond of his wife, he quite often wanted to escape, so the sheds played a part in that. Anyway, when he laid concrete slabs, they had to stay absolutely in position, and the idea of any weed coming up in between was unbearable, so the concrete was sunk to a depth of about a foot.

When I came, I got a couple of clearance guys (I can't remember where I got them, but they arrived in the morning, clearly already having had a drink) and they just got rid of everything. I don't know what I would have done if there had been any kind of real garden here before. I never did a proper plan; everything was very evolutionary. The first thing I wanted to sort was the mess and changes in levels round the house, and so I levelled everything with decking.

The next stage was to build the structure at the end of the garden, which supports the ceanothus and wisteria and solanum. Then I put in a curved path, which runs around the right-hand side, linking the end of the garden with the part near the house: so that was quite critical. Originally I had a circular lawn in the middle, where there is now the York stone, but lawns never do very well in small spaces with no light. I have also had real changes in terms of the planting. Initially, I had *Euphorbia mellifera* by the side of the arbour, but I have never seen anything grow so fast! I bought them when they were two feet high, and by the end of the first year they were already five feet. Also, they give out some sort of chemical, which means that everything around them dies, so those had to come out, which was rather sad, because they did look very effective.

In fact the garden was really at its peak about two years ago, and the structural plants are now beginning to get too big, so that the smaller flowering plants can't really establish themselves. It actually makes me feel quite nervous and hysterical, because I don't really know what to do. The trouble is that as soon as you decide to take something out, it becomes a massive undertaking because of the implications on everything else. It is *much* easier to do it for other people. If you are an outsider to a space, you see things much more clearly, and you have less emotion, and no sense of ownership, so it is much easier to make decisions.

My own garden is mostly for looking at. I hardly ever go out there, except to work in it. I'll show it to people, but mainly I look at it from the kitchen window, or from the dining-room, and just contemplate. I love it for that. About once every two months I have a kind of

Unusually, Kim sits amidst her plants. But in the main, hers is a visual garden, looked at and loved from inside.

blitz and spend a whole day gardening – mainly tidying up. And if it is hot, I will go out every morning and water the whole thing, but the thinking behind it is low-maintenance. There is an evergreen structure, with a few tall flowers planted amongst it or in pots; things like foxgloves, hollyhocks and aconites that come to eye-level. Some things like irises, lilies and scabious come through each year, but to lift the effect, I just buy more. Foxgloves should come every other year, but I have so many problems with slugs that things just disintegrate. Also if you have quite a lot of plants in pots, they may be happy for one year, but because there just isn't anywhere for their roots to go, they don't like it the next year. So it is a continuous process.

When I plant, for myself or others, I do not have a plan in advance but just go to a nursery on a particular day and put together combinations that seem to work well. I have always loved flower arranging, and I think that may have been my way into gardening, although I also always loved pot plants at home, too, when I was a child. As a child we had a house in London and a cottage in the country and my parents spent endless hours gardening, but I never really understood why. I love doing window boxes, and when I started, I was quite happy with a window box, and the thought of a border was just too big and frightening. Of course over the last ten years I have overcome that and am now very happy in a border, but I still haven't worked in the countryside very much – I think you have to have the confidence to work in a bigger scale, which comes with time and experience.

My first training was in social research and I worked for various different charities. Then when I got to the point when I knew I wanted to give that up – and I might have become a doctor, or anything really – it was a crisis point when I really didn't know what to do. So I thought I would do something that had always been in the background from an early stage, and gardening came to mind, and everything gradually fell into place. I did a course in horticulture and another one in design at the English Gardening School, and got started in my new career. Now I design and maintain town gardens. I am very familiar with the rectangle, the L-shape and the square. Urban gardens are distinctive in that they are almost all very clearly bounded, and, by virtue of that, you don't have to negotiate the transition between what is cultivated and what is wild. It is all created structures around the garden.

Part of what I enjoy is wanting to sort out spaces, wanting to make them beautiful, as well as organized. I really believe in clear, underlying structure in terms of the hard landscaping and strong geometric patterns. The planting then softens the clear shapes, and the process of choosing the plants and putting together combinations is something that I absolutely adore. When you go to a nursery it is like having a massive palette with all the different plants, and each time you do it, it is a different experience, but you are looking for combinations and things which unite plants. So you might find a plant with a red flower, and a different one that has a bit of red in the stem, and because of that you recognize a unity, and it is this which gives pleasure to the eye. The other important thing is repetition, like tapestry, repeating a small combination of planting.

Another thing I get pleasure from is the physical process of planting and having my

It can often be a mistake to have a lawn in a small town garden. Kim has done away with hers, but retains a lush greenness through her planting, particularly with tree ferns.

hands in soil. I sometimes forget the pleasure of this until after I have done it! You dig holes, put plants in, make them happy, and you are outside. You come home at the end of the day, exhausted, and have a bath, but you have worked hard and made a space green, and it is a wonderful feeling. It amazes me in London how many endless spaces there are which have never been touched and are just let go to ruin. I suppose people just don't have the time to garden themselves, and maybe cannot afford someone to do it for them.

When I design gardens there is one thing which both amuses and depresses me, and it happens so many times. Usually, I work for couples, but it is normally the woman who phones me, because she is organizing everything, and I go to see her. We will have an initial consultation, when I will ask her how she wants to use the space and what kinds of things she likes in terms of colour and that sort of thing, and I will do a site survey. Then I go away and do a design. And part of the reason that she has brought me there is because she hasn't got the time or inclination, but she wants a beautiful garden. But the interesting thing is that as soon as we have come together and met and talked, it has started her thinking about what she wants, so in a sense, I no longer have a free reign, although I may not have a great deal to go on.

Then the next time you go back with a design, the whole thing has really got to be renegotiated, because by that stage she has opinions. The other complication is that when I present the design, because the husband is often paying, he has to be there. It is usually on a Saturday morning, and it is the first time he has seen his kids properly all week, and he is often more used to dealing with figures or words than two-dimensional plans. So on a regular basis, I will get comments about 'this little drawing' or questions like, 'Where's the house?' even though it is marked in very big letters; or 'What did you do before you were a garden designer?' Also he is distracted by the kids and everything, but usually, during the course of the meeting, he engages, and the kids start to become a bit tedious to him, and then a bit fractious, and so the wife starts having to deal with that.

At this point, the husband often starts getting more interested in the garden and will say things like, 'Hang on a minute, where are the architect's plans that we had for the extension?' or whatever – in other words he engages intellectually and becomes quite excited by the project. Then, because I frequently design for tall, thin houses, where you look down on the garden, I will mention that aspect, and the fact that it often rains, so you may not go out there all the time, and it has to look good from the house. Now the wife, picking up the pieces with the children, is being sidelined from what was actually her project that she initiated. But the husband, taking over, will quite often say, 'Well, why don't we go and have a look at it from upstairs?'

Basically, I will end up in *their* bedroom, looking down at the garden with him, and when I come back downstairs, she is furious. The next stage is quite often a meeting with her, in which I have to work incredibly hard to smooth everything over, and also she will quite often start actually putting a spanner in the works, saying things like, 'For the *children*, this isn't going to work, and I want the garden to be like *this*.' So the politics, and the whole thing of dealing with people, becomes more time-consuming and more important in many ways than the creation of a beautiful garden. It happens virtually every time.

The other problem is the politics with the contractors. As a woman dealing with the construction industry, sometimes I just walk away and think, 'Why do I play the game?' I am having to flirt, to pretend I am stupid – all the stereotypical sexist things. The only way I have found of dealing with it is to be humorous about it. But sometimes you just think, 'All I want is for us to work together to build a beautiful garden, so why go through all this rigmarole?' I want to do the planting and have someone get on and just lay the York stone, and we both want to please the client. So I sometimes feel that I am not able to put my artistic vision into practice because of dealing with all these politics.

The other thing which people sometimes lose sight of, is that I hope more than anything that I am creating a space in which people will find it easy to *be*. I'd like to think of it as a process where beauty is encouraging either social interaction or else the ability to contemplate and be alone and be at peace. Sometimes I find it difficult to acknowledge that something I created is beautiful. I lose the ability to see it. Although actually there was a border I planted for someone eighteen months ago which just came exactly into its own. That is an amazing thing, to see something grow, literally from ground level. There was a fantastic *Acer griseum*, which has a very brown flaky bark, and that colour picked up on some pinky-brown foxgloves. I hadn't even seen the possibility of that combination, and then there it was.

Another thing which happened to that particular border was that lots of white symphytum came up, which I never planted, but which gave it a whole new character. It is lovely when a mixture of the unanticipated happens with the planned. I would love to have the opportunity to work with seed, and not have to battle with bugs and lack of sun. But actually, when clients want instant gardens, it doesn't really bother me. I think my love of flower arranging makes me very well suited to the creation of instant beauty. The trouble with instant gardens, though, is that they go over very quickly, and it makes me very, very stressed worrying about whether things are going to die and if they will get watered enough. I would much rather create something instantly beautiful which only had to last for a week.

If I were giving advice to people I would encourage them to have an irrigation system where possible. I also think, in urban gardens, a relatively small number of plants works best – a mixture of evergreen shrubs and herbaceous, repeated all the way through. Also in a town garden, because of the surrounding buildings, there is a fairly short time in which you have light, so you have to accept that basically you are working with shade and go with things like box and bay and tree ferns. Putting in some annuals and perennials will usually be an ongoing process. But just experiment and try. Don't worry for a moment what anybody else thinks, or about fashion, or tradition, or history. We need to reinvent all that in a contemporary way. I wish people who garden would be in touch with themselves and be truly creative. Gardening is undoubtedly strangely obsessive. Yet running parallel is the whole thing of nurturing and caring and observing and creating spaces to be at peace; to be at ease.

PHOTOGRAPHY CREDITS

Barbara Baker: Pages v-xv (all taken from her own garden). Pages 1, 3, 4, 8 (bottom), 11-17, 20-30, 34, 44-55, 71-76, 83-97, 100, 102, 105-118, 123, 134 (left), 135, 149, 164 (left), 167-170, 175-179, 186-193, 198, 199-209

Robin Baker: Pages 5-7, 8 (top), 9, 10, 18, 31-33, 37-43, 57-59, 78, 98, 99, 103, 121, 122, 125-133, 134 (right), 136-148, 150, 155-162, 164 (right), 165, 173, 181-185, 195-197, 211-214

Taken by or belonging to Miriam Rothschild: Pages 61-70